Speech, Music, Sound

Speech, Music, Sound

THEO VAN LEEUWEN

First published 1999 by
MACMILLAN PRESS LTD
Houndmills, Basingstoke, Hampshire RG21 6XS
and London
Companies and representatives
throughout the world

ISBN 0–333–64288–0 hardcover
ISBN 0–333–64289–9 paperback

A catalogue record for this book is available
from the British Library.

This book is printed on paper suitable for recycling and
made from fully managed and sustained forest sources.

Printed and bound in Great Britain by
Antony Rowe Ltd, Chippenham and Eastbourne

To Tobias Icarus, the other musician in the family

Contents

Acknowledgements

This book would not have existed without the students who took my courses on music and sound at Macquarie University and the London College of Printing. Some are mentioned by name, others will recognize the examples to which they first drew my attention.

Many writers on music and sound have inspired me. Their names are in the bibliography. But two must be singled out, Murray Schafer and Philip Tagg. Those who know their work will recognize their influence throughout the book.

Exactly the same goes for my teachers in the field of linguistics and semiotics, Michael Halliday and Jim Martin, and for my collaborator of many years, Gunther Kress. Their influence is everywhere, and without them none of this could have been written.

Over the years I have also benefited from discussions about speech, music and other sounds with Joyce Belfrage, Philip Bell, John Bernard, Jennifer Biddle, Maria Casas, Michael Chanan, John Clarke, Carolyn Craig, Arthur Delbridge, Laura Lopez-Bonilla and Radan Martinec.

Experimental music adventures with Linda Berry, Rigel Best, Rudi Homburger, John Shand and others were another key source of inspiration and ideas.

The London Institute generously supported the research for this book as part of a three-year grant for work on 'multimodality and the languages of multimedia'. Thanks also to Catherine Gray of Macmillan for her support.

And to Laura for being there and putting up with it all.

Chapter 1

Introduction

Integrating speech, music and 'noise'

It is the project of this book to explore the common ground between speech, music and other sounds. These three have usually been treated as separate, in theory as well as in practice. They have been talked about in different ways and with different terminologies: linguistics to talk about speech; musicology to talk about music; not much at all to talk about 'sound effects'. And they have been practised as separate disciplines too, especially in dominant modes of communication and high culture art forms. This kind of semiotic purism has not always existed. In the Middle Ages and the Renaissance the voice was still a musical instrument and music was embedded in every aspect of everyday life, just as many 'less developed' cultures had and still have songs for grinding grains, songs for harvesting crops, songs for constructing houses, songs for carrying goods, toilet training songs, puberty songs, news bulletin songs, political comment songs, and so on (cf. Merriam, 1964). But as clergical plainsong, the cries of night-watchmen, and the chanting of the ABC in schools were replaced by reading aloud, speech was divorced from music, and much flattened in the process. And as the musical sounds in our cities (church bells, the postman's horn, and so on) were replaced by mechanical noises, with music moving indoors, into the concert hall, music and 'noise', too, became separate categories: 'The string quartet and urban pandemonium are historically contemporaneous' (Schafer, 1977: 103).

Thus music and the rest of life went their separate ways. Much effort was spent in trying to underpin the separateness of music with watertight arguments. The most common argument was based on acoustics. Musical sound results from regular, periodic vibration, non-musical sound from irregular, non-periodic vibration: 'Music is a play of tones, that is, of fixed, clearly defined quantities. Other sounds, glissandoes, cries, noises, may occur as inserts. If they are numerous, the result is only partially musical. If they predominate, it is no longer music' (Wiora, 1965: 191–2). But many of the sounds of music (including 'classical' music) do not fit this definition, and that applies not just to percussion instruments: all conventional musical instruments have their irregularities and granularities. Another common argument was based on the effect of music. Musical sound is beautiful, it pleases us. But again, not all music is beautiful, and many of the sounds we do not normally regard as music can be and are called beautiful, for instance certain human voices, and certain of the sounds of nature.

In this century, all this has begun to reverse. Recording technology has brought music back into everyday life – through muzak, the transistor radio, the car stereo, the walkman. The boundaries between speech, music and other sound have weakened. Composers have experimented with combinations of musical instruments, singing and speaking voices, and non-musical sounds. Satie added a typewriter to the orchestra, Gershwin a taxi-horn, Antheil a propeller, Zappa a cash register, Reich car alarms. Schoenberg, Berio and others wrote Sprechgesänge ('speech songs') – and so, in a different way, do contemporary Rap artists. The Futurist composer Russolo created a noise orchestra consisting of noise makers, boxes cranked by a handle: buzzers, bursters, a thunderer, whistlers, rustlers, gurglers, a shatterer, a shriller and a snorter. And, most significantly, he redefined noise as music:

> Let us walk together through a great modern capital, with the ear more attentive than the eye, and we will vary the pleasures of our sensibilities by distinguishing among the gurglings of water, air and gas inside metallic pipes, the rumbling and rattling of engines, breathing with obvious animal spirits, the rising and falling of pistons, the stridency of mechanical saws, the loud jumping of trolleys on their rails, the snapping of whips, the whipping of flags. We will have fun imagining our orchestration: of department stores' sliding doors, the hubbub of the crowds, the different roars of railway stations, iron foundries, textile mills, printing houses, power plants and subways (Russolo, 1986 [1913]: 3–8).

The pioneers and early theorists of the sound film saw it the same way:

> It is the business of the sound film to reveal for us our acoustic environment, the acoustic landscape in which we live, the speech of things and the intimate whisperings of nature; all that has speech beyond human speech, and speaks to us with the vast conversational powers of life and incessantly influences and directs our thoughts and emotions, from the muttering of the sea to the din of a great city, from the roar of machinery to the gentle patter of autumn rain on a window-pane. The meaning of a floorboard creaking in a deserted room, a bullet whistling past our ear, the death-watch beetle ticking in old furniture and the forest spring tinkling over the stones. Sensitive lyrical poets always could hear these significant sounds of life and describe them in words. It is for the sound film to let them speak more directly from the screen (Balasz, 1970: 197–8).

Not only 'noise', but also the word began to be treated as music, for instance in the 'concrete poetry', pioneered by Dada poets of the 1920s such as Kurt Schwitters:

> priimiititttiii   tisch
> tesch
> priimiititttiii   tesch
> tusch
> priimiititttiii   tischa
> tescho
> (*and so on*)

We can now hear words as *sounds* again, whether in the 'nonsense word' conversations of young children (cf. for example, Keenan, 1974), in the magic chants and songs of many of the world's religions, or in the virtuoso 'scat' singing of singers like Ella Fitzgerald and the electronic manipulation of snippets of speech in Steve Reich's 'Come Out'. Murray Schafer makes the point with a telling example in a small book called *When Words Sing* (reprinted in Schafer, 1986):

> I have just been listening to two tape recordings I made of Miranda, age seven. In the first she reads a story from her reader; in the second she makes up a scary story of her own. The first sounds flat and stupid. I wish you could hear the second.
>
> > Once there was a little old man. He wanted to get a piece of volcano rock. So he got all his hiking equipment ready. Then he hiked up the mountain. It took him twenty years. When he got to the top he took off the lid. Oooooahooooo! Inside there was a ghost and he mo-aned and he gro-aned. The man ran away as fast as he could and he said, 'I'm never going to climb volcanoes again!'

Miranda recites her unusual story with intense emotion. Words like 'moaned' and 'groaned' are so highly inflected and attenuated they are almost chanted. The 'Oooooahoooo' is a pure glissando melody. Miranda knows that words are magic invocations and can cast spells. So she exorcizes them with music. Of course her teachers will correct all this in another year or two by muzzling her to the printed page (Schafer, 1986: 198).

This book tries to do on a *theoretical* level what many contemporary musicians, poets, film-makers, multimedia designers and so on, already do in practice (and what children have always done): *integrate* speech, music and other sound. It tries to foreground the integration of these three, rather than to talk about their specifics, and to contribute to the creation of a vocabulary for talking about this integration, and for exploring its ramifications and potentials. Above all, it tries to make you listen. Listen to the city as though it was music and to music as though it was the city, or to speech as though it was music and to music as though it was speaking to you. This listening can, in the end, only be done by you, the reader. But I hope my book will be able to give you a helping hand. It is not always going to be easy, incidentally. Not through our own fault we have, most of us, ill-educated ears. Re-educating them may take some effort.

Some principles of semiotics

Although I have not used this term in my title, this book is about semiotics. But what is semiotics? Or rather, what do semioticians do? Three things, I think.

Describing semiotic resources

Semioticians describe the semiotic *resources* people use in communication. Narrowing this down to sound, the semiotics of sound concerns itself with describing what you can 'say' with *sound*, and how you can interpret the things other people 'say with sound'.

Why the term 'resource'? This needs a little background. In the past the dominant semiotic understanding and explanation of communication derived from a particular conception of language which saw language as a set of rules, a *code*. Once two or more people have mastered the same code, it was thought, they would be able to connect the same meanings to the same sounds or graphic patterns, and hence be able to understand each other. The question of how this code came about, of who made these rules, and of how and why they might be changed, was not high on the agenda. The rules were treated as simply being there.

In some contexts communication actually works like this, for example, in bureaucracies. There the use of words, the shape of documents and so on, are laid down in impersonal rules that simply must be followed to the letter and are not open to interpretation – if they do turn out to be open to interpretation that means there is some kind of 'loophole' in the system which should be plugged as soon as possible. But in other contexts, say poetry, or advertising, or conversations between children, things work differently. No hard and fast rules exist. Any bit of language you might lay your hands on could come in handy for the semiotic job at hand, whether it is grammatical or not, whether it represents a standard variety of English or not, indeed, whether it is English at all. So long as it does the job. In yet other contexts, in music for instance, either approach (or some mixture of the two) is possible. Some musicians are bureaucrats in spirit, or rather, they have to earn their living in a context where music is practised in this bureaucratic spirit, and so must play according to a definite code, a musical grammar. Anything else is frowned upon: 'That is not how Bach should be played'; 'That is not jazz' and so on. Others work in less strictly regulated contexts. They have their ears wide open and use any sound they can lay their hands on if it suits their purposes, frequently crossing generic boundaries, or even the boundaries between music and speech, or between music and 'noise'. The same applies to interpretation. There are viewers, listeners and readers who view, listen and read 'according to the book' – in educational contexts you usually have to do this if you want to get a good grade. And there are viewers, listeners and readers who use whatever resources of interpretation and intertextual connection they can lay their hands on to create their own, new interpretations and connections.

In public (in the workplace, for instance) only people with a large amount of cultural power are allowed to break or make rules. Most of us must have to follow them. In private, in the smaller groups and subcultures we live in, we may have more freedom, but our semiotic productions and interpretations are not likely to spread beyond these contexts. They will remain relatively marginal. Sometimes, however, society *needs* something new, and there is a chance for new and adventurous modes of production and interpretation to break through. Sound (sound-*as*-sound, that is, rather than 'sound-as-music' or 'sound-as-language') belongs in this category. There is an increasing interest in it. A new discipline of 'sound design' is emerging. But the code-books have not been written, and the production and interpretation of sound have not been taught and policed in the 'bureaucratic' spirit. Sound design has remained, so far, a little bit marginal perhaps, but free. A semiotics of sound should therefore not take the form of a code book, but the form of an annotated catalogue of the sound treasures Western culture has collected over the years, together with the possible uses to which they might be put, as gleaned from past and present experience. A semiotics of sound should describe sound as a semiotic resource offering its users a rich array of semiotic choices, not as a rule book telling you what to do, or how to use sound 'correctly'.

To create a usable catalogue you need usable headings, and that means classifying. I will do a fair bit of classifying in this book, although I hope to bear in mind that 'classification is only justified if it leads to the improvement of perception, judgement and invention' (Schafer, 1986: 133). In doing my classifying I follow a 'systemic-functional' approach (cf. for example, Halliday, 1978; Martin, 1992). This means that the 'choices' which make up the 'resource' are set out as (a) *binary opposites*, (b) *ever more 'delicate' choices* (moving from left to right in a system network one moves from the broadest headings to the finest subdivisions) and (c) in terms of their *semiotic value* for the production and interpretation of sound events. Let us take these points one by one in terms of an example that will be discussed in more detail in Chapter 3.

This fragment of a system network is concerned with a particular sound 'resource'. It tries to map how sound events can be structured in terms of their *timing*. The key distinction it introduces is the distinction between 'measured' and 'unmeasured' time. Measured time is time you can tap your feet to (ONE-two ONE-two and so on, or ONE-two-three ONE-two-three and so on). This is not possible with unmeasured time. The physical reaction to unmeasured time is more likely to be a slow swaying of the body. To give some examples, a long wail is unmeasured, and so is medieval plainchant; the reciting of metrical poetry is measured, and so is dance music. The distinction is a binary distinction: sound is either measured or unmeasured. There is no in-between. Other contrasts, for instance the contrast between 'loud' and 'soft', are not binary and admit of many 'in-between' gradations – a notation for this will be introduced later. The 'metronomic' system is more 'delicate' than the 'measurement' system: 'metronomic' and 'non-metronomic' time form a subdivision of 'measured time'. 'Metronomic time' is governed by the implacable regularity of the machine, whether or not a metronome (or a drum machine or stopwatch) is actually used. It is the time of the machine, or of soldiers on the march. 'Non-metronomic time' is also measured, but it subverts the regularity of the machine. It stretches time, it anticipates or delays sounds and so on. It is the time of human speech and movement, or of Billie Holiday singing a slow blues while 'surfing on the beat'. Clearly it would be possible to go further and distinguish several kinds of 'non-metronomic' time. But these two distinctions are enough to illustrate the idea of a system network.

What is the semiotic value of these distinctions? What can be expressed by their use? To answer this question, we need to put the system in its social, cultural and historical context. The 'high art' of the Middle Ages was the music of the Church. Its favoured mode of timing music, its favoured 'choice' from our 'system' was 'unmeasured time', because unmeasured time is a particularly apt signifier for 'eternity' – it literally negates time and goes 'on and on'. When, in northern Europe, cultural dominance moved away from the Church and gradually passed into the hands of the emerging merchant class, with its interest in secular art and science, measured time became the favoured mode of timing for the new 'high art' music, that is, for what we now refer to as 'classical music'. This 'choice', too, had its semiotic value. First of all it elevated a secular mode of timing to the status of 'high art', for 'measured time' had previous been 'low art' and associated with secular life, with dance and popular song. Second, it was an apt signifier for the values of calculability and quantification which were so important in both science and capitalist enterprise. The Church saw it as desecration. 'The new school occupies itself with the measured dividing of time and pesters every composition with semibreves and minims', declared the Pope, 'We hasten therefore to banish these methods, and put them to flight, far from the House of God. Let nothing in the authoritative music be changed' (quoted in Harman and Mellers, 1962: 123).

'Non-metronomic' time became more important as a result of the influence of Afro-American music. It too was seen as a form of 'desecration' because it subverted the discipline of the clock which had been such a key value of the industrial age, and it heralded a time of changing social relations and less severe affect control. Merriam (1964: 242–3) cites some of the reactions it met with in the 1920s:

> The composer, Sir Hamilton Harty, worried that future historians 'will see that in an age which considers itself enlightened we permit groups of jazz barbarians to debase and mutilate our history of classical music and listen with patience to impudent demands to justify its filthy desecration', and a Dr Reisner added that 'Jazz is a relic of barbarism. It tends to unseat reason and set passion free.'

All this will be discussed in more detail in Chapter 3. The point here is, the 'choices' offered by semiotic resources have *semiotic value*. They carry with them a potential for semiosis, for meaning-making. This is why certain 'choices' may become mandatory, conventional or traditional in certain contexts: the kinds of meaning they allow are mandatory, conventional or traditional in those contexts. In this case there is no real choice, and this should be remembered even when, from now on, I will no longer put the word 'choice' in inverted commas. Other contexts, on the other hand, do not, or not yet, operate on the basis of strict rules, conventions or traditions, and in such contexts there is choice. It is then again the semiotic value of a given choice which makes people recognize it as an apt choice for expressing what they want to say.

It is important to *contextualize* semiotic systems, to put them in their historical and social setting. Some semiotic disciplines have neglected this, especially linguistic ones. Even now that the idea of 'context' has gained an important place in some forms of linguistic theory (for example, Halliday, 1978; Martin, 1992), it is still not always fleshed out in sufficient cultural and historical detail (the 'discourse-historical' method of Ruth Wodak and her associates is an important exception, cf. Fairclough and Wodak, 1997). Other semiotic disciplines, on the other hand, for instance art-historical iconology, are so tied up with the specificities of individual artists and schools, that the idea of a common 'language of art' is never worked out systematically. I want to combine these two approaches and profit both from the systematicity of linguistics and from the focus on social, cultural and historical detail which characterizes semiotic disciplines such as art-historical iconology.

'Describing semiotic resources', the first of the three things semioticians do, will be the main focus of this book. I will discuss six major domains, sound perspective, sound time and rhythm, the interaction of 'voices' (for instance by taking turns or speaking, singing, playing or sounding together in different ways), melody, voice quality and timbre, and modality. All are aspects of sound common to speech, music and other sounds, and in each case I will attempt to investigate how they can be used to say and do things with sound, and to interpret how people actually say and do things with them. In this my overall focus will be on the semiotics of sound as it has developed in Western culture. Yet I will often draw on sounds from 'other cultures'. This is only an apparent contradiction. Once sounds from other cultures have been written up by Western anthropologists, or (for example, in the case of 'World Music'), distributed through Western distribution chains, they have been already transformed and incorporated into Western culture and its frame of reference. My references to 'other cultures' are to be taken as references to other cultures *as they have been incorporated in Western culture and its frame of reference.* I do not pretend to be able to look at them as a member of that culture might look at them in an intracultural context.

Explaining how semiotic resources are used

Describing semiotic resources provides the means for describing and explaining how these resources are actually used. In this book I do this, not as an end in itself, but only to try and show that my descriptions can be used in this way. Every chapter ends with an extended example in which I show how the resources I have described in that chapter are used in articulating a particular sound event, and what kinds of socially and culturally relevant ideas might arise from the analysis of its use of these resources. I have used a variety of sound events to try and demonstrate that my ideas can be used in a number of different areas of cultural studies, media studies and film studies. This includes extracts from popular songs, radio and television programmes, commercials and film soundtracks.

There is of course a degree of artificiality to the way I have done this, because in each case I analyse a sound event according to one articulatory parameter only, whereas every sound event in fact incorporates 'choices' from *all* the resources described in the book – it is the interaction between all these choices, the total 'mix', that matters in the end.

Also, when I try to formulate the semiotic values of the 'choices', I do not provide a *code*, with definite and fixed meanings, but a *meaning potential* which will be narrowed down and coloured in the given context. The importance of context cannot easily be overstated. The same sound can be used to mean one thing in one context and another in another context. Take the example of 'unmeasured time'. In a science fiction film it might be the time of a background track made up of densely shimmering electronic sounds, and come across as signifying a sinister primeval chaos. In church it might be part of a musical setting of the words 'peace on earth', sung by a choir of boy sopranos, and coming across as signifying something like 'eternal peace'. Yet both meanings derive from the same meaning potential. In both cases the idea of 'out of time', of 'eternity' is a definite part of the total meaning and effect.

Exploring how semiotic resources can be expanded

There is yet another contribution semioticians can make: they are particularly well placed to explore how semiotic resources can be *expanded*, so as to allow more options, more tools for the production and interpretation of meaningful action. In other words, semiotics can be a tool for design.

In the past this was a by-product of semiotics. Semiotics was supposed to be 'the science of signs' and science, in turn, is supposed to be about 'what is', not about 'what could be' or 'what might be'. Still, when you systematically describe 'what is' you find gaps, you find yourself wondering why certain options are not available and why certain things cannot be done in certain semiotic modes. Which is only one step away from *unlocking semiotic doors*, from asking: Could it be done? Does it have to be impossible? And if we are going to do it, how shall we do it?

Film-makers in Soviet Russia in the 1920s were faced with the task of bringing a propagandistic message to people speaking many different languages, and they wanted to do this through film, a medium which, they thought, could be understood universally – movies were still silent at the time. In other words, they wanted to convey ideas in a medium which so far had only been used to tell stories and provide entertainment, and which therefore had not developed any resources for conveying ideas. So they asked themselves: Why can't we use metaphors in film? Why has film been so literal-minded, while metaphors are perfectly possible in other semiotic modes? And they studied semiotic modes which could convey more abstract or generalized ideas, for instance hieroglyphics and Japanese Noh theatre (cf. Eisenstein, 1949, 1975). In times of rapid change and new communicative challenges, semiotics and design, theory and practice, can work hand in hand.

In this book I concentrate on inventorizing 'what is'. But I hope that my 'catalogue' will trigger ideas and be of some use to the people who are now pioneering the new discipline of sound design, whether in relation to the design of objects or in relation to music and the computer media, and I do believe that making theory-and-practice links of this kind, and learning to describe 'what could be' is the single most important job now facing semiotics.

Exercises and discussion points

Write a 'system network' (see Appendix) to describe the main choices available in choosing a doorbell, knocker or other device or method for announcing your presence in front of a closed door or gate, concentrating of course on the sound, rather than the look of the devices.

What is the semiotic value of these choices? You might approach answering this question by thinking about the kinds of places (shops, office, apartments, houses and so on) or people who tend to make a particular choice, or by asking people why they chose the 'doorbell' they chose, and what they think about various other kinds of 'doorbell' which they did not choose.

Does your 'doorbell' system integrate speech, music and other sounds? If so, why? If not, why not?

Is the 'doorbell' a historically and culturally specific phenomenon? If so, how and why did it arise? How was its function fulfilled in other times and places?

Can you think of a new kind of 'doorbell'? What kind of sound would it have? Who might want to buy it and why?

Chapter 2

Perspective

Perspective and social distance

Every semiotic mode can create relations between what is being presented or represented and the receiver, the reader or viewer or listener of the message. Images do it through two slightly different and complementary ways of spatial positioning, *size of frame and perspective*.

Sizes of frame such as the close shot, the medium shot, the long shot and so on create a certain *distance* between the viewer and the people, places and things represented in the picture. The relations expressed by these distances derive from our everyday experience, from the distances we keep from different kinds of people, places and things in everyday life. Edward Hall (for example, 1966: 110–20) has described this in relation to our interactions with people, but the same applies to interactions with places and things. According to Hall, we carry with us an invisible set of boundaries beyond which we allow only certain people to come. The zone of 'personal distance', the distance at which you can touch the other person, is for those who are close to us – if others enter it this will be experienced as an act of aggression. 'Social distance' is for more businesslike and formal interactions. At this distance we keep people 'at arm's length'. 'Public distance' is for larger and more formal group interactions. It is the distance we keep from people 'who are and are to remain strangers'. To all these distances correspond different fields of vision. At personal distance only head and shoulders are in sharp vision, and as it happens this corresponds to the close shot, as usually defined in the world of film and television. At social distance we see a little less than the whole figure, which roughly corresponds to the medium shot, and at public distance we see the whole figure with space around him or her, which corresponds to the long shot. In this way close shots position viewers in a relation of *imaginary* intimacy with what is represented, while medium shots create more formal kinds of imaginary relations, and long shots portray people as though they fall outside the viewer's social orbit, either because they are strangers or because they are much lower or higher in social status. In reality this may not be the case. The people we see in long shot may be people like us. But that is not the point. The point is that viewers are addressed *as though* these people are not part of their world.

Perspective creates horizontal and vertical angles. Vertical angles can make us literally and figuratively 'look up at' or 'down on' what is represented in a picture – or make us see it from the position of an equal, at eye-level. The vertical angle is therefore connected to imaginary *power* relations, be it the power of the viewer over what is represented, or the power of what is represented over the viewer. The glamorous role models in advertisements, for instance, tend to be shown from below, so that we look up at them, while the products are shown from above, so that they seem within reach of our hands, and under our control. Horizontal angles can be frontal, confronting us directly and unavoidably with what is represented, *involving* us with what is represented, or profile, making us see it from the sidelines, as it were, in a more detached way – and there are of course many in-between possibilities.

These concepts can be used to ask what *attitudes* a given image expresses towards what it represents. Who or what is positioned close to or far away from us, and why? Who or what are we made to look up to or down on, and why? Who or what are we brought face to face with, and who or what do we see in the more detached side-on way? The answers to these questions are usually found in the context. In a Dutch junior high school geography textbook two pictures appeared side by side as part of a double page headlined 'The Third World in Our Street'. The picture on the left showed three women with headscarves, in long shot, on the other side of the street, and turned away from the viewer. In other words, these women were portrayed as strangers, as people outside the social orbit of 'us', Dutch high school students. The picture on the right showed a young couple, a white girl and a black boy, sitting at an outdoor café table, the girl's hand on the boy's arm. They were shown in a much closer shot and from a more frontal angle. A different imaginary relation was suggested here. The couple was portrayed, if not quite as 'our' friends, sitting at the same table, then at least as 'people like us', frequenting the same café. This school book therefore addresses Dutch high school students as though they are all white and *autochtoon* ('native') as the Dutch say, even though in reality many of them are not white and/or *allochtoon* ('non-native').

Perspective and the picture frame were invented in the Renaissance, when it became important to make pictures mobile by detaching them from their environment (for example, the walls of the church), and to encode specific, individual points of view in them. That the Renaissance also invented *musical* perspective is less well known. In 1597 the Venetian composer Giovanni Gabrieli (1557–1612) wrote a piece called *Sonata pian'e forte*. The piece was not, as might be thought, written for a keyboard instrument, but for two groups of instruments, the one consisting of a viola and three trombones, the other consisting of a cornet and another three trombones. When they played together, the music was loud (*forte*), when either of the two sections played alone it was soft (*piano*). This was quite an invention. Even today many types of modern popular music do not use dynamics as a means of expression, and many digital keyboard instruments do not allow for it. Particular genres of music may have a characteristic overall loudness level, or perhaps use different levels for different types of song, but they do not make much use of dynamics within songs, as a means of expression. In the polyphonic music of Gabrieli's time, too, the instruments all played at the same level throughout. It was not until some 100 years after Gabrieli wrote his 'Sonata' that Bartolomeo Cristofori developed the first keyboard instrument that allowed dynamic variation, the *gravicembalo col piano e forte*, better known as the piano, and another 50 years before dynamic marks became common in classical music scores. For my piano teacher the composer's marks were not enough. As his annotations in Figure 2.1 show, he taught me to carefully *hierarchize* the three voices of Grieg's 'Arietta', with the melody loudest (*p-mf*), the sustained bass notes second loudest (*p*), and the undulating broken chords very soft (*ppp*). I will return to the significance of this later in the chapter.

Sound and image are distinctly different media. There is, for instance, no equivalent of the 'frontal' and 'side on' angle in sound. Sound is a wrap-around medium. But there are also similarities. Both can create relations between the subject they represent and the receiver they address, and in both this is related to distance, in two ways. The first is the way of *perspective*, which hierarchizes elements of what is represented by placing some in the foreground, some in the middle ground and some in the background, either literally, as in a landscape, or figuratively, as on the cover of a book, which may have letters in the

Figure 2.1 Annotated score of Edvard Grieg's 'Arietta' (*Lyrical Pieces*, Op. 12, No. 1)

foreground and a photograph in the background, or as in the soundtrack of a film, which may have dialogue in the foreground and music in the background. The second is the way of *social distance*, which creates relations of different degrees of formality between what is represented and the viewer or listener, such as intimacy (the very close shot, the whispered voice), informality (the close or medium close shot, the relaxed, casual voice), formality (the medium long or long shot, the louder, higher and tenser voice which 'projects' the message).

Perspective and the soundscape

Sound dubbing technicians in radio and film divide the soundtrack into three zones – close, middle and far distance. Murray Schafer (1977: 157) quotes the radio engineer A.E. Beeby:

> The three-stage plan divides the whole sound scene (called 'Scenic') into three main parts. These are 'the 'Immediate', the 'Support' and the 'Background'. The chief thing to bear in mind is that the 'Immediate' effect is to be *listened* to, while the 'Support' and the 'Background' effects are merely to be *heard*... The 'Support' effect refers to sounds taking place in the immediate vicinity which have a direct bearing on the subject in hand, leaving the 'Background' effect to its normal job of setting the

scene. Take for example the recording of a commentary at a fun-fair. The 'Immediate' effect would be the commentator's voice. Directly behind this would come the 'Support' effects of whichever item of fairground amusement he happened to be referring to, backed, to a slightly lesser degree, by the 'Background' effect of music and crowd noises.

Walter Murch, key sound technician on most of George Lucas' and Francis Ford Coppola's films, expresses the same idea (Weis and Belton, 1985: 357):

> The thing is to think of the sound in layers, to break it down in your mind into different planes. The character lives near the freeway, so you've got this generalized swash of traffic sound, but then occasionally a plane flies over: these are the long, atmospheric sounds. On top of these you then start to list the more specific elements: the door closes, the gunshots, the bats that live in the attic – who knows? Isolated moments. Once you've done that, once you can separate out the backgrounds from the foregrounds, and the foregrounds from the mid-grounds, then you go out and record... Since each of the layers is separate, you can still control them, and you can emphasize certain elements, and de-emphasize others the way an orchestrator might emphasize the strings versus the trombones, or the tympani versus the woodwinds.

The terms differ. Beeby has 'Immediate', 'Support' and 'Background', Murch 'foreground', 'mid-ground' and 'background'. Murray Schafer (1977: 157) uses yet another set of terms and definitions. He defines 'Figure' as 'the focus of interest, the sound 'signal', 'Ground' as the setting or context, the 'keynote sound', and 'Field' as 'the place where the observation takes place, the soundscape'. The ideas, however, are essentially the same. The 'three-stage plan' means dividing the sounds which are heard simultaneously into three groups and then *hierarchizing* these groups, treating some as more important than others. *What* is made important in this way will vary, but it will always be treated as a 'signal', as something the listener must attend to and/or react to and/or act upon, while background sounds are 'heard but not listened to', disattended, treated as something listeners do not need to react to or act upon. We will adopt Schafer's terms, but with the proviso that they do not only apply to places in the literal sense, but also to symbolic places or positions, for instance in music, and that sometimes there might be just two layers, a foreground and a background, instead of three.

Schafer also distinguishes between *hifi* and *lofi* soundscapes. Hifi soundscapes allow discrete sounds to be heard from a great distance because of the low ambient noise level. Think of a very quiet library, where you can hear someone pick up a pen or turn a page from twenty-five metres away. In lofi soundscapes, on the other hand, individual sounds get blurred, obscured in a tangle, a wall of sound which may be as close to the listener as the other side of the street. In such soundscapes perspective is lost and amplification becomes necessary if one wants to be heard. They have become so common in the contemporary urban environment that acoustic engineers deliberately create walls of 'masking noise', even in libraries, because they believe people find discrete noises distracting, or even disturbing:

> If a masking noise is uninterrupted and not too loud, and if it has no information content, it will become an acceptable background noise and will suppress other objectionable intruding noises, making them sound psychologically quieter (Doelle, 1972: 6).

As already mentioned, any sound may be Figure, Ground or Field. Even sounds which are clearly intended to stand out, such as bells, alarms and sirens, may become Ground, for instance in the big city. It all depends on the position of the listener. In my workroom the tapping of the keys of my computer keyboard and the hum of my computer are Figure, a car starting up outside and the sometimes raucous voices of the men drinking beer outside the pub across the road are Ground, while the 'swash of traffic noise' in the High Street, a little further away, is Field. If a car alarm went off outside it would simply mix in with the Ground and not form a 'signal' for me.

Anne Skelly, a student participating in my sound seminar at Macquarie University, drew my attention to the use of perspective in BBC sound effects collections. A track of a two-horse brake on a hard road, from the collection *Vanishing Sounds in Britain* had the rumble of the wheels and the creaking of the springs as Figure, the gallop of the horses as Ground, and rural sounds such as cows, roosters and church bells as Field. It thereby positioned the listener in that world of vanishing sounds as a kind of country squire, rather than, say, as a farmhand. In other words, what is Figure, what Ground and what Field, depends either on the listener's relation to the represented world (my real position as a writer working at home), or on the way such a relation has been *created* for the listener in sound mixes, musical compositions and so on (my imaginary position as a country squire in the world of yesteryear). I may then enjoy my vicarious ride in the horse-drawn carriage or distance myself from it, dismissing it as typical of the BBC's glorification of England's past, but in either case I will know that the track has been designed to make me identify with the country squire, even if I subsequently do something with it which it was not designed for.

In all this we should also remember that sound is dynamic: it can move us *towards* or *away from* a certain position, it can *change* our relation to what we hear. A Dutch television documentary showed a Christ statue on top of a hill, to the accompaniment of choral church music. The camera then tilted down to the busy expressway at the foot of the hill, and the roar of the expressway faded in to drown the music. This distanced the audience from the religious sentiments evoked earlier.

Here are two further examples. The first is a track from a French 'ambient sounds' recording by Eloisa Mathieu, *Ambient Sounds at Costa-Rica: Afternoon at the La Selva Biological Station.* Three distinct groups of sound can be heard. The Field is the sound of cicadas, hence a continuous 'broadband' sound, a kind of drone. The Ground is formed by a variety of birdcalls, hence by more discrete, individual sounds which nevertheless continue without noticeable gaps throughout the track. The Figure is the cry of a single howler monkey, more intermittent, and only entering after a while. The sleeve notes state that sound mixer Jean Roche 'had the task of mixing the recordings, to recreate atmospheres unique to each habitat'. But perhaps Roche has done more than that. Perhaps he also adapted the scene to a fit a design schema more typical of the modern city than of the tropical forest. To anyone who has heard the deafening noise of cicadas on a summer afternoon it is immediately clear that the level of the cicadas on this track is far too low relative to the other sounds. They are turned into a background, a Field, like the 'masking noise' in the library, or the traffic on the High Street nearby my work room. It is also clear that the aural point of view created by the mix is physically impossible. No one could simultaneously be so close to so many different birds that the sound of each and every one of them would dominate that of the cicadas to the extent it does on this track – and then be closer still to the howler monkey. This is not a recreation of the sounds of the forest. It recreates the three zones of the social world of the modern city dweller – the zone of the significant others whose utterances we must react to or act on (the monkey, closest to our own species uttering specific and rather dramatic howls), the wider support group or community, whose members are still individually recognizable but less closely known, and whose actions we perceive as predictable and repetitive (the birds – or the men in the pub across the road), and the mass of strangers, who all blur together in one indistinct whole (the cicadas – or the cars on the high street nearby).

In other words, we have here a typical 'schema' which can be realized in different types of sound environments and soundtracks. But there are schemas and then there are the things you can do with the schemas. In Hollywood films action and dialogue are usually in the foreground and the music which creates the mood and the emotional temperature of the scene in the background – a typical schema in which emotion must be 'held back' and remain subservient to the action. As the film composer Leonid Sabaneev put it:

> In general, music should understand that in the cinema it should nearly always remain in the background: it is, so to speak, a tonal figuration, the 'left hand' of the melody on the screen, and it is a bad business when this left hand begins to creep into the foreground and obscure the melody (quoted in Gorbman, 1987: 76).

But in a climactic scene from Jane Campion's *The Piano* (1993) the pattern is reversed. It is the scene in which Stewart (Sam Neill) chops off Ada's (Holly Hunter) finger with an axe. In this scene the *music* is Figure, more specifically, the musical theme which, throughout the film, has been associated with Ada's inner emotions of loss and longing – emotions which, as a mute, she cannot express in words. The sounds of the gushing rain and of Stewart's violent actions and screaming, on the other hand, recede into the background, as if her inner world has, for her, and hence also for us, the audience, more reality and more relevance than the outside events, however cruel and oppressive they may be (cf. Van Leeuwen, 1998 for a more elaborate analysis).

This is just one example of the way dynamics can hierarchize speech, music and other sounds, whether on film soundtracks or in the environment (think of the muzak and public announcements in railway stations, airports, supermarkets and so on), and whether in conventional or less conventional ways. In John Cage's piece *4' 33"* ('a piece in three movements during which no sounds are intentionally produced') the pianist sits at the piano for 4 minutes and 33 seconds without playing. All he or she has to do is to indicate the three movements by means of arm movements, and then to close the lid of the piano at the end of the piece. Thus the background (sniffs, coughs, the rustle of clothes, the traffic outside the concert hall) becomes foreground, and the audience must consciously attend to what they normally disattend: 'My favourite piece', Cage said, 'is the one we hear all the time if we are quiet' (Cage, 1968: 59).

Groups of people speaking (or chanting, or singing) simultaneously may also be perspectivally hierarchized. In Dutch Protestant churches, as no doubt in many other churches, the Lord's Prayer is spoken by the whole congregation in unison. But the minister's amplified voice projects the words carefully and stands out clearly against the unamplified voices of the members of the congregation, who mostly mumble. In many advertising jingles and pop songs the voice of the male solo singer is foregrounded while the female 'back-up' vocalists are re-recorded at a lower level, so that they will act as accompaniment, background, support.

In music, as in painting or photography, perspective can be used to depict landscapes. A beautiful example is Charles Ives' 'Housatonic at Stockbridge', part 3 of his *Three Places in New England*. The Housatonic is a river and Stockbridge is a town – Ives himself described the scene on which the music is based:

> A Sunday morning walk that Mrs Ives and I took near Stockbridge the summer after we were married. We walked in the meadows along the river and heard the distant singing from the church across the river. The mist had not entirely left the river bed and the colours, the running water, the banks and the trees were something one would always remember (quoted in Mellers, 1965: 45).

When the music begins, we hear the strings play very soft, misty chords and patterns that drift along irregularly and seemingly haphazardly, with a piano adding twinkles of light. After a while we hear a distant melody, a hymn melody, played on horn and lower strings. Gradually this melody gets louder, but the sounds of nature, instead of being overwhelmed by it, pushed into the background, also become louder and the two kinds of sound begin to clash, in a conflict between the unpredictable and ever-shifting rhythms of nature and the world of order and communal values expressed by the hymn – a conflict also expressed in many other American cultural products, for instance in Westerns.

But musical perspective can also be used in less pictorial ways, to represent, indeed, to enact and celebrate, key aspects of the social structure of modern life. When I practised Grieg's 'Arietta' according to the instructions of my teacher, I learnt an important lesson about the use of perspective in Western music: the melody must be Figure and the accompaniment Ground. The melody thus acts as the individual, asserting him or herself, and standing out from the background as an individual, while the accompanying voices act as the 'community' around the individual, serving and supporting him or her in more or less predictable and repetitive ways – through patterns whose modulations follow the lead of the melody. As Tagg (1990: 108) has pointed out, this is by no means a general feature of music:

> Few of us really comprehend the interaction and symbolism of the various voices in Renaissance polyphony or medieval motets. Even fewer of us comprehend Afro-Sudanic polyrhythms or the Tunisian nouba. This is because we use the dualism of melody-accompaniment as a common basis for constructing musical meaning, whether the creator's name be Haydn or AC/DC. The melody-accompaniment dualism has parallels in other European modes of thought; with the figure/ground of visual arts, the hero/story of novel writing, the particular/general of natural sciences, etc. These foreground/background relationships seem to make clear distinctions between the individual and the rest of social and natural reality.

Tagg has also interpreted the typical perspective of 'hard' rock 'n' roll along these lines. The modern urban environment, he says, is a lofi soundscape characterized by broadband noises such as car engines, air conditioning and refrigerator hums and so on. This kind of sound is rare in nature – only some insects (for instance cicadas!) produce it. Another one of its characteristics is the absence of reverberation and distance perception. In an empty street you would hear the sound of a car reverberate for a long time. But our streets are not empty, and by the time the softer sound of a car's reverberation could be heard it would already be drowned by the louder sounds of many other cars: 'by drowning discrete reverb in this way, the overall impression of acoustic space is that it is crowded and close' (Tagg, 1990: 111). Rock 'n' roll accompaniment is similarly characterized by broadband sound and reverb, so much so that the sound as a whole becomes 'crowded' and 'homogenized', with 'the long sounds filling up all the holes to create a wall of sound'. The singers or solo instruments must then scream and shout to be heard across the din (ibid.: 112).

The perspective of more recent dance music is quite different. 'Drum 'n' bass' tracks such as, for instance, Dual Fusion's 'Anything

Goes', Art of Noise's 'Something Always Happens', or Love Corporation's 'Give Me Some Love', reverse the traditional pattern of European
music. They have the melody (the individual) in the background and
the accompaniment (the group) in the foreground. The complex and
shifting rhythms of the drums and the bass constitute the Figure, the
drums with the breakbeat, a clean, clear and close rustle of snare drum
taps, sticks on closed hihats and so on, the bass at a more steady tempo,
with short, deep and dampened notes. Both drums and bass in fact
sound as though they are not played in an actual space at all, but inside
the head or the body, with all the sound absorbed inside. The Ground
is usually some kind of keyboard sound, an organ playing sustained
chords that alternate rather than progress, or a piano playing repetitive
patterns which shift from one phase into another every once in a while.
The Field, finally, is made up of intermittent snippets, natural and
'techno' sound effects, voices, fragments sampled from the history of
black music – all very soft, very distant, completely backgrounded by
the prominent rhythms in the foreground. When the track begins we
usually hear the Ground and/or the Field only – the Figure does not
enter until after a while. In other words, the intro gives us the *context* –
the immediate context, as represented by the keyboard playing repetitive patterns and/or chords (chords are simultaneously sounding
sounds, the 'community of sounds'); and the wider cultural context,
consisting of faint echoes from the real world (the ocean, all sorts of
human grunts and groans) and/or from the musical traditions of the
recent and not so recent past (jazz solo phrases, snippets of song and so
on). The drum and bass, the rhythm we can *dance* on, becomes the
foreground, the text. *Action*, tuning into the world, becoming part of
it, moving the body in tune with it, following a rhythm which seems to
come from within and yet joins us to others, as rhythms always do –
that is what is foregrounded here, not a melody, not a musical
statement sung or played by some individual soloist, some lone star
admired from afar and imaginarily identified with by individual fans
who must keep their bodies still in chairs.

We can now summarize:

1. The semiotic system of aural perspective divides simultaneous
   sounds into groups, and places these groups at different distances
   from the listener, so as to make the listener *relate* to them in
   different ways.
2. The sound may either be divided into three groups (positioned as
   Figure, Ground and Field) or two groups (positioned as Figure and

Ground or as Figure and Field). When there is no perspective, there is only a Figure. The significance of these positions can be glossed as follows:

Figure

If a sound or group of sounds is positioned as Figure, it is thereby treated as the most important sound, the sound which the listener must identify with, and/or react to and/or act upon.

Ground

If a sound or group of sounds is positioned as Ground, it is thereby treated as still part of the listener's social world, but only in a minor and less involved way. We are to treat it as we treat the familiar faces we see every day and the familiar places we move through every day, in other words, as a context we take for granted and only notice when it is not there any longer.

Field

If a sound or group of sounds is positioned as Field, it is thereby treated as existing, not in the listener's social, but in his or her physical world. We are to treat it as we would treat the people that crowd the streets through which we walk, or the trees that populate the forest past which we drive.

3. The meanings of Figure, Ground and Field, as described above, are made more specific by the context in which they occur, as the examples in this section have hopefully illustrated.

4. The system of perspective can be *played with* in different ways, for instance by *not* placing one sound in the foreground and the other in the background, as in 'Housatonic at Stockbridge', or by reversing conventional patterns, as in the case of *The Piano* and 'drum 'n' bass' music.

5. Perspective is *realized* by the relative loudness of the simultaneous sounds, regardless of whether this results from the levels of the sounds themselves, from the relative distance of the people or objects that produce them, or from the way a soundtrack is mixed.

6. Perspective has been a key system in the semiotics of sound, as historically evidenced by the increasing importance of dynamics in European music, and more recently by the increasing importance of the role of the sound mixer, first in radio and film, and now also and especially in many forms of popular music, where the mixer is considered as much of an artist as the musician, and may even perform live.

Sound and social distance

When we are close to people (literally and figuratively) we speak more
softly than when we have a more formal relation with them or speak to
them in the context of a more formal occasion. As distance grows, the
voice not only becomes louder, but also higher and sharper. The same
applies to musical instruments – think of the difference between the
blaring trumpets of a military brass band and the muted intimacy of
Miles Davis' trumpet.

In the beginning of this chapter we made a link between 'social
distance', as mapped out by Edward Hall, and 'size of frame'. Hall
relates social distance also to the voice (1964, 1966: 184–5). At 'very
close' range (3 in. to 6 in.), he says, the voice will be a soft whisper, and
the message 'top secret', for the ears of one (very special) person only.
At 'close' range (8 in. to 12 in.) it will be an audible whisper, still
sounding 'very confidential', still meant to be heard by one person
only. At 'near' range (12 in. to 20 in.) the voice will be soft indoors and
'full' outdoors, carrying an effect of confidentiality. At 'close neutral'
range (20 in. to 36 in.) we speak in a soft voice at low volume, about
'personal subject matter', while at 'far neutral' range (4.5 ft to 5 ft) we
speak in a 'full voice', about 'non-personal matters'. At 'public distance'
(5.5 ft to 8 ft) the voice is 'full with slight overloudness', conveying
'public information for others to hear'. When we speak 'across the
room' (8 ft to 20 ft) our voices will be loud, and we will no longer be
talking to one or two people, but to a whole group. When, finally, we
'stretch the limits of distance' (20 to 24 ft indoors, and up to 100 ft
outdoors) we are probably hailing people from a distance or shouting
farewells. Hall stresses that these distances are culturally specific. At 'far
neutral' range, for instance, 'the American voice is under that of the
Arab, the Spaniard, the South Asian Indian and the Russian, and
somewhat above that of the English upper class, the South East Asian
and the Japanese' (1964: 44).

So long as there is no selective amplification by means of
microphones or mixing, the scale running from the intimate whisper of
the lover to the hysterical scream of the demagogue remains
interlocked with the scale running from soft to loud. The only difference between the system of 'perspective' and the system of 'social
distance' is that social distance applies to single sounds, while perspective applies to simultaneous sounds and has relative rather than
absolute levels. But the technology of amplification and recording has

uncoupled the two, and allowed them to become independent semiotic variables. As a result a soft breathy whisper can now stand out clearly against loud drums or brass sections, and is no longer only for the ears of one very special person, but audible by thousands. Conversely, the screams of rock singers can be played at a comfortable level, to be heard by one person only, as he or she walks along with headphones on. Social distance is uncoupled from real distance, and from voice level, and now conveyed primarily by *voice quality*, on a scale running from the voiceless whisper, via the very soft and low voice in which we can hear the breath and other signs of the speaker's close presence, to the high, tense voice, and, ultimately, the rasping scream. The same scales could be constructed for musical instruments and non-musical sounds such as engines – compare the put-put of a boat to the screaming racing car or jet. The close miking of voices and instruments, finally, can further enhance closeness, while adding reverb can enhance a sense of space and distance.

In music this led to new styles of singing which soon made earlier music-hall and vaudeville styles seem quaint and antiquated. The 'crooning' style of Bing Crosby pioneered this, suggesting the 'intimate, personal relationship with fans that worked best for domestic listeners' (Frith, 1988: 19). The word 'suggest' is crucial – amplification allows singers to address us *as though* they have a personal relationship with us, even though they are in reality as distant from us as can be. The close relationship is imaginary. The opposite is also possible, bringing the public world into the private world, for instance by listening to the rasping voices of 'hard rock' singers in the intimacy of our living rooms. These voices are not only hard and loud but also high, on average an octave above the normal speaking level of the singers. As Tagg (1990: 112) has described it, they shout and scream to be heard over the noise of the city, in which:

> shouting to a friend on the other side of the street becomes impossible because there is a wall of sound between the two of you. The rock singer must therefore raise the volume, pitch and sharpness/roughness of timbre of his or her voice to be heard, just as the instrumental soloists must 'cut' and 'bang' their way through the ambient sound of the environment.

In Skylab's drum 'n' bass track 'The Trip', a voice sings in whispers, almost next to our ear, while we hear the much louder drums *at the same level*, and equally closely miked. It is a physically impossible aural vantage point. Perhaps the drums, with their exceptionally close presence and lack of reverb, must be heard as being 'in our head' rather than out there in space, and the female singer as whispering words in our ears – 'I start to dream', 'Close your eyes': on much of the track there is no other sound, as if the rest of the world has ceased to exist.

Not only singers and instrumentalists, also speakers began to exploit this new tool for engineering imaginary social relations. Politicians became aware of it in the 1930s, when Roosevelt initiated his 'fireside chats', in which he replaced oratory with 'calm, measured statements' and addressed his audience 'as though he were actually sitting on the front porch or in the parlour with them' (Barnouw, 1968: 8). In the same period the BBC talks department encouraged radio speakers to speak more casually and adopt a low-key, conversational manner (Cardiff, 1981), and Goebbels urged German radio announcers to use local dialects and speak more informally and colloquially, to 'sound like the listener's best friend', as he put it (quoted in Leitner, 1980). By today's standards the commentators and radio speakers of that period were still barking at their audiences, but the idea had taken hold, even if its full fruition had to wait till the breakthrough of television, in the early 1960s.

Radio and television speakers change their voice (and microphone distance) according to the genre of the broadcast or the type of station for which they work (Van Leeuwen, 1982, 1984, 1992). Newsreading, for instance, is a relatively formal genre and as a result most newsreaders' voices become higher and tenser when they read the news. The disc jockeys of some commercial radio stations seek to 'energize' the listeners through the way they speak. According to the breakfast announcer of a Top 40 station in Sydney, Australia:

> You've got to sound 'up', but there's a thin line between that and sounding a bit mindless, spewing out those words, you know, spilling them out and screaming… Your sound has got to be a 'hey let's get it happening' sort of approach, like 'we're here having a good time' (quoted in Van Leeuwen, 1992: 238).

The announcers of a Sydney 'easy listening' station, on the other hand, aimed at a 'relaxed', 'muted' and 'gentle' sound, and used closely miked, soft, low and breathy voices. The same contrasts can be observed between the voices in commercials – think of the difference between the excited pitch of the hard-sell second-hand car salesman and the seductive breathy whisper of the voice in a perfume ad.

We can now summarize:

1. The sound of the voice is an important factor in the system of social distance, alongside other factors such as potential for touch and field of vision. In the age of amplification and recording it becomes an independent semiotic system, the system of (aural) social distance, able to create imaginary social relations between what is presented or represented by a sound and the listener. These distances form a continuum, but the significance of the key points on the scale can be described as follows:

Intimate distance
The relation between the sound and the listener is one of real or imaginary *intimacy* – what is presented or represented by the sound is regarded as one would regard someone with whom one is intimate. In speech, intimate distance is realized by whispering or maximally soft voices.

Personal distance
The relation between the sound and the listener is a real or imaginary *personal* relation – what is presented or represented by the sound is regarded as one would regard a friend with whom one can discuss highly personal matters. In speech it is realized by a soft, relaxed voice at low pitch and volume.

Informal distance
The relation between the sound and the listener is a real or imaginary *informal* relation – what is presented or represented by the sound is regarded as one would regard someone with whom one has a businesslike but nevertheless informal encounter. In speech it is realized by a full voice at somewhat higher pitch and volume.

Formal distance
The relation between the sound and the listener is a real or imaginary *formal* relation – what is presented or represented by the sound is regarded as one would regard people to whom one speaks in a formal or public context. In speech it is realized by an overloud, higher and tenser, 'projected' voice.

Public distance
The relation between the sound and the listener 'stretches the limits' and is regarded as one would regard someone who can only just be reached when one shouts at the top of one's voice – hence it is realized by the maximally loud sound.

2. These relations can also extend to places and things. We can, for instance, have an intimate relationship with the tools we use everyday (a handbag, a computer, a car) and a more formal relationship with the machine in the office we pass every day but never touch. Water can sound close enough to touch (softly lapping water, the rustle of a small stream), or far away (the surf, the roar of a waterfall). The saxophone of Archie Shepp can address us in a hoarse whisper, or sound like a foghorn in the mist.

3. The microphone and the mixing panel have turned perspective and social distance into independent variables, allowing the close and the distant, the personal and the impersonal, the formal and the informal, the private and the public, to be mixed in various ways and to various degrees.

4. Recording techniques can aid the perception of social distance. Close miking enhances a sense of close presence to the source of the sound, and adding reverb enhances a sense of space and distance.

Immersion

The opposite of perspective is immersion, wrap-around sound. Low frequency sounds (bass) are especially important here. They carry further (think of the foghorn) and fill spaces more completely. They are also harder to tie to a particular spot and seem to come from everywhere at once.

Evergreen forests produce this kind of perspective and so do medieval churches. The amplification of the low frequencies and the long reverberation time of these places submerge the listener in sound. Perspective and hierarchization disappear. The individual no longer feels separate from the crowd, but becomes fully integrated and immersed in the environment:

> The sound in Norman and Gothic churches, surrounding the audience, strengthens the link between the individual and the community. The loss of high frequencies and the resulting impossibility of localising the sound makes the believer part of a world of sound. He does not face the sound in enjoyment – he is wrapped up by it (Blaukopf, 1960: 180).

Interestingly, this is also the condition of the lofi urban environment which we discussed earlier – provided you give up trying to be heard above the noise and allow yourself to swim with the stream, as happens, perhaps, in the modern dance club:

> Low frequency sounds seek blend and diffusion rather than clarity and focus. The listener is not an audience which concentrates but is at the centre of the sound, massaged by it, flooded by it. Such listening conditions are those of a classless society, a society seeking unification and integrity (Schafer, 1977: 118).

Today this can also be achieved individually. The car, with speakers in every corner, can become a cocoon of booming bass sounds, literally vibrating the listener, and the walkman can achieve what Jane Campion achieved in the scene from *The Piano* I discussed earlier, the foregrounding of the inner emotions and the backgrounding of the sounds of the world around us. In Nada Yoga the same kind of effect is strived for, making the body vibrate with the sound of the mantra, and removing yourself from your immediate environment, in an attempt to find inner integrity.

Just as visual perspective has been challenged since the beginning of the twentieth century, first by new forms of modern art such as cubism and the collage, later by mass media forms such as magazine layout and television graphics, so aural perspective, too, has been challenged, by avant-garde composers like Xenakis, but, above all, by new forms and technologies of listening which aim at immersion and participation, rather than at concentrated listening and imaginary identification.

An example: perspective and social distance in the radio play

The distinctions introduced in this chapter can be summarized in the form of a 'system network' (Figure 2.2). The assumption is that any sound must relate to the listener in one of the ways mapped out in the network, in other words, that for any sound a 'choice' must have been made from the resources of the systems of perspective and social distance. 'Choice' does not mean 'intentional choice'. The 'choice' *may* be intentional, but it may also result from a convention followed unthinkingly, a habit acquired unreflectively, or an unconscious impulse. It depends on the context. The square brackets indicate 'either/or choice', for instance: ' if the perspective is dynamic, the proximity of the sound must either increase or decrease'. The curly brackets indicate 'simultaneous choice', for instance 'any sound must either be immersive or perspectival *and* have some kind of social distance'. The double-headed vertical arrow indicates a 'graded choice', a sliding scale for instance, 'to choose a social distance, choose some point on the scale that runs from intimate to public'.

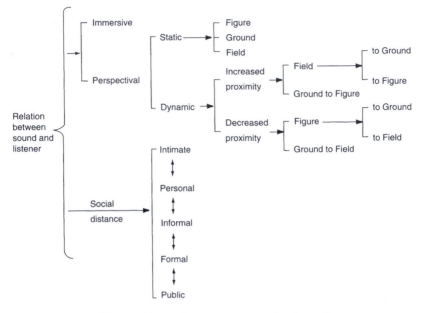

Figure 2.2   A system network of aural
perspective and social distance

The following extract shows the system in use in the analysis of an extract from *Wild Honey*, an Australian radio play, written and produced by Kaye Mortley for the ABC (Australian Broadcasting Commission) in 1992. An analysis of this kind can of course be laid out in many other ways – the main point is that all the sounds in the mix must be itemized separately so as to link them clearly to the analysis of their perspectival position and social distance in the right-hand column.

Even such a short piece of analysis already brings out interesting patterns. The excerpt illustrates, for example, how speech, sound and music are used in the play. Most of the action is conveyed by dialogue, or rather, monologue. Music is used at the beginning of the scene, to set the stage and convey the location. Sounds 'illustrate' the verbally told story, and also, because of their closeness, convey a sense of physical presence, of 'now-happening', that third-person, past-tense narrative cannot, by itself, provide. Goffman sees these uses of sound

	Perspective	Social Distance
1. The sound of a DIDGERIDOO fades in.	Figure	Close
2. The DIDGERIDOO fades down again as	Figure to Ground	Close
3. The voice of a YOUNG ABORIGINAL WOMAN enters:	Figure	Close
Many wet seasons ago, I went with my father to get sugarbag, wild honey. He used to climb on top of the trees and look for the bees going into or coming out of the cutting where the sugarbag is. He would make a cradle out of paperbark to get the honey syrup. We tasted the honey syrup which is like sugar. It is too strong and sour when you drink it straight. You have to drink it with water dew.		
4. The sound of the didgeridoo now fades down as	Ground to Field	Close
the buzzing sound of BEES fades up	to Figure	Close
and the sound of VOICES SPEAKING AN ABORIGINAL LANGUAGE also fades up	to Ground	Far
5. The buzzing of the bees now fades down and the Aboriginal voices fade out as	Figure to Field	Close
A WHITE FEMALE VOICE enters:	Figure	Mid
The ladies said 'Come hunting. Hunting for the wild honey. Tomorrow'.		
6. As the voice continues FOOTSTEPS fade up	to Ground	Close
'Follow us', they called, 'Come hunting for sugarbag.'		
7. And the footsteps continue after the voice stops	to Figure	Close

and music as typical of radio drama generally. Music, he says (1974: 147) often serves as a kind of 'bridge'. It then is:

> a signal that the scene is changing, music being to radio drama what curtain drops are to staged drama. Such music does not fit *into* a scene but fits *between* scenes, connecting one whole episode with another.

The use of sound, he says (ibid.: 145–6), often follows the convention that:

> spatial information is introduced at the beginning of a scene, then faded down or eliminated entirely. Unlike the everyday experience of reverberation in a kitchen, we cannot disattend reverberation running under the dialogue on radio. It is therefore introduced in the first few lines and faded out. The same rule operates for spatial transitions. Moving the scene from the country to the city might be suggested by

> *Man*: I'll bet Joe and Doris aren't so hot out there in the country. (Music fades in, SFX (sound effects) birds chirping, fade out music, birds chirping runs under dialogue)
> *Joe*: Well, Doris, this country weather sure is pleasant.

Within three lines the birds will be faded out, though they might return just before the transition back to the city.

> Similarly, there is the convention of allowing one or two low sounds to stand for what would ordinarily be the stream of accompanying sound... The audience is not upset by listening in on a world in which many sounds are not sounded and a few are made to stand out momentarily, yet if these conditions suddenly appeared in the offstage world, consternation would abound.

Or take the contrast between the English-speaking voices and the voices speaking an Aboriginal language. Not only do the Aboriginal voices all speak at the same time, they are also positioned at some distance from the listener. The English-speaking voices, on the other hand, speak in neat turns and are positioned much closer to the listener. Of the two, the voice of the 'young Aboriginal woman', telling the 'subjective' first-person story, the childhood memory, is closest and most intimate. The voice of the white female narrator, telling the 'objective' third-person story, sounds more formal, and conveys something of the authority of the omniscient narrator. So how is the listener positioned in relation to this story? As a white middle-class Australian woman who is not Aboriginal but nevertheless imagines a kind of kinship between her experience and that of an Aboriginal girl? Or imagines her childhood self to have been in some way like that of an Aboriginal girl? As someone who interprets being like an Aboriginal girl as an *individual* experience of being close to nature – to the bees, the wild honey, the footsteps in the long grass – but who feels less close to, and more excluded from, the Aboriginal languages and communities which remain part of that same landscape?

Exercises and discussion points

1. Record the sound of two contrasting environments or events (for instance a street market and a weekday church interior, or a whispered conversation in a quiet bar and a conversation at a party with loud music). Transcribe a section from each recording, using the 'script' format introduced in this chapter (see Appendix), and analyse the perspectival patterns of the two excerpts.

   How do these perspectival patterns reflect the 'point of view' ('point of hearing', would be more apt) from which you made the recordings? What other 'points of hearing' might you have chosen, and how would they have changed the perspectival patterns?

2. Choose a piece of contemporary music which makes important use of perspective and social distance. Transcribe its beginning, using the 'script' format introduced in this chapter and describing the sounds in words (for example, 'soft tinkling piano chords', 'a repetitive bass pattern'). Then analyse how perspective and social distance are used in the performance and recording.

   How would you interpret this use of perspective and social distance?

3. Using the script format introduced in this chapter, write the script for a sound recording based on the following scene from 'Children on a Country Road', a short story by Franz Kafka (1978: 89). Indicate (a) which sounds you would make Figure, which Ground and which Field, and (b) what social distances you would choose for the individual sounds.

The moon was already some way up in the sky, in its light a mail-coach drove past. A small wind began to blow everywhere, even in the ditch one could feel it, and near by the forest began to rustle. Then one was no longer so anxious to be alone.

'Where are you?' 'Come here!' 'All together!' 'What are you hiding for, drop your nonsense!' 'Don't you know the mail's gone past already?' 'Not already?' 'Of course, it went past while you were sleeping.' 'I wasn't sleeping. What an idea!' 'Oh shut up, you're still half asleep.' 'But I wasn't.' 'Come on!'

We ran bunched more closely together, many of us linked hands, one's head could not be held high enough, for now the way was downhill. Someone whooped an Indian war-cry, our legs galloped us as never before, the wind lifted our hips as we sprang. Nothing could have checked us; we were in such full stride that even in overtaking others we could fold our arms and look quietly around us.

At the bridge over the brook we came to a stop; those who had overrun it came back. The water below lapped against stones and roots as if it were not already late evening. There was no reason why one of us should not jump on to the parapet of the bridge.

From behind clumps of trees in the distance a railway train came past, all the carriages were lit up, the window-panes were certainly let down. One of us began to sing a popular catch, but we felt like singing. We sang much faster than the train was going, we waved our arms because our voices were not enough, our voices rushed together in an avalanche of sound that did us good. When one joins in song with others it is like being drawn on by a fish-hook.

Try to explain the reasons for your choice of perspectival pattern and social distances.

Chapter 3

Time

The rule of the clock and the rule of the metronome

In the previous chapter I avoided the word 'meaning' and instead used the phrase 'what is presented or represented by the sound'. This distinction derives from the work of Martinec (1996). I use it here to indicate that sounds can both present their source (identify who or what their source *is* and *does*), and convey what it *means* to be that source, or to be like that source. The linguist J.R. Firth (1957: 225) wrote: 'Surely it is part of the meaning of an American to sound like one.' In other words, by 'sounding American', Americans present themselves as Americans to others, whether these others are also American or not, *and* wittingly or unwittingly signify what 'America' stands for in the eyes of those others) – what this is will of course depend on the context, for example, on whether the 'others' are also American or not, and if not, on what they know about Americans and how they feel about them. In other cases *non*-Americans can select features of American English to *represent* Americans or 'American-ness' – British actors playing an American, for instance; or the disc jockeys of Australian commercial radio stations at the time when American-style radio music formats were first introduced in Australia (Sussex, 1977); or young Swedish musicians trying to sound like Elvis Presley (Lilliestam, 1990).

Another example. If a church minister chants a blessing and the congregation responds with a chanted 'Amen', minister and congregation *enact* the social relation that helps organize what goes on in a church service. Call–response patterns alternate a line sung by a soloist, the leader of the group, and a line sung by a chorus, the 'followers'. In church the minister is the leader and the members of the congregation the followers. By using the call–response pattern they not only present this relationship, but also represent it, to each other, and

35

to outsiders who are not participating in it, but observe and interpret it. They 'dramatize' their relation, as Goffman would have it (1959). Advertising jingles also make use of call and response patterns, usually with a male voice as the leader and a choir of female voices as the followers. The leader then represents the seductive salesman or role model, and the choir members repeat the brand name or slogan in a catchy chorus, to represent the customers who are seduced by the salesman or follow the lead of the role model. As always when there is a lag between the moment of articulation and the moment of the actual exchange of meaning, the 'sender' of the message cannot present himself in person to the 'receiver' (or to bystanders) and must therefore represent both himself and his audience *in* the message. The sound of 'Americanness' and the call and response pattern are hence available as, on the one hand, marks of identity or modes of enacting a relation, and on the other hand as signifiers for *representing* such identities or relations. The same applies to natural sounds. The roar of a waterfall or the whine of an engine can disclose the presence of an actual waterfall or engine nearby, but may also be used to signify 'waterfall' or 'engine' in the absence of an actual waterfall or engine, for instance in a radio play.

Musical time, similarly, can be the time that regulates our activities, or *represent* the characteristics of that time and, being musical, make us rhythmically tune into and affectively identify with those characteristics. To appreciate this, we need to consider time, not as a phenomenon of nature, but as a human activity, as the result of the activity of tim*ing*. As Norbert Elias (1992: 43) put it:

> The reifying character of the substantival form 'time' disguises the instru-
> mental character of the activity of timing. It obscures the fact that the
> activity of timing, e.g. by looking at one's watch, has the function of
> relating to each other the positions of events on the successive order of two
> or more change continua.

These 'change continua' can be natural (the cycles of days and nights, moons, seasons) or artificial, manufactured by human enterprise, as in the case of the movements of the hands of the clock.

The clock was pioneered in Benedictine monasteries. In the seventh century Pope Sabinianus had decreed that Benedictine monks should pray seven times every twenty-four hours (the 'canonical hours'). Some means of keeping time became necessary. The water-clock, already known to ancient Rome, was reintroduced. Around 1345 the division of the hour into minutes and seconds became common. In 1370 the first mechanical clock was built. In Lewis Mumford's words (1934: 13):

> Benedictine rule gave human enterprise the regular collective beat and rhythm of the machine; for the clock is not merely a means of keeping track of the hours, but of synchronizing the actions of men.

Outside the monastery, clocks were initially an object of cultural fascination. There were elaborate clocks in the churches and on the market squares of the towns, showing not only time but also the movements of the moon and the planets. And there were clocks in the houses of the new merchant class, often decorated with mannikins performing stiff, robotic movements in perfect synchrony with mechanical time. In the Industrial Revolution the clock became a major tool for the control, first of labour, then also of other human activities. In industries such as weaving, the guilds which had traditionally controlled labour had had to increasingly rely on merchants, as they alone could supply the capital and raw materials needed, or provide insight into what the market demanded. The merchants resented the guilds' control over labour and started to 'farm out' work, which they could do because the guilds' rule did not extend to the country. But that was unsatisfactory too, as the rural workers worked more or less when they pleased and were difficult to discipline. Thus the factory was conceived, where workers could be under the watchful eye of an overseer, and where constant attendance and punctuality could be enforced. Soon the discipline of the clock would extend to other major social institutions, the school, the hospital, the prison and so on and punctuality would become a key virtue of bourgeois society. As Mumford put it (1934: 14):

> Time-keeping passed into time-serving and time-accounting and time rationing. As this took place, Eternity ceased gradually to serve as the measure and focus of human actions.

I am telling this story because the same thing also happened in music. In the high music of the Middle Ages, the music of the Church, the 'eternal' time of plainchant had dominated. Now musical time, too, began to be divided and measured. The bar line was introduced, and the concomitant subordination of all the voices and instruments playing a piece of music to the same metronomically regular beat. No wonder that in the fourteenth century Pope John XXI was worried, and wrote:

> Certain disciples of the new school, much occupying themselves with the measured dividing of time, display their method in notes which are new to us, preferring to devise ways of their own rather than to continue singing in the old manner; the music, therefore, of the divine offices is now performed with semibreves and minims, and with these notes of small value every composition is pestered... We now hasten therefore to banish these methods... and to put them to flight more effectually than heretofore, far from the house of God. And if any be disobedient, let him... be punished by a suspension from office of eight days (quoted in Harman and Mellers, 1962: 122–3).

But he was fighting a rearguard action. Western music was to become overwhelmingly dominated by the principle of a regular, unvarying, machine-like beat, to which all voices and instruments had to submit.

In time music itself would take on the function of timing human activity, as in the case of using Muzak to 'accompany' repetitive work (cf. Tagg, 1984), a thoroughly modern version of the work song. A worker may for instance have to spend 90 minutes on a repetitive task that takes 20 seconds to perform. These 90 minutes will be divided into six 15-minute slots, in which 15-minute segments of music alternate with 15 minutes without music. The music segments themselves consist of five 3-minute tracks, each of which therefore accommodates nine of the repetitive operations. The segments also contain 'a rising stimulus which provides a sense of forward movement', to prevent 'boredom or monotony or fatigue' (Muzak Corporation publication, quoted in Schafer, 1977: 97). This is of course quite a different thing from the way workers may themselves rhythmically coordinate their actions by means of work songs, as happens in many societies (cf. Merriam, 1964).

In other cases characteristic *qualities* of Western time are musically represented. According to Tagg (1984: 32), the regular beat of 'disco' music thus 'represents a high degree of affective acceptance of and identification with clock time, digitally exact rhythm and hence with the system in which this time sense dominates'. We will return to this subject later. For the moment, the main point is that the way a given society handles musical time can present or represent the way that society handles the timing of social activities generally, in other words, its 'order of time'. This will apply also to non-musical sound. Many modes of contemporary media speech (newsreading speech, for example) must be timed very precisely to fit in short slots, and as a result have become much more regular in rhythm and tempo than ordinary conversational speech (Van Leeuwen, 1984). As for other kinds of sound, the industrial age has contributed a plethora of new machine rhythms, from the sewing machine to the steam engine, and it is only now, in the electronic age, that these are increasingly replaced by the much softer hums and buzzes of electronics.

The anatomy of measured time

Measured time divides the flow of time into measures which are of equal duration and which are marked off by a regularly occurring explicit pulse ('accent', 'stress', 'beat') which comes on the first syllable or note or other sound of each measure and is made more prominent than the surrounding sounds by means of increased loudness, pitch or duration, or some combination of some or all of these (cf. Meyer, 1956: 102ff.; Van Leeuwen, 1982, 1992). Tempo results from the duration of the measures. On metronomes the slowest tempo is 40 pulses per minute, the fastest 208 pulses per minute. An average speed would therefore be about 90 pulses per minute. This range corresponds closely to that of the heartbeat, which ranges from 50 beats per minute to just over 200 beats per minute. Ninety beats per minute is the pulse rate of an average male adult walking at an easy pace – the musical term *andante* comes from the Italian word *andare*, 'walking'. According to Tagg (1984: 22) 'we should therefore expect tempo in music to be an important parameter in determining the human/biological aspect of an affective relationship to time'.

In the example below, two lines of dialogue from Hitchcock's *North by Northwest* (1959), the measures are separated by oblique strokes and the pulses emboldened and italicized. The measures with three syllables are spoken faster to make sure they will be equally long as the ones with two syllables:

THORNHILL: But/ *where* will I/ *find* you/ -
EVE: I've/ *got* to/ *pick* up my/ *bags* now//

Pulse plays an important role in making (and receiving) meaning, because it carries the key information of each measure: 'where' and 'find' in Thornhill's line, for instance, and 'got', 'pick' and 'bag' in Eve

Kendall's line. If you just heard these syllables you might still get the message, if you just heard 'I've to up my now' you would not. The non-pulse syllables flesh out the information in more or less predictable ways, and help construct the melody line that conveys its emotional temperature.

Figure 3.1 gives a musical example, the opening of the first movement of Tchaikovsky's Fifth Symphony. The pulses (indicated by arrows) fall on the main notes, the notes that are most indispensable for getting the musical message across. The first falls on a minor third, the note that causes the music to sound 'minor', or 'sad'. The second pulse moves up by one step, trying to 'rise above it', but the third falls back to the minor third again: the attempt to lift the music out of the gloom has failed.

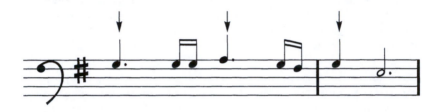

Figure 3.1   First two bars of Tchaikovsky's Fifth Symphony

The example below attempts to represent an (intentional and communicative) sound effect, repeated knocks on a door. There are two silent measures: the timing of the wait between the knocks continues the regular beat (ONE two three/ONE two three) set up by the knocking, and the pulses in these measures are felt rather than heard.

/*knock* knock knock/ (*silent pulse*) – – / (*silent pulse*) – – / *knock* knock knock/

It is also possible to integrate sound effects and speech in this way ('creak' is meant to stand for the creaking of a door):

/*knock* knock knock/ (*silent pulse*) – – /'*Yes*' – – / (*silent pulse*) – – / *creak* – – //

The pulses again carry the key information – and that includes the silent pulses: the duration of the wait between successive knocks can carry a lot of information.

Measured time also groups measures (up to seven) into *phrases*. These are also known as breath groups, as their length is similar to that of the cycle of breathing, on average 9 to 25 syllables, or 3 to 5 seconds (longer during sleep, when it is 6 to 8 seconds, which, incidentally, is also the average rhythm of the surf). Between phrases there is usually a short pause, or a drawing out of the last syllable or note or other sound, or perhaps a change of tempo – some kind of audible break or change to indicate the 'boundary' (Van Leeuwen, 1982, 1992). The reason why measures are grouped together in this way is to indicate that they are meant to be understood as belonging together in some way or other, that they form a musical statement, or a move in the ongoing speech act, or a unit of action. The boundaries between them may be slight, allowing the phrases to flow together without much interruption, or more emphatic, causing the sound to be more parcelled up, something which happens in didactic speech, but also, for instance, in hesitant speech. A phrase may begin with a short, incomplete measure, known as the 'anacrusis'. One of the pulses, usually the last one, will be stronger than the others, and carry the crux of the message – for instance the note that signals the failure to 'rise above it' in Figure 3.1. In the example below, three lines of dialogue from Howard Hawks' *The Big Sleep* (1947), the phrases are enclosed in square brackets, the boundaries indicated by a double oblique stroke, and the main pulse by capitals:

CARMEN: [You're/ *not* very/ *TALL*//] [*ARE* you//]
MARLOWE: [Yeah/ *WELL* I er//] [I/ *TRY* to/ *be*//]
CARMEN: [Not/ *BAD* looking//] [though you/*pro*bably/ *KNOW* it//]

To explain how the phrasing delimits the 'moves in the ongoing speech act', a little background is needed. Marlowe (Humphrey Bogart) has been called to the house of General Sternwood (Charles Waldron) to help him deal with a case of blackmail involving his youngest daughter Carmen. As he waits in the hall to be shown in, Carmen (Martha Vickers) confronts him in a flirtatious manner. Now Carmen could have pronounced the whole first line as one phrase, connecting her provocative remark and the tag question. But she does not. She pauses for effect, and then provokes a little more. And Marlowe, in his reply, makes an incomplete phrase, a hesitation, into a separate move in the speech act, thus conveying more clearly that he is momentarily taken aback, for once at a loss for words.

For a musical example, think of the way jazz musicians transform the phrasing of the well-known 'standards' they often choose to improvise on. The saxophonist Archie Shepp, for instance, transforms the phrasing of the 'bridge' (middle section) of the Fats Waller ballad 'Ain't Misbehavin'' in this way on *Black Ballads* (Timeless Records, 1992). In most renditions it has four phrases, clearly marked apart by the pauses at the beginning of each phrase. The four phrases are identical, except for the last one, in which the top note moves up by a half tone, from a 'dark' minor third interval to a 'brighter' major third interval. Shepp retains only three phrases. The first two lose their up and down, 'saw-tooth' shape and are turned into plaintive cries with a long-drawn-out first note, the last is an extended series of short, almost stuttering notes which then finally and triumphantly move up by a half tone to the brighter tonal zone and a long-drawn-out note. A completely different phrasing – and a completely different musical statement.

To summarize:

1. Measured time divides the stream of sound into *measures* of equal duration. *Tempo* results from the duration of these measures.
2. Each measure begins with a *pulse*, a sound which is 'stressed', made more prominent by means of loudness, pitch, relative duration or some combination of these. The pulses mark the sounds (syllables, tones and so on) which carry the greatest information value in the given context.
3. Measures are grouped together in *phrases* of up to seven measures. The phrases are marked off from each other by *boundaries*, breaks or changes in the regular rhythm of the pulses. Boundaries may be unobtrusive or strongly marked. The phrases delimit units of interaction – units of action, or moves in the ongoing speech act or musical act.
4. Each phrase has a key pulse, the *main pulse*. This main pulse is the culmination of the 'message' of the phrase.

Degrees of regularity: speech

Like all human action, speech has rhythm, a regular pulse. In conversation speakers even attune to each other's rhythm, so that the same pulse underlies the speech (and gestures) of both (cf. Hall, 1983: 140–1). In other respects, however, conversational speech is less regular than for instance most forms of Western music:

1. The number of syllables per measure varies within each phrase. If there are many syllables in a measure, they will be pronounced rapidly, squashed together, if there is only one it will be drawn out. This ensures that the measures will be of equal duration and the pulses evenly spaced, or at least *perceived* as evenly spaced, because psychologists have discovered that human perception regularizes what 'objectively' (according to instrumental measurements) is not completely regular (Lehiste, 1973).
2. The number of measures per phrase will also vary from phrase to phrase. Some phrases consist of just one measure of one syllable, for example

   [*AH*//]

Others, like the commercial radio traffic announcement below, have measures of up to six or even seven syllables, and phrases of up to seven, or even eight measures. The announcer in the example is the one I quoted before, and here he is rushing the syllables as fast as he can, literally 'spewing out those words', in an attempt, perhaps, to create a style to fit the genre of the traffic announcement, a kind of 'rush hour speech':

> [and/ *that* accident on the / *BRIDGE*//] [is/ *still* causing/ *BIG* problems this/ *mor*ning//] [the/ DMR/ *tow* trucks are having/ *BIG* trouble/ *get*ting to the/ *ac*cident near/ *Mil*son's Point Station//] [so if you/ *see 'em/ co*ming/ *let* 'em/ *THROUGH*//] (quoted in Van Leeuwen, 1992: 246).

In radio speech genres the tempo remains more or less constant, except for special moments of (feigned) excitement, as in this example, where the announcer's voice slows down dramatically on the words 'Rain Brings People Together':

> [in that/ *last*/ *bracket* of/ *SONGS*//] [we/ *HEARD*//] [*Rain*/ *Brings*/ *Peop*le to/ *GETH*er//]

In ordinary conversational speech the tempo changes quite often. The following excerpt comes from an informal interview with a newsreader (Van Leeuwen, 1984: 88). The number of syllables per measure varies from one ('em') to five ('not just because I'm'); the number of measures per phrase varies from one (again, 'em') to three; and after the fourth phrase ('far easier to read'), the tempo suddenly speeds up, to slow down again in the sixth phrase. It is also clear that his phrasing does not follow the grammatical rules of written language, but is motivated by the communicative needs of the moment, by what the speaker needs to make into separate 'moves in the speech act' to get his meaning across best. Hence a hesitation ('em'), indicating that he is carefully considering what he is going to say, and an emphatic assertion of the truth of what he is about to say ('certainly') are both made into separate phrases, separate 'moves in the speech act':

[*I*'ve read/ *news* at all/ *SORTS* of/ *pla*ces and the the//] [*blokes* that/ *write* the news/ *HERE*//] [*EM*//] [*CER*tainly//] [*far*/ *EA*sier to/ *read*//] [and that's/ *not* just because I'm/ *wor*king here/ *NOW*//] [than/ *A*ny news I've/ *read* anywhere/ *else*//]

When the same speaker changes to newsreading his speech becomes more regular in every one of these respects. The number of syllables per measure becomes more regular (three in most measures, except at the end of a phrase); the number of measures per phrase becomes more regular (four); the tempo becomes not only a good deal faster (an average of 4.7 syllables per second, as opposed to 3.9 in his conversational speech), but also more constant; and the phrase boundaries more clearly follow formal rules rather than that they are given in by the communicative needs of the moment. They may even hinder optimal communication – the word 'leave' in 'due to leave', for instance, should surely have carried more weight than the word 'due':

[the con/ *tai*nership/ *A*sian Re/ *NOWN*//] [is /*due* to leave/ *BRIS*bane to/ *day*//] [with a con/ *sign*ment of u/ *ra*nium/ *YELL*owcake//]

In a textbook of broadcasting techniques, a former head of radio training at the BBC (Evans, 1977: 50) condemned this kind of rhythmic regularization: 'Newscasters sound monotonous simply because their speech rhythms are too regular.' But all newsreaders do it, so there must be a reason. Perhaps the reason is that newsreading, like other formal, solemn or official forms of speech, must sound impersonal, neutral. In reading, intonation and rhythm always add the reader's interpretation of the written word. To stress a syllable means to single it out as important. To put words together as one phrase means to make them belong together as one unit of meaning. These decisions add the reader's interpretation to the meaning of the written word, just as a musical performance adds the musician's interpretation to the music written by the composer. But newsreaders are not supposed to add their own interpretation. They must be neutral. Their speech should be as devoid of any expression by means of intonation and rhythm as the written language itself. Hence they subject their speech to formal, more or less 'mechanical' rules, including the rule of 'rhythmic regularization'. Such rules are not explicitly stated. But if any newsreader violated them he or she would not last long in the job. On some commercial radio stations, however, human interest matters more than impartiality. On such stations newsreading often becomes more informal, and announcers hardly modify their speech when they switch from music announcements or advertisements to the news (cf. Van Leeuwen, 1982, 1992).

There is a form of speech in which regularization can go even further, metric poetry. Metric poetry can have exactly the same amount of syllables in each measure, for instance two, as in 'The Piper', from Blake's *Songs of Innocence*:

[*Pi*ping/ *down* the/ *val*leys/ *wild*//]

Or three, as in 'The Garden of Love', from the same source:

[I/ *went* to the/ *Gar*den of/ *Love*//]

or four, as in Kipling's 'Mandalay':

[And the/ *dawn* comes up like/ *thun*der outer/ *Chi*na 'crost the/ *Bay*//]

Note that the terminology of traditional prosody differs from the one adopted here. Prosody has the 'foot' instead of the measure and the foot may either begin with the main accent (pulse) or both. Thus measures of two syllables are either 'iambs (short-long) or 'trochees' (long-short) and measures of three syllables either 'anapaests' (short-short-long) or dactyls (long-short-short). Metric poetry can also have exactly the same amount of measures in every phrase, for example, two ('dimeter'), three ('trimeter'), four ('tetrameter'), five ('pentameter'), or six ('hexameter') – the range is the same as in speech examples. Here is an example of a pentameter, from Gray's 'Elegy':

[The / *plough*man/ *home*ward/ *plods* his/ *wea*ry / *way*//]

The social semiotics of metre goes back to Aristotle's *Rhetoric* and *Poetics* (1954 [4th century BC]). For Aristotle metre carried semiotic value. Some metres were 'high' and 'noble', others 'common' and 'ignoble'. The dactylic hexameter was the 'heroic' metre, 'the gravest and weightiest of metres', 'more tolerant than the rest of strange words and metaphors', while the iambic and the trochaic were 'metres of movement, the one representing that of life and action, the other that of a dance' (1954: 258). In the *Rhetoric* (1954: 180–1) he said:

> The heroic has dignity, but lacks the tones of the spoken language. The iambic is the very language of ordinary people, so that in common talk iambic lines occur oftener than any others: but in a speech we need dignity and the power of taking the hearer out of his ordinary self. The trochae is too much akin to wild dancing: we can see this in tetrameter verse, which is one of the trochaic rhythms.

Nowadays the meaning of metrical patterns is rarely commented on. But perhaps Aristotle's insights are as relevant as ever. The meaning of a metrical pattern (and, as we will see, many other meanings as well) derives from two sources. The first source is the *provenance* of the pattern, 'where the pattern comes from' (for example, 'the language of ordinary people') and hence also 'what we think about the place where the pattern comes from' (we might find it 'wild', for instance). The second source is the *experiential meaning potential* of the pattern, the meaning potential given by what we are actually *doing* when we produce the pattern (cf. Lakoff and Johnson, 1980). By using one syllable per measure, for instance, we are stressing everything, we are making everything equally important. That is the 'meaning potential'. The actual meaning is then formed by the context in which we put the meaning potential to work. In one context (a radio music announcement, for instance) we might stress every syllable to convey excitement. In another we might do the same thing to make our speech more didactic. The Rap artist Grandmaster Flash, in 'The Message', uses it to convey exasperation, in a line whose long-drawn-out monosyllabic rhythm clashes with the rhythm of the bass and the drums and contrasts with much of the rest of the song in which most measures have four syllables and a pulse which coincides with the main pulse of the drums (some/ *times* it makes me/ *wonder* how I/ *keep* from going/ *un*der//)

[*Don't*/ *push*/ *me*/ I / *am*/ *close*/ *to*/ *the*/ *EDGE*//]

Using three syllables per measure is rather artificial, rather 'different from the everyday'. Most of the things we do (walking, running, shivering and so on) have a binary rhythm. This 'being different from the everyday' is then coloured in, as it were, by the context. It can for instance become 'noble' and 'dignified' – high status is often signified by artificiality.The same line of argument can be applied to speech tempo. Fast speech derives its meaning potential from what it is we do when we produce it: speeding. The meaning then becomes more precise in context. In the case of radio news, for instance, it helps convey the values of news as a genre of speech. As described by Raymond Williams (1974: 116):

> Over much of the actual newsreporting there is a sense of hurried blur. The pace and the style of the newscast take precedence over the items in it. This sense of hurried transmission from all points is then in sharp contrast with the cool deliberation of the commercials. The flow of hurried items establishes a sense of the word: of surprising and miscellaneous events coming in, tumbling over each other, from all sides...

In another context fast speech can help paint a sound picture, for instance in the reading of a poem about a hunting expedition, as analysed by Fonagy (1976: 15):

> The rhythmical structure conjures up the picture of a merry chase. The anacrusis, the levelness of the tone, the repression of stress and the relatively fast tempo symbolize the first part of the chase.

Degrees of regularity: music

The timing of most Western music is regularized in two ways:

1. The tempo remains constant during the whole of a song, piece, movement of a symphony or sonata and so on.
2. The number of measures per phrase is regularized, to four measures per phrase, or some multiple of it. The amount of notes per measure may be regular, for instance in syllabic songs such as 'My Favourite Things', which has a 'dactylic' metre, with three notes (and three syllables) in every measure:

Rain drops	on	Ro	ses	and	whis kers	on	kit	tens
1	2	3	1	2	3	1	2	3	1	2	3

But this need not always be the case. In 'Meditation', an Antonio Carlos Jobim bossa nova song, the amount of notes (and, as it happens, also the amount of syllables) in the first measure is 1, the second measure 2, the third measure 3, the fourth measure 2, and the fifth measure 7.

In							my	lone	li	ness
1	2	3	4	1	2	3	4	1	2	3	4

				you're gone 'n I'm all by myself						
1	2	3	4	1	2	3	4	1	2	3	4

However, even when the number of notes per measure varies, or when the different parts that are played simultaneously have different amounts of notes, there is still a common metre or 'beat', followed by all the voices and/or instruments, even if it is sometimes only *felt* (or tapped out with the foot), rather than actually played. 'Meditation', for instance, is counted /ONE two three four/ ONE two three four/. In measure 2 and measure 4 the pulse is not sounded. Nothing happens on the 'ONE'. But the pulse will still be felt.

Two kinds of 'counting', two 'time signatures', have dominated 'high' Western music since measured time was introduced (in dance music they already existed): *duple time*, counting in two (ONE two/ ONE two), or in four (ONE two THREE four), and *triple time*, counting in three (ONE two three/ ONE two three). The meaning of this contrast again derives in part from 'provenance', and here it is useful to look at the dances with which these time signatures have been associated. Duple time had been associated with *collective* dances, especially procession dances, such as the *allemande* and the *polonaise*. In the Baroque era collective dancing went into decline, and 'the variety of the concrete types of movement (dance) narrowed down to a walk or promenade where only the mechanical continuity of the steps existed as the organizing force of the community' (Marothy, 1974: 239). Collectivity thus became a matter of public parades and military marches, that is, of the expression of national ideals rather than community values, as is the case, for instance, when people dance in a circle.

Triple time, on the other hand, the more 'articifial' metre, had been associated with the 'closed couple dance'. In older forms, such as the *volte* or the *minuet*, the couple was still involved with the group as a whole, opening out towards the group and gesturing towards it, but in the *waltz*, the couple became a world of its own, physically together with others in the ballroom, yet no longer communicating with these others, in the way that neighbours in a suburb might live close to each other yet not communicate. In addition the waltz was seen as replacing the 'stiffness' and 'artificiality' of the court dances, and creating space for self-expression (Marothy, 1974: 233). So there was on the one hand the procession dance, with its forwards movement, symbolizing progress, exploration, expansion, and nationalistic values, and on the other hand the closed couple dance, expressing the ethos of individualization, self-expression and privacy. Two tendencies, the 'heroic' and the 'sentimental', as Marothy says, the one associated with the public, the other with the private side of the industrial age, the one with work, the other with leisure, the one with the public ceremony, the other with the *salon*, the one, also, as McClary (1991) has very convincingly demonstrated, with constructions of 'masculinity', the other with constructions of 'femininity'.

The time structure of the blues, in the form in which it has become one of the key sources of and formats for Western popular music, the urban blues, is quite highly regularized. The lyrics have two or three syllables per measure and five measures in each of the three lines of each verse:

> [my/ *man* don't/ *love* me/ *treats* me/ *oh* so/ *mean*//]
> [my /*man* he don't/ *love* me/ *treats* me/ *aw*ful/ *mean*//]
> [*he's* the/ *low*est/ *man* that I've/ *ev*er/ *seen*//]

Musically a blues consists of three units of four bars (or eight measures, in our terminology), each containing a line of the song and an instrumental response. The lyrics as well as the melody of the first two lines are identical or near-identical, although a different chord is used in the accompaniment of the second line. Time signature and tempo remain constant and regular throughout. Certain types of country blues, however, were much more irregular. They could have different numbers of lines for different verses (for example 8 or 10 or 13 or 14, instead of the standard 12 bars), different numbers of measures per line, and changing time signatures. This is because they were narrative songs, sung by one man with a guitar. There was no need of a regular rhythm, because the song was not meant for dancing and there were no other players whose timings had to be synchronized with that of the singer. Urban blues, on the other hand, were usually performed by groups and played in clubs where people danced. Still, it is perhaps no accident that the blues, as a musical form, became rhythmically a good deal more regularized when the performers moved from the country to the city. As Tagg (1984: 29) describes it:

> In changing his folk tradition, the black Southerner was influenced by experiences of time and new feelings of movement and space in his new environment. Having to live in a four-square tenement block, take the bus or train at specific clock times through the right-angled grid of the city streets to the rectangular factory building where rectilinear assembly lines moved at a regular rate and machines made metronomically regular noises, having to clock in and clock out, travel back home at another given time past traffic lights, through grid streets again and so on and so on, the black working immigrant required music which would reflect his new life at an affective level of perception. On the other hand we could say that the performer or listener could be preparing himself affectively for the rhythm and sounds of the life he has to lead in an attempt to master it on an emotional level.

In other words, musical time can reflect the way time is lived in the lifeworld where the music is made as well as people's affective relationship to that time, whether they embrace it or struggle with it.

We can now summarize:

1. There are three kinds of rhythmic regularization: (1) regularization of the tempo, (2) regularization of the amount of sounds per measure, and (3) regularization of the amount of measures per phrase.

    Any combination of these is possible, in speech as well as in music or in semiotic productions using 'non-musical' sounds, and intricate patterns can be produced by alternating different degrees or types of regularization.

2. The meaning of different metrical patterns is in part based on *provenance*, on 'where the patterns come from' (and on the associations we have with that 'place'). In Western music triple patterns have a history of being associated with 'sentimental' rather than 'heroic' music, for instance. But there is another factor as well, *experiential meaning potential* – our knowledge of what we do when we produce the pattern can be the basis for giving it a specific semiotic value in a specific context. In producing a triple pattern we

know that we are doing something relatively artificial and unusual. Most human actions have a duple rhythm, and in music, too, triple rhythm is the exception rather than the rule – almost all popular music has duple rhythm. This 'being different from the everyday' can then be given a more specific value in a given context. It can, for instance, mean 'noble' and 'dignified', as in Aristotle, or 'individuality' and 'emotive expressivity', as in the Romantic era.

Unmeasured time

Medieval Church music was unmeasured. Rather than a regular pulse you could tap your feet to, it was characterized by a slow, meditative time *fluctuation* to which you might at best sway your body to and fro. In the Netherlands of the 1950s, and perhaps still, the congregations of the stricter Protestant denominations sang the psalms (and they only sang psalms) in this way: very slowly and sustaining all the notes for exactly the same time. This literally created the absence of a sense of a regular pulse, a 'beat', and could therefore set sacred time apart from profane time, from the rhythms of everyday life and work, for instance, which, especially before the advent of the machine, produced so many different kinds of recurring rhythmic patterns – the pattern of the blacksmith and his assistant for instance (Figure 3.2):

Figure 3.2 The sound of a blacksmith and his assistant at work
(quoted in Schafer, 1977: 54)

We have already seen how measured time at first mainly occurred in 'folk' music, for instance dance music and 'work songs', and how it then became incorporated in the 'high' music of the Renaissance, replacing the eternal time of medieval high music, to celebrate the values held sacred in the new era – the work ethic, the synchronization of activities, the clock-like regulation of life, and, as people came to conceive of it, the clock-like regulation of the universe itself: it was in this era that God changed from an Eternal Being to a kind of clockmaker.

Classical Indian music contrasts measured and unmeasured time within the same piece of music. The _raga_ begins with a continuous sound, a _drone_, on which, after a while, the measured time of melodic phrases is superimposed. This drone is played on the tampura, a string instrument, and

> is not supposed to be 'interesting' like the piano accompaniment to a modern song but is the medium in which the melody lives, moves and has its being... It is heard before, during and after the melody: it is ageless and complete which was in the beginning, is now and ever shall be. The melody itself, however, is the changeable character of Nature which comes from the Source and returns there (Coomaraswamy, quoted in Tagg, 1984: 25).

In other words, Indian music opposes (and at the same time brings together) the principle of eternity and the principle of human activity, which _does_ have a beginning and an end, and which _does_ have its timings and periodicities.

There are at least two reasons why the drone is an apt signifier for the concept of 'eternity': (1) it is a continuous, never-ending, never-changing sound, and (2) it is a sound which cannot be produced by the human voice without special techniques, because humans need to breathe, and their speech and song are normally divided up in what we have called 'phrases'. Producing a drone therefore needs a string instrument rather than human breath, or special techniques such as the circular breathing which Aborigines use in singing (Kartomi, 1984: 76) and in playing the didgeridoo; or special technologies such as the organ or the modern synthesizer. The drone is therefore 'not human' and its quality of being 'not human' is then available for the production of more specific meanings in the specific contexts in which drone sounds may be used.

In contemporary Western music, unmeasured time is often used for signifying the grandeur of nature. The opening of the film _The Piano_, for instance, takes place against the backdrop of the impressive scenery of the New Zealand coast. The music of Michael Nyman enhances this with misty, mysterious chords, fluctuating in waves of increasing and decreasing dissonance, resting on deep, sonorous organ tones, and all lasting equally long and progressing without any clear sense of a regular pulse, just like the singing in Dutch *zwarte kousen* ('black stocking') churches. It is a film music convention for portraying nature as eternal, timeless and unchanging (cf. Tagg, 1983). A melody is then added to this, precisely as happens in an Indian *raga*. It soon begins to climb in pitch, announcing events to come and setting up expectations of an emotively stirring human drama – but always against the backdrop of the 'eternal' nature of things.

'Not human' can also come to mean 'supernatural'. The musics and sound effects that signify supernatural events not only tend to use 'non-human' instruments, electronic instruments for instance, or instruments that can play much higher or lower than the reach of the human voice, but also 'non-human' forms of timing. The work of the BBC Radiophonic Workshop provides telling examples. John Baker's 'Spectres in the Wind', included on a BBC Science Fiction Sound Effects collection, features a sound which seems to blend a deep male voice with the sound of the wind, lined with a metallic shimmer. The sound of this spectral 'voice' is continuous (the 'spectre' clearly does not need to breathe) and fluctuates in pitch, sliding up and down slightly at irregular and widely spaced intervals, and gradually climbing higher, no doubt to increase the suspense.

'Not human' time can also be used to signify the vastness of space. When the ABC (Australian Broadcasting Commission), in 1985, replaced the 'Majestic Fanfare' tune they had used for almost 30 years with a new 'news signature tune', they still included something reminiscent of a trumpet bugle call. But the trumpets no longer sounded 'majestic' and they played a muted minor melody against a new background, a slightly wavering synthesizer drone. The meaning of this was anchored by a picture of the starry sky, with a revolving satellite in the foreground. The human activity of announcing the news was now set against the vastness of space. Thus different contexts (nature, spectral beings, space) colour in just how the basic experiential meaning potential (what we know about the sounds from our experience of producing them, or, in this case, the knowledge that we *cannot* produce them) is made more specific, to signify the sacred, the supernatural, the eternal and so on.

In our everyday urban environment recurrent rhythmic patterns and periodicities such as the sound of the smithery, of brass-bound wheels on cobblestones, of horses' hooves and so on, are less and less common. The new key sound is not that of rhythmically structured human activity, but the soft and continuous hum of the electromotor, and it has apparently become so important and indispensable to us that acoustic engineers deliberately provide it in libraries and that we want to hear something like it even on recordings of natural environments such as the *Ambient Sounds of Costa Rica* CD discussed in the previous chapter. As the inevitable replacement of the combustion engine by the electromotor proceeds, this change in our soundscape towards softer, but more continuous and unchanging sounds will become even more profound. In the absence of other sounds, and in the right context, a large hall, for instance, this kind of sound can acquire a near-sacred character, a sense of the unseen presence of an awesome power quite unconnected to the world of human activity. In the meanwhile more and more of our music and other sound productions celebrate this kind of sound, placing it in the ancient tradition of the sacred drone. As we have seen, such drones are usually a backdrop, a setting for human activity. But the reverse is at the very least possible. When we are close to the pounding of the surf or the loud hum inside the power station, the drone becomes foreground and makes the sound of human voices and human activities quite small and insignificant by comparison.

To summarize, there are two main kinds of unmeasured time: *continuous time*, which lacks any form of phrasing and either does not vary in pitch at all, or wavers in pitch in slight and irregular ways, and *fluctuating time*, which also lacks phrasing, but does shift between different pitches, at more or less regular intervals which are, however, too long to produce a clear sense of regular pulse or periodicity, a rhythm listeners could tap their feet to. The meaning potential of both is given by their opposition to the characteristics of human productive work or dance, both of which have the regular rhythmic patterns and periodicities that are also expressed and celebrated in the repetitive rhythmic motifs of many forms of musical accompaniment. Thus the resulting meaning potential of being '*not* human' and '*not* timed' can become available to signify 'God', 'nature', 'the universe', the 'supernatural' and so on, depending on the context.

Polyrhythms

The Western approach to time is divisive. Time is divided in hours, minutes and seconds, so as to synchronize activities by reference to the objective authority of the clock, the schedule, the calendar and so on. As a result people often experience a contradiction between objective (clock) time and subjective ('lived', 'felt') time. Western music follows the same pattern. Musical activity is synchronized by reference to the objective authority of the metronome or the drum machine, or by reference to the authority of the conductor with his baton – the role of the conductor dates from the early nineteenth century, and at that time was explicitly compared with that of the overseer in the factory (cf. Koury, 1986). I will have to qualify this picture later, because in music, too, there is tension between 'objective' and 'subjective' time, but, still, the dominant form of musical time has been one in which the members of the musical group must all synchronize to the same beat, in the same way soldiers, or rush-hour commuters in a narrow London Underground pedestrian tunnel, must march in step.

In polyrhythmic music, on the other hand, each member of the musical group follows his or her own internal clock. Compare it, not to an underground pedestrian tunnel, but to a large open square with people crossing in all directions and at their own pace, yet perfectly coordinated with each other as they weave in and out without ever colliding with anyone – musicians from various African cultures in fact refer to rhythm as 'weaving in and out' (Chernoff, 1979: 201). In such situations it is impossible to say what 'the' rhythm is – there are always several rhythms going on at once. Not surprisingly, societies where this approach to rhythm is dominant are what Hall (1983) has called 'polychronic' societies, societies where the regime of the clock has never gained as much of a foothold as it has, for instance, in North America and (especially northern) Europe, and where people are capable of attending to several things at the same time, prioritize people and networks over procedures and schedules, and find many things more important than getting somewhere on time (cf. Hall, 1959, 1983).

Let us look at two of the key differences between 'monorhythmi-cality' and 'polyrhythmicality'. In groups or societies where clock time is dominant, important social gatherings (school, work, church, public performances and so on) begin and end at a precise time which must be adhered to by all concerned. The same applies to the dominant musics of these groups or societies. The conductor or leader counts in and every member of the musical group starts at exactly the same time. At the end a baton signal or drum roll ensures a perfectly synchronous ending. Other societies take a more casual view of beginnings and endings. For a time I lived in a London street which had a Jamaican Pentecostalist church at the corner. The services went on all morning – and all morning people kept entering and leaving the building, a total contrast with the Dutch church I grew up in, which had the minister and the elders wait at the door till it was exactly ten o'clock before solemnly proceeding through the church to the foot of the pulpit. Entering after the opening blessing was a serious disruption, frowned upon by all, and leaving before the final 'Amen' was out of the question. In polyrhythmic music, on the other hand, starting at the same time is not only undesirable, it is just about impossible. As Chernoff describes it (1979: 45, 47):

> Instruments must find their entrance, not by counting from the main beat, but in relation to other instruments. The use of 'staggered' independent entrances in the cross-rhythmic relationships of the music indicates an important characteristic of African music.

More fundamental still is the fact that in this kind of music playing together, cooperation, does not require synchronization. The rhythm of any given player may coincide with that of one other player every 16 beats, with that of another player every 24 beats and so on, so that each player rhythmically interacts with each other player in a different way. As a result the players cannot 'follow' either a basic beat or any other player. If they did, they would soon lose their place. They must concentrate only on their own playing, in what Thompson (1966) called 'apart-playing'. Polyrhythmic music thus celebrates individuality and difference, 'pluralism as a source of vitality' as Chernoff says (1979: 158) – and he also notes that this kind of pluralism is a key value in many African societies, which see the world as a place where multiple forces act together in determining what should and does happen. ·

Yet, despite this emphasis on individuality and on following one's own, internal rhythm, the part played by any given player is meaningless by itself. Without the whole it would 'give the impression of a rhythm tripping along clumsily or meaninglessly accented' (Chernoff, 1979: 52). The same would be true of the path followed by pedestrians crossing the square – their variations in tempo and direction would be incomprehensible without seeing the people they circumnavigated in this way. Thus polyrhythmic music suggests a relationship between the individual and the group in which one's own unique identity, one's individuality, cannot be seen as threatened by the need to conform to a group. On the contrary, a distinct and unique individuality cannot exist without the group. It follows that the principle which keeps a group together is not something imposed from the outside, for instance by a clock or metronome, but something that can only be produced by the concerted action of the group: 'The music consists of many rhythms and the "beat" emerges from the way these rhythms engage and communicate with each other' (Chernoff, 1979: 157). This 'beat', moreover, is never explicitly stated, and must be 'found' by listeners whose 'listening' is in fact more a matter of active participation than of the concentrated perception of and imaginary identification with the communicated message:

> In African music, it is the listener or dancer who has to supply the beat: the listener must be *actively engaged* in making sense of the music; the music itself does not become the concentrated focus of an event, as at a concert. It is for this reason that African music should not be studied out of its context or as 'music': the African orchestra is not complete without a participant on the other side. The drum ensemble is an accompaniment, a music-to-find-the-beat-by (Chernoff, 1979: 50).

There is no doubt that polyrhythmic forms of music such as salsa and other Latin and African musics are finding increasing response in societies where the time of the clock used to dominate and to a certain degree still dominates, and that the rhythms of contemporary popular music such as drum 'n' bass are becoming increasingly rich and complex. If it is true that forms of musical timing are in an active relationship with forms of social timing generally, that musical timing reflects, enacts, celebrates, critiques, subverts, or proposes forms of social timing, this interest in polyrhythmicality perhaps points towards a society in which synchrony will lose its grip. Although the remaining state institutions, schools for instance, and the public media, continue to enforce punctuality and fixed hours of attendance, many companies no longer require their employees to all keep the same hours or to all take their holidays in the same period, and round the clock news on cable or satellite has put an end to the need for switching on the television at exactly seven or eight o'clock so as to catch the news or the favourite soap. In 'postmodern' society time will become increasingly fragmented and heterogeneous and multiple (cf. Paolucci, 1996). As a result the emphasis on conformity will make place for an emphasis on diversity and heterogeneity. Communication will no longer require a similarly constituted sense of identity and a common cultural heritage, but can become a complex network of coinciding moments of shared activity, a meeting of travellers from many different countries on the crossroads of their travels, rather than a meeting of countrymen abroad, amidst 'foreigners'. Our changing conceptions of and attitudes towards the environment point in the same direction. The rhythms of nature, from the babbling of the small brook to the pounding of the surf, are complex and apparently 'chaotic', determined by the shifting coincidences of many simultaneous rhythmic cycles, and yet result in sounds with a distinct clarity of character:

> While variable rhythms were transformed into an invariable, metronomic beat, nature became formalized and subject to calculation. Unlike technology, however, nature is complex and in its complexity not amenable to scientific description or calculation... In nature there are no events which undergo exact reproduction: there is no metronomic beat... The rhythms of nature are marked not by monotonous repetition of the same, but instead are a kaleidoscope of individually differentiated limited time-scales (frequencies): they are thus characterized by 'polyrhythmic' structures (Kummerer, 1996: 226–7).

A subtle treatment of the complex layering of speech rhythm can be found in Martinec (1995).

Subverting metronomic time

So far I have given the impression that monorhythmic music is always strictly 'metronomical'. But this is not the case. Although monorhythmic music will always have a main beat, it is possible for notes in the melody to anticipate or delay the beat, so as to recreate or enact a tension between objective and subjective time. In nineteenth-century *Lieder* or romantic piano music (and still in the bulk of romantic pop, film and advertising music), suspension, delaying the beat, is one of the key affective devices – *stretching* time, so as to escape its rigidities, if only for a moment, and only within the context of leisure time and the private sphere, in the way that dinner parties need not start quite as punctually as board meetings.

The influence of Afro-American music has challenged the classic Western order of time more profoundly. In popular music inspired by the Afro-American tradition the beat is often anticipated or delayed, and triple and duple times may be superimposed on one another in limited polyrhythmicality. The examples in Figure 3.3 are an attempt to show the differences in timing between two blues performances, one by Billie Holiday, in a 1939 version of 'Long Gone Blues', the other by the Australian singer and trumpet player Vince Jones in 'When You Get Up To The City', a jazz blues recorded in 1988. The calibrations

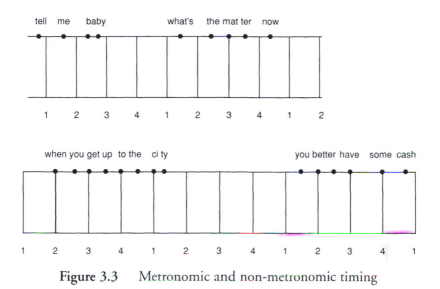

Figure 3.3   Metronomic and non-metronomic timing

on the bottom line represent the regular ' ONE two three four' beat, the dots on the top line (and the words) the timing of the melody. In the case of Billie Holiday only one note (on the first syllable of the word 'matter') coincides with the beat. All other notes displace the beat, creating a dialectic between her own subjective time and the objective 'time of the city'. In the case of Vince Jones the notes of the melody come mostly on the beat, with the exception of the last notes of each of the two lines. He 'falls in' with the time of the city, gives himself over to it. But this kind of contrast must really be heard to be appreciated. Tap on the beat of the music and then concentrate on the voice or the solo instrument – are the notes of the melody placed 'against' the beat or in exact synchrony with it?

Music can thus either align itself with the time of the clock, enact it, celebrate it, affectively identify with it – or struggle with it, rebel against it, subvert it. Philip Tagg has described the timing of rock music in this vein, seeing it as an attempt to 'gain some control over time through musical expression', in a context where any real control over time is lacking and where mechanical time remains dominant 'at work and in other official realms of power' (1990: 112). 'The bass drum and bass guitar', he says, 'are responsible for stating clock time, the bass drum generally playing every or every other beat, the bass guitar emphasising every fourth one (explicit pulse)' (ibid.: 112). Other instruments use syncopation to 'pull time hither and thither':

> Pulse beats can be missed out and strong beats in the metre anticipated by either half a beat, one beat or even two beats, this causing agogic effects which subvert the implacable exactitude of natural science, computers and clock time. Over this already partially rehumanized version of humanly produced regularity, other instruments (for example, cymbals, hi-hats, rhythm guitars, keyboards) perform riffs including accentuations at microcosmic loggerheads (out of phase by a quaver usually) with the implicit or explicit beat (pulse). These riffs create a weave of rhythm making patterns of coincidence and non-coincidence with each other and with the bass drum and bass guitar. The rhythms and sounds of our times are in this way brought to a higher degree of stylisation through this musical resocialization (Tagg, 1990: 112).

In disco, on the other hand, there is, according to Tagg, 'not the same extent of subversion of clock time, not the same human appropriation of the mechanical pulse' (Tagg, 1984: 31–2).

An example: news signature tunes

To end this chapter, I first present an overview of the main distinctions I have made in this chapter, and then an example analysis in which all these distinctions are used. The superscript letters 'I' and 'T' in Figure 3.4 mean 'if' and 'then', for example: 'If there is no regularized *pattern*, then there must be a regularized *tempo*':

    The example is the already mentioned ABC (Australian Broadcasting Commission) television news signature tune, dating from 1985. No detailed technical knowledge of music is necessary for studying the timing of music along the lines I have proposed here. All that is required is an ability to listen to each element of the composite soundtrack in turn, and to each 'sound event' in which that element is involved, and to ask, for each element and each sound event, 'Is it measured or unmeasured?', then, if, for example, it is unmeasured, 'Is it fluctuating or continuous?' and so on, following Figure 3.4 and using the definitions provided in this chapter.

    This is how the news signature unfolds. As we see an image of the universe, with a revolving satellite in the foreground, we hear an amorphous synthesizer drone. This sound continues as Ground for two

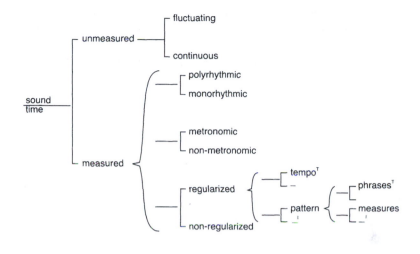

Figure 3.4   A system network of timing

'call and response' dialogues between a solo trumpet and a brass ensemble. The solo trumpet sounds a somewhat muted 'bugle call' in a minor key. The brass ensemble responds. Then follows a new section, in which three sounds are heard at the same time, (1) a rhythmic pattern played by a synthesizer voice sounding a bit like the plucked strings of a cello and suggesting the staccato of a teletypewriter or some similar instrument, (2) very short melodic phrases, played by two different alternating synthesizer voices, with quite a bit of space between them, and (3) a voice reading the news headlines. Finally we return to another 'call and response duet' between the solo trumpet and the brass ensemble, ending on a loud, high and very abrupt unison note. I will again describe the sounds in 'script' form, and provide the analysis in a separate column, on the right.

1. **SYNTHESIZER DRONE enters**	Unmeasured (continous)
2. **SOLO TRUMPET CALL** (**as drone continues**)	Measured (monorhythmic; non-metronomic; regularized in tempo and no. of tones per measure)
3. **BRASS ENSEMBLE responds** (**as drone continues**)	Measured (monorhythmic; metronomic; regularized in tempo and no. of tones per measure)

4. 2ND SOLO TRUMPET CALL (as drone continues)	Measured (monorhythmic; non-metronomic; regularized in tempo and no. of tones per measure)
5. BRASS ENSEMBLE responds (as drone continues)	Measured (monorhythmic; metronomic; regularized in tempo and no. of tones per measure)
6. Drone fades out as	

7.   NEWSREADER'S VOICE enters:
 	
      [*To/ NIGHT//*] [*Syd*ney on pa/
      RADE//] [as the/
	Measured (monorhythmic;
	non-metronomic;
	regularized tempo;
	semi-regularized number of
	syllables per measure
	(preponderance of
	'staccato' monosyllabic
	measures) and measures per
	phrase (all headlines start
	with very short, again
	'staccato' phrases)

8.   REPETITIVE RHYTHMIC
     'CELLO' PATTERN
     SUGGESTING
     TELETYPEWRITER
     (as voice continues:)
 	
      *Na*vy's/ *big/ GUNS//*]
      [*turn/ OUT//*]
	Melody measured
	(monorhythmic;
	metronomic; regularized
	tempo and pattern).
	Speech as above

9.   TWO-NOTE MELODY IN
     'BRASS' VOICE
     (as 'cello pattern' continues)
	Measured (monorhythmic;
	metronomic; regularized
	tempo and no. of measures
	per phrase (with reference
	to other phrases)

10. Repetitive rhythmic 'cello pattern' continues	'Cello pattern' as above
11. FIVE-NOTE MELODY IN SYNTH-VOICE enters as	Melody is measured (monorhythmic; metronomic; regularized tempo and no. of measures per phrase

12. NEWSREADER'S VOICE re-enters (and 'cello pattern' continues)	Speech and 'cello pattern' as above
[Aus/ *TRA*lia//] [*POISED*//] [for a/ *Da*vis Cup/ *win* over the U/*S*/]	
13. TWO-NOTE MELODY IN 'BRASS' VOICE re-enters (as 'cello pattern' continues)	All elements as above
14. THREE-NOTE MELODY IN 'SYNTH' VOICE enters (as 'cello pattern' continues)	All elements as above
15. TWO-NOTE MELODY IN 'BRASS' VOICE re-enters as	Two-note melody as above
16. NEWSREADER'S VOICE re-enters;	Speech as above
[*and*/ *T*/*J*//] [TAKES//] [*Ep*som day *Ho*nours at/ *RAND*wick//]	
17. 'Cello pattern' fades out as	
18. SOLO TRUMPET CALL re-enters	Measured (monorhythmic; metronomic; regularized tempo and no. of notes per measure)
19. BRASS ENSEMBLE responds (as last note of trumpet call continues)	Measured (monorhythmic; metronomic; regularized tempo and no. of notes per measure)
20. ABRUPT UNISON END NOTE OF SOLO TRUMPET AND BRASS ENSEMBLE	

This tune replaced a signature tune which had preceded and followed the news for more than 30 years (cf. Van Leeuwen, 1989). It was called the 'Majestic Fanfare' and opened with a group (a 'we') of unison trumpets playing an energetic and optimistic 'anthem'-like 'call', in strict and metronomic march tempo, a tune, therefore, which very much supported the rule of clock time and asked listeners, as it were, to stand at attention at the exact moment at which the official voice of the newsreader began to read the bulletin. Introducing unmeasured time in this context was no small change. Against the background of the vastness of the universe, the imperial self-importance of the trumpet call was much diminished, much muted, and it was now played by only one trumpet – a *piccolo* trumpet! This trumpet also 'jazzed up' the march-like timing, just as the ABC, in this period, 'jazzed up' the content of the news itself, introducing more human interest values and more sport.

Also new was the middle section. It drew a musical picture of the news itself. The rapid teletypewriter rhythm conveyed the *urgency* and the *recency* of the news, suggesting that news items were coming in even as the news was being read – on other channels something similar is often done visually, by showing a busy newsroom, with people working behind computers, as the newsreader is reading the news in the foreground. The contrasting melodic fragments suggested the *variety* of the news, with its alternation of 'hard' and 'soft' news, of items from the world of politics and finance and items from the world of human interest. The news, finally, was also *dramatic*. The voice read the headlines with a dramatic staccato, a 'headline rhythm' (try it out!), and the polyrhythmic relation between voice and music was one which until then had been more typical of film and television drama, at least in the ABC.

In all these ways the change of news signature tune reflected the changing nature of the ABC news, and of the ABC itself, in a period during which this publicly funded broadcaster moved further and further towards types of programming and styles of presentation that had previously been more characteristic of commercial radio and television.

Exercises and discussion points

1. Collect at least two signature tunes or examples of title music from the following types of television programmes: current affairs, police series and nature programmes.

   What are the main characteristics of their approaches to musical time, and why, do you think, were these approaches chosen?

2. Record examples of rhythmically regularized speech (children's ditties, market vendors' chants, religious chants and so on). What kinds of rhythmic regularization are used, and why?

3. Listen to the rhythms of the city, and of nature. Transcribe them as 'sound scripts', and analyse their mode of timing.

4. It has often been noted that rhythmic regularity helps recall. This is why the lore and knowledge of oral cultures were remembered in the form of metrical poetry (cf. Ong, 1982). Advertising jingles also make use of the principle.

   Take a section from some school textbook (for instance a page about the circulation of the blood from a science textbook) and turn it into a rhythmically regularized chant (or a song, if you know how to).

   Afterwards, reflect on the reasons for your choice of regularization patterns.

Chapter 4

Interacting sounds

Sequentiality and simultaneity in speech

In 'conversation analysis' there is a rarely challenged assumption that people speak in turns. Harvey Sacks, who originated the most widely practised form of conversation analysis, sees it as a key rule of conversation: 'At least and not more than one party talks at a time' (quoted in Coulthard, 1977: 53). If people do talk at the same time, this is either a momentary slip, which will be corrected immediately, or a rude interruption. If no one talks, one of the speakers will fill the silence with 'ems', 'ers' and other 'filler noises', to claim it as part of his or her turn. The underlying rule of conversation, Western conversation at any rate, is that dialogue is strictly sequential, strictly linear – one speaker at a time. Hence conversation analysts pay particular attention to the way speakers get their turns, start their turns (for example do they interrupt the previous speaker, leave a gap after their utterances and so on), end their turns, and nominate the next speaker (cf. Pomerantz and Fehr, 1997), that is, to the whole 'management' of turn-taking. An important aspect of this is that the first speaker in what is known as an 'adjacency pair' is always to some degree at an advantage, simply because all speech acts have an 'expected' response (Halliday, 1985), and thereby constrain to some degree what the next speaker can reasonably say: a greeting must be followed by a greeting, a question by an answer, a statement by agreement and so on. It is possible to respond in other ways, but there will be a price to pay. The relationship with the other participant in the conversation will suffer. To ignore a greeting is impolite, not to answer a question is less than cooperative, and to disagree with a statement is to put the interaction on an adversarial footing – which is, of course, the norm in 'adversarial' kinds of speech interaction, for example in political interviews, debates, arguments and so on (cf. Bell and Van Leeuwen, 1994, Ch. 4).

In sequential interaction of this kind either one speaker dominates the other, as in the example below, or each speaker attempts to dominate the other, as for example in political interviews or debates. The aim is to 'have the floor', to silence the other and assert the self. Feminist conversation analysts have shown that men do it all the time in conversation with women, yet consider women who do it 'aggressive' and 'pushy'. Cate Poynton (1985: 27) quotes a telling example from the American linguists West and Zimmermann. I quote it here with all the typical conversation analysis annotations, to show how conversation analysts attend to the space (or lack of space) between turns. Square brackets [ ] indicate that the participants are overlapping (in this case that the man is interrupting the woman). An equal sign = means that two subsequent turns butt together without any gap. A hash sign # indicates a pause of one second or less and a number (for example 1.8) indicates the time between turns in seconds. Colons ::: indicate a prolonged speech sound and a dash - at the end of a word indicates that that word is cut short. Double brackets (( )), finally, enclose descriptions of actions.

Woman:	How's your paper coming?=
Man:	Allright I guess (#) I haven't done much in the past two weeks.
(1.8)	
Woman:	Yeah::::know how that ⌈can ⌉
Man:	⌊Hey⌋ ya' got an extra cigarette?
(#)	
Woman:	Oh uh sure ((hands him the pack))
	Like my ⌈pa- ⌉
Man:	⌊How⌋ 'bout a match?
(1.2)	
Woman:	Er ya go uh like my ⌈pa- ⌉
Man:	⌊Thanks⌋
(1.8)	
Woman:	Sure (#) I was gonna tell you ⌈my- ⌉
Man:	⌊Hey⌋ I'd really like ta' talk
	but I gotta run (#) see ya
(3.2)	
Woman:	Yeah.

And Poynton comments (1985: 26)

One of the persistent stereotypes of women as language users is that they are indefatigable talkers... A number of recent studies demonstrate that this is a gross caricature and that in conversational interaction between men and women, far from men never being able to get a word in edgeways, they usually have the upper hand. Topics are determined by, or in deference to, men – by men interrupting, or talking over women in order to get the floor if women do not automatically yield the right by 'asking him about himself and his interests'... Such behaviour can clearly be seen as dominance display on the part of males.

Another linguist, Deborah Tannen, critiques the kind of research Poynton invokes here, arguing that researchers have too often merely counted interruptions, without taking into account 'what was being talked about, speakers' intentions, their reactions to each other, and what effect the "interruption" had on the conversation' (Tannen, 1992: 189–90):

> Claiming that an interruption is a sign of dominance assumes that conversation is an activity in which one speaker speaks at a time, but this reflects ideology more than practice. Most Americans *believe* one speaker ought to speak at a time, regardless of what they actually do. I have recorded conversations in which many voices were heard at once and it was clear that everyone was having a good time.

According to Tannen, some conversations, for example conversations between children, or between friends, especially women friends, are in the first place about 'enthusiastic involvement', about '*rapport* talk' rather than '*report* talk'. In such conversations 'interruptions' are not seen as rude, but as a sign of involvement. In other conversations, for example conversations between men and women or otherwise 'different' and/or unequal parties, or in adversarial conversations, conversations which are about asserting yourself, as are many conversations between men, interruptions *will* be seen as rude or aggressive.

Here is an example of 'cooperative overlapping' cited in Tannen. It comes from a conversation recorded at a kitchen table by linguist Janice Hornyak, who also takes part in the conversation. Jan and her mother Peg are visiting Jan's aunt Marge who lives in the North. Peg and Marge discuss bringing up children in a cold climate, something of which Jan, who has always lived in the South, has no experience. In this transcript only the overlaps are shown.

PEG: The part I didn't like was putting everybody's snow pants and
         boots ⌈and
MARGE: ⌊Oh yeah that was the worst part
PEG: ⌈and scarves
MARGE: ⌊and get them all
         bundled up in boots and everything and they're out for half
         an hour and then they come in and they're all covered with
         this snow and they get that *shluck* all over⎮
PEG: ⎮all that wet stuff
         and
JAN: That's why adults don't like snow, huh?
MARGE: That's right.
PEG: Throw all the stuff in the dryer and then they'd come in and
         sit for half ⎮ an hour
MARGE   ⎮ and in a little while they'd want to go back out
         again.
PEG: Then they'd want to go back out again.

Tannen comments that Peg and Marge 'play a conversational duet:
they jointly hold one conversational role, overlapping each other
without exhibiting (or reporting) resentment at being interrupted'.
Indeed, they often 'end a comment with the conjunction *and*, creating
the appearance of interruption when there is none, as when Peg says,
'All that wet stuff and' (ibid.: 204). Instead of holding the floor until
they have finished what *they* want to say, they deliberately hand over to
let *the other* finish their thought.

Drama scripts also follow the rule that conversation happens in
turns. Yet expert scriptwriters know that interruption is not always
aggressive, and simulate it by means of what is known as the 'dialogue
hook'. As described by a Hollywood scriptwriter (Herman, 1952:
205ff.), this includes ending lines with '*and*', so as to 'tie a series of
speeches together', creating a joint production of meaning in precisely
the way described by Tannen:

                    TONY
We can take in the Riviera, Sue and...

                    SUE
              (interrupting)
And Cannes, and Paris, and...

                    TONY
              (interrupting)
The whole works, yes!

Actors, too, know about conversational overlapping. Goffman (1974: 141) quotes an actor who explicitly links it with 'being interested in each other':

INTERVIEWER:	What is the secret of your teamwork?
LUNT:	I don't know. I guess each of us is interested in the other. That's one thing. And, of course, there is our way of speaking together. We started it in *The Guardsman.* We would speak to each other as people do in real life. I would, for instance, start a speech, and in the middle, on our own cue, which we would agree in advance, Lynn would cut in and start talking. I would continue on a bit. You can't do it in Shakespeare of course. But in drawing-room comedies, in realistic plays, it is most effective. (...)
INTERVIEWER:	This interaction is presumably what every actor dreams of.
LUNT:	They thought it couldn't be done. And when we first played *Caprice* in London, they were outraged because we talked together. Really outraged the press was. But it was a great success.

Hollywood director Robert Altman, in films like *Nashville* and *A Wedding*, introduced new sound-recording techniques specifically to allow overlapping dialogue. Rather than having the boom operator swivel the microphone from one actor to the next between turns, which necessitated elaborate cueing and rehearsing of any overlapping lines of dialogue, he gave each actor a separate microphone. This also gave him more control over turn-taking during editing and mixing. Charles Schreger, in a discussion of important postwar innovations in film sound, comments (1985: 340):

> It was another way of making movies like life – where a conversation is carried on in bursts of words and grunts, where people interrupt each other's sentences, where the participants are straining to be heard above the noise of the subway, the TV or other people's voices.

In other cultures the value of overlapping speech may be more openly recognized, also by men. Anthropologist Stephen Feld has described how the Kaluli of New Guinea enjoy conversations in which the speakers interlock, overlap, quickly alternate and so on. The word they use for this kind of speech means 'laying together sticks to make a fire'. As Feld says (1982: 251):

> The Western normative concepts of individual speaker turns, floor rights and turn-taking etiquette, notions rationalized in speech act philosophy and conversation analysis, are absent from Kaluli conversation and narration. What might be heard as regular 'interruption' is not that at all, but rather the collaborative and co-creative achievement of *dulugu salan*, 'lift-up-over-speaking'.

To summarize, speech interaction can take place in two ways: *sequentially*, by speaking in turns, or *simultaneously*, by speaking at the same time. This is not an 'either-or' contrast, but a sliding scale, with on the one end the *monologue*, which silences one of the interactive participants altogether, and is minimally oriented towards interactivity, and on the other end the *duologue*, the continuous simultaneous speech of two speakers, or the *polylogue*, the continuous simultaneous speech of more than two speakers, forms which are maximally oriented towards interactivity. In between are different forms of turn-taking, ranging from forms with a respectful gap between speakers and/or strong constraints for the second speaker in adjacency pairs (they may for instance be restricted to giving signs of approval to the first speaker, or answering 'yes' or 'no' to a barrage of questions) to forms which use overlapping deliberately and/or minimally constrain the utterances of the second speakers in adjacency pairs. The scale therefore moves from forms which are oriented towards the 'report' function of speech and involve unequal power between the participants (or a struggle for power, a view of conversation as contest) to forms which are oriented towards the 'rapport' function of speech and involve equality, cooperation, collaboration and the joint production of meanings. We will see that the same range exists when speech and music merge in song, and even when music becomes wordless.

Sequentiality in music

In musicology, turn-taking is called *antiphony* – the term brings out that the form can present or represent a sense of difference or opposition between two individual voices or groups of voices, or between an individual voice and a group of voices.

Worldwide, the musical monologue occurs, not only in unaccompanied lullabies or in the songs of herdsmen in the fields, but also to express dominance. Alan Lomax has correlated styles of singing from across the world with key characteristics of the political and social contexts in which they are embedded, and concluded that 'as social differentiation increases along with alienation and exclusivity of leadership function, there is usually a concomitant rise of explicit solos' (1968: 158):

> The solo wordy style stands for exclusive dominance and reaches its peak in large states where political organization has always depended upon a powerful centralized government and a strong leader of some kind, be he premier, president, emperor, khan, lama or god (Lomax, 1968: 161).

In Western music the single unaccompanied voice or instrument is relatively rare and tends to express extreme isolation and loneliness rather than 'exclusive dominance'. In Western music solo performers either accompany themselves, or play an instrument that allows a single player to produce several voices at once, so as to internalize social interaction, as it were. Perhaps this is because the leadership of which Lomax speaks is enacted between actual leaders and actual subjects, and therefore accompanied by the actual awed silence of these subjects, just as the flute of the lonely herdsman is accompanied by the actual silence of the vast plain. As soon as dominance or leadership is *represented*, it becomes necessary to *hear* the support of the leader's followers or the silence of the vast plain in the accompaniment, if only through a soft wavering drone, as for instance in 'Landscape', the third part of Vaughan Williams' *Sinfonia Antarctica*.

Not only is musical turn-taking very common across the world, it also has a long history in Western music. In early Christian psalm singing two forms were recognized, the 'responsorial' form, in which the cantor sang the lines of the psalm and the congregation answered after each verse with a single word, like 'Alleluiah' or 'Amen', and the 'antiphonal' form, in which the congregation sang a whole line before the psalm, between the verses, and at the end. The words and the music of the solo part therefore varied continuously, while the responses were formulaic and repetitive. The solo singer imparted information, both verbally and musically, the chorus confirmed and conformed. The antiphonal relation is therefore fundamentally unequal, an inequality which can be further enhanced by respectful silences between 'call' and 'response', or somewhat diminished by overlapping.

In smaller societies, musical turn-taking tends to become a favoured form when leadership becomes more remote, so that leaders are no longer 'first among equals'. But distance may diminish as the song proceeds. In the kingly assemblies of the Zulus, for instance, the King reached his decisions in public, with the whole tribe voicing its approval. The song would begin with the parts only just touching, but gradually the chorus would 'encroach upon the leader's time, until at last both are singing without letup in exciting rhythmic relationship to each other' (Lomax, 1968: 158). The same interactive structure can be observed in many contemporary advertising jingles, and also in the duet from Gershwin's *Porgy and Bess* which I will discuss at the end of this chapter.

Who is the leader and who are the members of the chorus? In the examples given so far they are the King and his subjects, or the priest and his congregation. But there are many other possibilities. In representational music the leader can be a heroic, brassy instrument like the trumpet in the 'Majestic Fanfare' news signature tune, or a softer and more sentimental instrument, a cello, for instance. In many forms of contemporary popular music the leader is a male singer and the chorus a group of female 'back up' vocalists, which enacts (from the point of view of the musicians) and represents (from the point of view of the audience) a relationship of male dominance. In advertising jingles the leader is someone who can act as a role model for the 'target' audience. In jingles directed at children, for instance, the solo singer tends to be either another child, the 'opinion leader' of the peer group, or an adult who sings in a 'funny' clown's voice, that is an adult who is *not* a parent or teacher and deliberately plays down his (it is always a him) adult characteristics, acting out the funny-uncle-who-always-brings-a-present role. These are the types of leader to whom the children's choirs in jingles respond, and to whom the advertisers no doubt hope the children who watch their commercials at home will also respond, by buying the advertised goods or begging their parents to do so.

As already indicated, responses can take different forms. The forms most common in advertising jingles are as follows:

1. The chorus repeats what the leader has sung line for line, in a kind of 'say after me' fashion. Let us call this *imitation*. The following jingle from a Ski yoghurt advertisement has a 'funny uncle' leader, a male voice singing in clownesque style, and a chorus of children's voices:

LEADER:	You take a spoon on your lips
CHORUS:	Take a spoon on your lips
LEADER:	And then you lick your lips
CHORUS:	Then you lick your lips
(…)	

2. The chorus repeats the final line of each verse. Let us call this *emulation*.

3. The response differs from the call and is brief and *formulaic*: 'Yes', 'No', 'So be it', 'Hurrah', 'Go, Johnny', 'Long live the King', 'Down with the Dictator'. In songs it may be the 'Amen' or the 'Alleluiah' of the church service, the 'Oooh' or 'Yeah Baby' of the pop song, or the sung brand name of the advertising jingle. The jingles below are from a toy commercial in which the brand name is affirmed by the chorus (both leader and chorus are children), and from a commercial for 'Move' flavoured milk which has a male soloist and woman singing 'Ah' in an erotically charged sigh.

LEADER:	Toys from Kidco go and go
CHORUS:	Kidco, Kidco
(…)	

LEADER:	Tell me with your lips
	The things I'm gonna taste now
	Take me to the stars
	And shoot me into space now
	Move…
WOMAN:	Aaah…

4. The response differs from the call and is a more *fully stated* response, such as the antiphone in the psalmody, the brass section riff punctuating the saxophone solo in a big band performance, or the sung slogan in an advertising jingle. 'Talkin' 'bout my generation' from The Who's 'My Generation' and 'Take a shot of Comfort' from a Southern Comfort whisky commercial are examples of such response choruses. In the latter a male solo voice is responded to by a small group of women's voices.

LEADER:	People try to put us down
CHORUS:	Talkin' 'bout my generation
LEADER:	Just because we get around

CHORUS: (…)	Talkin' 'bout my generation
LEADER:	So listen to me baby, Got a new plan, Why don't we
LEADER + CHORUS:	Take a shot of Comfort
LEADER:	Gonna show you when you see
CHORUS:	Take a shot of Comfort.

It should be noted that both kinds of responses may be positive, supportive, affirmative, or disagreeing, opposing, contrasting, dissenting.

The various forms of musical turn-taking can present or represent all kinds of unequal relations, including the relation between persuasive salespeople or role models and targeted consumers, and an analysis of these forms can bring out, not only who the leader and the chorus are (a child, a choir of other children), but also how their interaction is represented (the message of the child is repeated and affirmed by the other children). According to Rösing (1982: 34) such representations constitute 'manipulation models'. The 'socio-psychological model', for instance, has 'a "good" wife, a scientist, a famous football star and so on take on the adviser and authoritarian function' and 'mostly uses forms of march music and fanfare' of which 'the affirmative character supports the declaration of the authority figure', while the 'identification model' 'has a special affinity to choral music with jubilation motives so that the listener can identify himself with the choral singers'.

It should finally be pointed out that these relationships can exist, not only between an individual voice or instrument and a group of voices or instruments, but also between two individual voices or instruments, as in duets, or between two groups, as, for instance, in the big band arrangements of 1930s swing bands which often had the bands' sections do battle with each other – Wilfrid Mellers (1964: 312) described it better than I can:

> The swing bands tended to separate a technically drilled brass section from a reed section,… so creating a brazen, big-city version of the traditional antiphony of African ritual music and of the gospel hymn. Since little

room is given for *melodic* extemporisation, sheer physical power comes to stand in lieu of creation... and the barking riffs of the massed trumpets, trombones and saxes epitomize the city's energy; although the effect may be one of well-being it is also, significantly, belligerent.

In the Dutch Protestant church I grew up in, communal singing was sometimes divided between the men and the women, who first sang in alternation, and then, in the final verse, together. It was a proud feeling for a little boy to be able to sing with the men – but it was also a little alienating for him *not* to be allowed to sing with his mother and sisters.

These turn-taking patterns are, again, not restricted to music. The study of language has been so strongly influenced by writing, and hence by the 'solo voice', that the possibility of a communal voice, of a group speaking, commonplace as it may be in music, has been overlooked. Bramstedt (1965: 226–7) describes an 'antiphonal' speech event, a radio broadcast by Joseph Goebbels, who began by saying:

> Thus you, my listeners, are representing the nation at the moment. And to you I should like to direct ten questions which you should answer with the German people before the whole world.

Then he put the questions (for example 'Are you and are the German people determined to give your ultimate for victory?'). Each question was answered by shouts of approval and thunderous applause. Goebbels concluded:

> I asked you – you gave me your answers. From your mouth the attitude of the German people has been made manifest.

To summarize:

1. *Adjacency pairs* consist of two sequentially ordered and complementary moves in the ongoing speech or music or sound activity, for instance a question and an answer, a call and response, a door bell and the buzzer that opens the door. The two moves are normally performed by two different interactive participants. The first of these is the *initiator*, the second the *reactor*.

2. The greater the *segregation* between the initiator's move and the reactor's move (for example the longer the pause between the two),

the greater the real or symbolic distance (for example power difference) between them. The greater the *overlap* between the two
moves, the less the real or symbolic distance between the
participants.

3. The complementary relation between the moves in an adjacency
   pair can take two forms, *repetition* and *response*. *Imitation* involves
   the repetition of all, *emulation* the repetition of part of the
   initiator's move (of what the lead singer of a jingle sings, the teacher
   in a classroom says and so on). *Responses* are more or less independently formulated, and may either be *formulaic* or more *fully stated.*
   Both types of response can be *supportive* of (or otherwise similar to)
   the previous move of the adjacency pair, or *opposing* (or otherwise
   contrasting) to that move.

4. Both initiator and reactor may either be an individual or a group. A
   dialogue between two individuals is a *sequential duet.* The idea can
   be extended to three individuals (*trio*), four (*quartet*) and so on. The
   upper limit is usually six (*sextet*), sometimes seven (*septet*).
   According to Joos (1967: 35) 'a group size of approximately six sets
   the limits on the size and composition of a 'committee' in the
   English-speaking sense. Beyond that parliamentary law is requisite,
   that is, a division into active and chair-warming persons.' It is so
   also in (Western) music.
   A dialogue between groups is a *sequential group dialogue,* and a
   dialogue between an individual and a group is a *leader–group
   dialogue.* Leader–group dialogues are always sequential.

Simultaneity in music

The voices and instruments in music are usually heard
simultaneously – maybe because music is so overwhelmingly about
'rapport' rather than 'report', to use Tannen's terms. The various
possible *modes* of simultaneous interaction again reflect (emotively
celebrate, struggle with and so on) modes of interaction in daily life
and work. They form the 'immediate affective expression of social
identity or cultural collectivity' (Tagg, 1984) which are the special
strength of musical (and dance) expression.

Interlock

So far we have assumed that musical groups are involved in a common activity, in singing or playing the same piece. But this is not necessarily the case. People may be involved in the same kind of musical activity at the same time and in the same place without actually playing or singing together, and they may in fact derive pleasure from this, and a sense of belonging to a larger whole. Think of an orchestra tuning up, or of Charles Ives' inimitable composition *General Putnam's Camp*, in which:

> Several military and ragtime tunes are played together in different rhythms and tempi, and often in different keys, mixed with the huzzaing of the crowd and various a-rhythmic, non-tonal sounds of nature. The music evokes, with astonishing immediacy, the physical and nervous sensation of being present at a vast outdoor celebration (Mellers, 1964: 46).

It is tempting to think of this kind of sound as 'cacophonic', yet sound events of this kind are not necessarily ugly or anarchic, and neither are the equivalent speech events, for example the simultaneous talking of many small groups of people at a large reception or party, or the equivalent sound events, for example the simultaneous singing of many different birds, or the simultaneous sounds of many different hammers, saws and drills in a workshop or at a building site. Lomax has a coined a term for this kind of interaction, 'interlock':

> Everyone is singing so independently in melodic, rhythmic, and/or harmonic terms that it is impossible to ascribe a dominant role to any part. The effect may be one of integrated, contrapuntal unity, or extreme heterogeneity and diffuseness (Lomax, 1968: 156).

And he notes that, worldwide, it is often associated with female singing – in the same way that 'rapport talk' is often associated with female talk:

> Perhaps it is more than idle speculation to suggest that this style, where everyone phonates at once, suits the feminine group which, in most societies, is essentially egalitarian. Thus interlock may represent the first, or one of the earliest and most egalitarian nodels of all human interaction – the basic interaction model of the feminine society (Lomax, 1968: 156).

Social unison

The case of 'social unison' or 'monophony' is quite different: all voices and/or instruments sing or play the same notes. What this can present or represent is, again, given by what we *do* when we sing or play in unison: the same thing. In context we can then give more precise meaning and value to this basic given. Where we value it positively, it can come to mean solidarity, consensus, a positive sense of joint experience and belonging to a group. Where we value it negatively, it can come to mean conformity, strict disciplining and a lack of individuality. Lomax (1968: 156) has found that small societies in which social unison is the dominant form tend to be 'leaderless societies' which are male-dominated and have an emphasis on consensus and conformity:

> North American Indians, Australian Aborigines and New Guinea Highlanders all structure their singing activities in this way, as do many societies in which males dominate ritual life… Our research indicates that this was an early communication discovery, probably more associated with male than female performance, and with dominance rather than with independence (Lomax, 1968: 157).

But in more complex societies, too, social unison can be an important means of disciplining joint activity – whether in the pub or the church, the school or the army, it allows no one to opt out or act out of step.

An additional factor is vocal (or instrumental) *blend*. This is a matter of degree. On the one end of the scale unison voices can be so well blended that individual timbres can no longer be distinguished. On the other end the singing or playing becomes what musicologists call 'heterophonic': each voice or instrument stands out from the whole through individual timbres, timings, embellishments and so on. Late-eighteenth-century hymn singing in the newly constituted USA was apparently of this kind, a musical enactment of the rights of the individual which was experienced as total musical anarchy by visitors from Europe. In teaching children to sing, Anglo-Americans tend to put little emphasis on blending and usually seem charmed by childish heterophony. Children of other cultures, on the other hand, appear to achieve vocal blend more or less spontaneously:

> Tonal unity is achieved among Anglo-Americans only by intensive rehearsal of carefully chosen personnel under the restrictive guidance of a director. Yet a casual assembly of comparative strangers in other cultures

can immediately form a harmonious choir of voices that seem to melt together into a big, unified, colourful sound.... Each chorus member, by submerging his individuality in the collective intent, adds his complement to the structure of the whole sound.... Every performance demands and brings about group solidarity (Lomax, 1968:171).

In advertising music vocal blend often becomes a resource for representing consumers as unique individuals or as united in their preference for the advertised product. The male choirs in beer ads are rough, with the individual voices clearly standing out, while the female choirs in many other ads are very well blended. This constructs men as more individuated than women – and as less oriented towards values of solidarity.

Social heterogeneity

In 'polyphony' several different voices and/or instrumental parts combine and intertwine. However, each of these also has musical interest and value as an individual voice and could stand on its own. As a result there is no sense of individuality as something in opposition to or irreconcilable with society, something that would need to be sacrificed or betrayed if one wanted to truly belong to society as a whole. Thus polyphony expresses the same kind of social values as polyrhythmicality, but now in respect of the melody, the musical 'speech act' which will be discussed in more detail in the next chapter: different people say their own thing, yet fit together in a harmonious (or occasionally disharmonious) sounding whole. They are 'equal but different', united in a musical pluralism.

Lomax (1968: 165) showed that two-voiced polyphony, in many of the smaller societies in which it is used, symbolizes gender roles, even when both parts are sung by men, and that the societies in which this occurs tend to be 'complementary' societies, societies with a distinct division of labour between men and women but no strong sense of women's work being of less value than men's work, or vice versa. Indeed, he believes that counterpoint and polyphony are 'very old feminine inventions':

> Subsistence complementarity is at its maximum among gatherers, early gardeners and horticulturists. Among gatherers, women generally bring in the major part of the food. In early hoe agriculture women outweigh or

equal men in productive importance, probably because it was they who domesticated the plants and even the animals. In such societies women are not so likely to be shut away from the public center of life; not so often are they passive witnesses of social events, but active participants at or close to the center of the stage. It is in such societies that we find the highest occurrence of polyphonic singing (Lomax, 1968: 167).

In Europe, early medieval music was monophonic. From the ninth century onwards polyphony began to develop, first in the form of 'parallel organum', which is what we would now call 'harmony lines', where the different voices still 'follow the same line', but no longer 'say exactly the same thing', because they can now sing at their own (pitch) level and acquire different identities as soprano, alto, tenor, bass and so on – identities which have had complex relationships to gender, and which at times already involved some hierarchizing, but, interestingly, of the 'middle' voice rather than the 'top' voice. From about 1100 onwards, 'counterpoint', or inversion, began to be developed, a form of music in which two voices 'say the opposite thing' (for example when the one goes up by two steps, the other goes down by two steps), yet fit together harmoniously. A century later full 'polyphony' began to develop and the different melodies gradually became fully independent, also rhythmically. The expression of heterogeneity was not restricted to the music, but also included 'polytextuality', the simultaneous performance of two or three different texts, sometimes in two different languages, for example French and Latin (Harman and Mellers, 1962: 108). In this period, you could say, Europe had lost some of its cultural unity, yet managed to incorporate difference in a more complex and multifaceted identity.

Social domination

In 'homophonic' music one voice (the melody) becomes dominant, the 'top voice', and the other voices accompaniment, support, 'back up'. The parts of these 'subordinated voices' do not have individual value and are not melodically interesting in their own right. They are meaningful only in relation to the whole. Their role is 'harmonic', they must 'harmonize with' the dominant voice, supply chordal pillars to prop up the dominant voice.

Homophonic music began to develop around 1600, in the work of the Italian opera composers. By the time of the Industrial Revolution it had become dominant to the exclusion of almost everything else, and it still is, in the vast majority of popular music. Its culmination was the symphony orchestra, which dates from the time of the Industrial Revolution and is a form of making music which relates to the small ensemble as the factory relates to the small workshop. A large number of musicians perform music which is, into the minutest details, master-minded, first by a blueprint, the score, then by an overseer, the baton-wielding conductor in front of the orchestra, the only one to have the full score in front of him (it still is almost always a him). What Andrew Ure, an early-nineteenth-century apologist of the then new factory system, wrote of factories, goes, *mutatis mutandis*, also for the symphony orchestra. Factory overseers, he wrote, had to learn to overcome the difficulties in:

> the distribution of the different members of the apparatus into one cooperative body, in impelling each man with the appropriate delicacy and speed, and in training human beings to identify themselves with the unvarying regularity of the complex automaton (quoted in Mumford, 1934: 173).

Arnold, in 1806, wrote in very similar terms about the then new role of the conductor:

> The fusion of the individual members to the reproduction of a single feeling is the work of the leader, concert master, music director or conductor (quoted in Koury, 1986: 61).

And Max Weber believed that 'one of the most highly developed types outside the factory (of the combination of specialized functions) is the organization of a symphony orchestra' (Weber, 1947: 227). The symphony orchestra thus enacts and celebrates discipline and control, the fragmentation of work into specialized functions, in short, the work values of the industrial age. It is perhaps significant that countries like Japan and China, as soon as they began to industrialize on a large scale, also began to play Western symphonic music, often with a great zeal to excel in it, and conceiving of it as a technical achievement.

However, with harmony comes the possibility of *disharmony*, of conflict, of clashes between the dominant voice and the subordinated voices, of muffled tension, dissonance, dissent – a dissonance which the music must then constantly try to resolve if it is to continue to progress forward (note the metaphorical resonance of the technical terms 'resolution' and 'chord progression'). This book is not the place for detailed technical explanations of harmony, but anyone with ears who has been sufficiently exposed to Western music can hear whether accompanying voices create harmony or disharmony, consonance or dissonance, and so begin to appreciate how and why the 'drama' of nineteenth-century orchestral music derived from the way it stretched the 'class struggle' between the dominant voice and the subordinated voices further and further. The composer Schoenberg, one of the key figures in breaking with traditional harmony and developing 'a-tonal' music, hints at this in his massive *Theory of Harmony*, when he speaks of 'transgressive dissonance' and compares dissonant voices to 'vagrants' who travel without a passport in a world ruled by the 'laws of the autocrat', and of a situation in which 'the supreme lord becomes weak and his subjects strong' (Schoenberg, 1983[1911]: 128–9).

In this light it is interesting that 'easy listening' adaptations of nineteenth-century music often strengthen the dominant voice and weaken harmonic conflict between the dominant voice and the subordinated voices. A Henry Mancini adaptation of Beethoven's 'Moonlight' sonata, from his *Award Winning Hits* (RCA SP-118, 1972) not only strengthened the metronomic pulse by adding light drums, but also (1) replaced the solo piano, an instrument for individual expression, with the symphony orchestra, a group 'instrument' requiring discipline and control, (2) simplified the chords in passages where the accompaniment threatened to assert itself over the melody, forcing it to change direction towards a different tonal region, and (3) added melody lines where Beethoven's melodies apparently were not dominant enough (these changes are discussed in more detail in Van Leeuwen, 1991).

'Classical' music was, and still is, the 'high culture' music of Western society. A well-developed taste for and interest in classical music constitutes what Bourdieu (1986: 16) called the 'legitimate taste' and is a 'mark of distinction' for members of the dominant class. Easy listening music, on the other hand, is targeted towards the lower middle class, the class which aspires to belong to the higher middle class, and so also aspires to its musical taste. Yet it receives the music in an adapted form which in fact helps draw the line between the two classes, and, like attempts to 'speak properly' by people with a socially stigmatized dialect, easily provokes the ridicule of people with 'good taste' in classical music. It is a form which removes from the music its harmonic complexity and hence also its ability to incorporate and resolve harmonic tension, the expression of plurality and dissent which may be allowed between fractions of the dominant class, but cannot be allowed between classes. It retains the dominance of the melody and adds the mechanical pulse of the drums, the discipline of time, as well as the symphony orchestra, the musical equivalent of the factory. Thus the easy listening audience is doubly dispossessed, denied access to both opposition and dominance.

To summarize:

1. Participants in the production of simultaneous sound may be either two or more individuals or two or more groups. The case of two individuals is that of the *simultaneous duet*, the case of three individuals that of the *simultaneous trio* and so on. An example of simultaneous *group interaction* is the interaction between the sections of a large band or orchestra.

2. When different participants are involved in the same simultaneous sound production activity and co-present in the same place, but not involved in producing one and the same 'piece' (piece of music, conversation, discussion and so on), the simultaneous dialogue is *unstructured*. This is the case which Lomax termed 'interlock'.

3. Structured simultaneous sound may be *unison*. In this case all participants produce the same sounds, either in such a way that all the sounds *blend* so that individual sounds no longer stand out, or in such a way that the individual sounds are *unblended* to a greater or lesser degree, so that they can still be picked out from the whole.

4. Simultaneous sounds may also differ from each other and in this case they are either hierarchized or not. In the case of *plurality* there is no hierarchy. All sounds would not only have value on their own, but also contribute equally to the whole.

   There is then the further possibility that they are *parallel*, 'saying' the same thing in a different way, or (literally or figuratively) 'at a different level', or *opposing*, 'saying' opposing things. Both principles can result in *harmonious*, cooperative interaction or in *disharmonious*, competitive and conflictual interaction.

5. Finally, when simultaneous sounds are hierarchized, there will be *dominance*: one sound (either an individual or a group sound) could stand on its own and will carry most weight in the interaction, while the other sounds could not stand on their own and make small contributions which acquire value only in their whole. This case is therefore the simultaneous equivalent of (sequential) leader–group interaction.

The relation between the dominant and the subordinated sound can, again, be *harmonious* and supportive, or *disharmonious* and conflictual.

Example: the duet

I will again conclude with an overview of the distinctions made in the course of the chapter (see Figure 4.1), and an example in which these distinctions are used in the analysis of a 'sound interaction'.

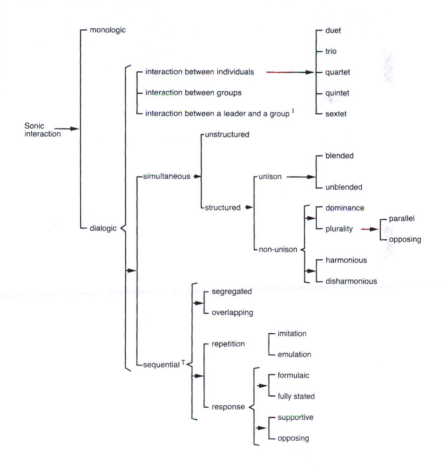

Figure 4.1   A system network of sonic interaction

Our example is the duet 'Bess, You Is My Woman Now' from Gershwin's opera *Porgy and Bess*. In this song Porgy and Bess celebrate their new-found love. The musical interaction therefore articulates the interaction between two new lovers, in the context of this particular story, with its particular setting and its particular characters. The setting is Catfish Row, a poor black harbourside community in the South. Bess, a beautiful woman, has been left to fend for herself after Crown, her husband, has committed murder and escaped to nearby Kittiwah Island. Sportin' Life, a drugs dealer and low-life character, has tried to persuade her to come with him to New York, but she has resisted. With nowhere else to go, she has moved in with Porgy, a cripple living in a miserable hovel, an 'innocent and good man, yet broken and unfulfilled' (Mellers, 1964: 398). The two become a pair and it is at this point that they sing the duet. As far as the plot is concerned, 'happiness has just begun'. But in the end Bess will not be able to resist the temptations of Sportin' Life, his 'happy dust', and his promises of life in New York.

1.	**Group melody** (**strings**)	parallel harmonious initiator	
2.	**Solo melody** (**cello**)	monologue reactor	relation to (1): segregated opposing
3.	**Porgy sings whole verse** *'Bess you is my woman now, You is, you is And you must laugh and sing And dance for two instead of one'* (etc.) PLUS	initiator	relation to (5): dominance harmonious
4.	**Group melody** (**strings**)	unison blended	relation to (3): unison; unblended
	PLUS		relation to (5): dominance harmonious

5.	**Group accompaniment** (rest of orchestra)	plurality parallel	relation to (3,4): subordinated
6.	**Group melody** (strings)	unison blend	(bridge to key of Bess)
7.	**Bess sings whole verse** *'Porgy I's your woman now,* *I is, I is* *And I ain't never going nowhere* *'less you'll go too'* (etc.)	reactor	relation to (3): fully stated response supportive segregated (by 6)
	PLUS		relation to (9): dominance harmonious
8.	**Group melody** (strings) PLUS	unison blended	relation to (7): unison
9.	**Group accompaniment** (rest of orchestra)	plurality parallel	relation to (7,8): subordinated
10.	**Porgy sings short verse** (melody as in (1)) *'Mornin' time and evenin' time* *and summertime and wintertime'* PLUS	reactor	relation to (7): fully stated response; supportive less segregated than (7)
11.	**Group melody** (strings) PLUS	unison blend	relation to (10): unison unblended
13.	**Group accompaniment** (rest of orchestra)	plurality parallel	relation to (10,11): subordinated
14	**Group melody** (strings)	unison blend	(bridge to new key)

15. **Porgy and Bess sing together** *'Bess you is my woman'* *'Porgy I's your woman now'* *'Now and forever. This life is'* *'I is, I is, and I ain't never'*	plurality parallel harmonious harmonious	relation to (18): dominance harmonious
PLUS		
16. **Group melody** **(strings)**	unison blend	unison with BESS
PLUS		opposing harmonious with PORGY
17. **Group accompaniment** **(rest of orchestra)**	plurality parallel	relation to (15): subordinated
THIS GRADUALLY **CHANGES TO**		
15a. **Porgy and Bess sing together** **(words also differ)** *'I know you mean it'* *'But I ain't going'* *'I have seen it'* *'You hear me saying'*	plurality parallel opposing disharmo- nious	BESS' relation to (17a): dominance harmonious
PLUS		PORGY's relation to (17a): plurality opposing disharmonious
16a. **Group melody** **(strings)**	unison blend	unison with BESS opposing disharmonious with PORGY
PLUS		

17a. Group accompaniment (rest of orchestra)	plurality parallel	relation to (15a): subordinated to BESS
18. Final 2 chords (strings)	dominance harmonious	

The short introduction (sound events 1 and 2) contains two opposing moves: a love theme played by the strings and a dark, mournful melody played by a single unaccompanied cello. The strings interact with each other in harmonious parallel, the cello is alone, and reacts to the love theme by opposing it with sadness and loneliness. Thus two themes are introduced and intertwined from the very start: love combines with the group and with harmonious togetherness, not with an individual who is set apart from the community.

Porgy, the man, initiates the love duet, addressing Bess in the second person, claiming ownership, as it were: 'You is my woman now.' The community (as represented by the orchestra) supports him in two ways: the violins, the community's 'heart strings' double the melody and play in unison with him, and the rest of the orchestra provides harmonious accompaniment. Next, Bess, the woman, responds, at first still keeping her distance from Porgy (there is considerable 'segregation' between the two moves). In her response she accepts Porgy's claim: 'Porgy, I is your woman now'. The community of instruments is behind her in this, supporting her in the same way as it supported Porgy in the first verse. Still engaged in 'sequential dialogue', still singing in turns, but already with less segregation between the moves, Porgy responds once more, again supported by the whole community. Their love will be for ever: 'Mornin' time and evenin' time, summertime and wintertime'.

Finally they begin to sing together, enacting their 'rapport', but they do not sing in unison. Unison is for the relation with the community. In love, the partners sing their own words and their own melodies. Initially these fit together harmoniously but as the duet proceeds, they start to diverge. By the end Bess has gained the upper

hand and sings the main melody, doubled by the strings and harmoni-
cally supported by the rest of the orchestra, while Porgy sings a
chromatically descending lament that hardly fits the words of hope and
trust he sings. What happened sequentially in the introduction now
happens simultaneously: Porgy's voice becomes a sad, solitary voice,
sharply counterpointing Bess and the community.

In the next scene Bess will be persuaded by the people of Catfish
Row to join them on a boat trip and picnic. Porgy, the cripple, will
have to stay behind, alone. During the picnic Crown will come to take
Bess with him to his hiding place on Kittiwah Island. She will return
to Porgy three days later, sick with fever and remorse. When they sing
the duet, none of this has happened yet. But in their musical interaction they already seem to have an inkling what fate will have in store
for them.

Exercises and discussion points

1. Study the interaction between the instruments and/or voices in
    examples of three genres of twentieth-century music.
    How might the differences be explained?

2. Record an hour or so of the goings-on in a nursery school. What
    patterns of speech interaction can be observed? If the patterns shift
    from time to time, what causes the shifts?

3. Turn the following poem by Natalya Gorbanevskaya (1977: 177)
    into a piece for at least three voices and/or groups of voices, with
    added sound effects.

    > We shall remember
    > – smoke rises from dry grass
    > We shall remember
    > – millstones grind to a stop
    >
    > We shall remember
    > each footstep, each sigh,
    > the blood, the blood-flecked sweat
    > and blood's heavy burden

The flame leaps through the grass
and reaches the trees,
and the one who lies in the leaves –
his time has come

A fanfare sounds in the dark,
a blade is drawn across the pane:
we shall remember,
we shall remember all

Which of the possibilities for interaction explained and exemplified in this chapter did you use and why did you choose them?

Chapter 5

Melody

The sound act

The Belgian linguist Jef Verschueren (1985) lists some 650 different speech acts, 'things people do with words', from 'abandon' to 'zip one's lip'. Such a list has not been compiled for 'sound acts', but that is not because we do not do things with sound. With sound we announce our presence, hail, warn, call for help, lull to sleep, comfort, and much more. Birds have their pleasure calls, distress calls, territorial defence calls, flight calls, flock calls and so on, but, as Schafer noted (1977: 34), so have people. In the right context, music can be a pleasure call, the car horn a territorial defence call, the police siren an alarm call and so on. In all this the dividing line between speech, music and other sounds is thin. Many of the same kinds of things can be done verbally, musically or by means of 'noises'. It is only recently that musical sounds such as the hunting horn, the postman's horn or the church bells have been replaced by non-musical sounds. And with the sound of the hunting horn much could be done. It could open and close the hunt, announce the different animals by means of little fanfares, cheer on the dogs, give warning, call for aim, utter special signs of pleasure, and more. Train whistles, similarly, not only allowed drivers to pass on many different messages between trains, but even to do so in a personal style (Schafer, 1977: 81). And if we can use sound to actually *do* things, to hail or warn or soothe, we can also use it to *represent* these things, to represent hailing or warning or soothing. Hunting horns lived on in music long after their language had gone in decline, and contemporary composers musically imitate or incorporate the sound of sirens (for example Bernstein, in *West Side Story*), car alarms (for example Steve Reich in *City Life*) and more. Speech can include all sorts of onomatopoeic sounds, not just the animal sounds that are usually quoted, but also mechanical sounds, as when children imitate cartoon sound effects such as 'WHOOOM', 'KA-BLAM', 'KRAASH' and so on.

As many of my examples have shown, sound can be used to represent our environment and to represent the actions and interactions of people (cf. the preceding chapter). Such representations imitate sounds, or, more abstractly, distil key qualities from them. But whether we use sound to *present* (to act or interact) or to *represent* (Martinec, 1996), sound is always dynamic. Sounds are not things, nor can they represent things. Sounds are actions and can only represent the actions of people, places and things: the cries of street vendors, not the vendors themselves, the rustling of the leaves of the trees, not the trees themselves, the lapping of water against the shore, not the lake itself. Sound messages only have verbs, so to speak. The nouns are inferred, not stated.

To speak about this in more detail we first need to return to our discussion of rhythm. In Chapter 3 we saw how rhythm segments the stream of sound into discrete sound events, discrete moves in the ongoing sound (inter)act, and how the rhythmic structure of these phrases creates the pulses that mark the moments of greatest communicative import within these phrases. Together the two elements, phrasing and pulsing, provide frames for sound acts. But if anything is going to be communicated, something will have to be fitted into the frame, a melody, for instance (cf. Zak, 1982). In Chapter 3 I used the first two bars from Tchaikovsky's Fifth Symphony as an example (Figure 3.1), and pointed out how the rhythmic pulses in these two bars mark the *spaces* for the most important sound signs, and how it is the pitches occurring in these spaces (and the resulting pitch *contour*, or melody) which outline the 'message' contained in the two bars. As discussed in Chapter 3, the first pulse carries a 'gloomy' minor third note, the second carries a slightly higher note, which lifts up the gloom a little (but only a little, and only briefly, as if melody is too heavy to be lifted any higher) and the third drops the melody again to the minor third, and then down to the tonic, the 'ground level' of the key in which the piece is scripted. In other words, the attempt to 'rise above it' fails, and the end result is a sound act of 'admitting defeat' in a downcast way (because of the low pitch level), of 'giving up trying'. *Who* gives up trying, or in respect of *what* defeat is admitted, we do not know. Like all abstract art, instrumental music leaves things open, to be filled in differently by each listener, unless professional interpreters or opinion leaders intervene to regulate or influence interpretation, or unless the meaning is made more concrete through the words it is set to, or through the images or dramatic actions it accompanies.

I am not saying here that the pattern of this melody (minor third–fourth–minor third) always 'means' 'admitting defeat', or that 'admitting defeat' is always expressed by this pattern. 'Admitting', 'of' and 'defeat' are words and words are both too precise and not precise enough for 'translating' musical meanings. But however people (composers, musicians, professional interpreters, audiences) interpret and experience this pattern, their interpretations and experiences are likely to be in the same broad area, and unlikely to include, for instance 'joy', or 'surprise'. And they will derive from and be concordant with an *experiential meaning potential*, with a knowledge of what it is we would physically have to *do* to produce this kind of pattern with our voice: starting on a very low point, increasing vocal effort to raise the pitch slightly, then dropping it again to the low level, as if it is too heavy. When and why would even such a small effort be too great? This too is common human experience. When you have no strength, no willpower left, not even to raise your voice. A possible explanation for why Tchaikovsky's music has many moments of this kind will be discussed later in this chapter.

For Fonagy and Magdics (1972: 304) melodies express emotions, in speech as well as in music: 'emotions are expressed in European vocal and instrumental music by a melody configuration, dynamics and rhythm similar to those of speech'. In comparing Hungarian and French data they found very similar patterns, and they concluded that these patterns are therefore not arbitrary: 'If a certain emotion is expressed by similar melodic patterns in non-related languages, then intonation must not be considered as arbitrary' (ibid.: 292). Here are some examples of how they characterize the realization of these emotions. The notation of the speech patterns is adapted from Delattre (1972) and uses musical staves to give a sense of the scale of the pitch steps, rather than to indicate precise pitches. For the music patterns I have used musical notation: even if you do not read music you can perhaps follow the ups and downs of the black dots, and appreciate the size of the jumps between them.

Joy

Wide pitch range at high pitch level. The melody rises, then falls sharply, then stays level (or descends slightly). Lively tempo. Pitch glides (Figure 5.1).

Figure 5.1 The intonation of 'joy' and its musical representation (in 'Joy Spring', Clifford Brown)

Tenderness

Voice at high pitch level but with narrow pitch range. Melody descending slightly and undulating. Medium tempo. Soft, slightly nasal and labialized voice (Figure 5.2).

Figure 5.2 The intonation of 'tenderness' and its musical representation (in 'Tenderly', Gross/Lawrence)

Surprise

Voice suddenly glides up (or up and down) to high pitch level, then
falls. Extent of the fall depends on degree of surprise. Medium tempo.
Breathy voice (Figure 5.3).

Figure 5.3   The intonation of 'surprise' and its musical
representation (in 'Sudden Samba', Neil Larsen)

Anguish

Voice at mid-pitch level. Extremely narrow pitch range. The melody of
the pulsed syllables rises about a semitone and returns to mid-high
level 'where it becomes, so to speak paralyzed' (Fonagy and Magdics,
1972: 289). Breathy, tense voice (Figure 5.4).

Figure 5.4   The intonation of 'anguish' and its musical
representation (in 'My Heart Cries For You', Ray Charles)

In these examples the titles and/or lyrics express the same emotion as the intonation or the music. But this is not always so. It is quite possible to say 'I'm so happy' while sounding decidedly unhappy. In many songs the emotions expressed by the lyrics contrast strongly with those expressed by the music. The lyrics of Simon and Garfunkel's 'I Am A Rock' begin on a note of wistful sadness ('A winter's day/In a deep and dark December/I am alone/Gazing from my window...') and then move to a refusal of love, based on the fear of being hurt ('I have no need of friendship/Friendship causes pain/It's laughter and loving I disdain/I am a rock/I am an island...'). The music, on the other hand, has a bright rhythm, a happily ascending melody, and, unlike the lyrics, is free of any sentimental devices. If the music had also expressed pain, you might have thought the 'disdain' a pose, to hide the pain underneath. As it is, the song becomes defiant, even cynical, perhaps. Like other intonation analysts (for example Crystal, 1969) and music analysts (for example Cooke, 1959) Fonagy and Magdics argue for the meaning of melodies on the basis of the words they go with. But melodies are not slaved to words. They form an independent meaning system, which can relate to the verbal meaning system in many different ways. The same words have been set to many different melodies, and the same melodies have carried different words, often changing, in the process, from gospel songs into teenage love songs, from nursery rhymes into advertising jingles and so on.

Do melodies only 'express emotions'? I think not, and hope to show so in the rest of this chapter. And even when they do, are emotions only 'expressed'? Do they not have an active as well as a passive side, a side of *touching* people as well as a side of being in a certain state or experiencing a certain feeling? Again I would like to stress the dynamic and interactive character of sound here and correct a too one-sided emphasis on representation and expression. To quote some of the 'feelings and attitudes' on Fonagy and Magdics' list, melodies do not only 'express tenderness', they also and at the same time *caress*, they do not only 'express scorn', they also and at the same time *mock*, they do not only 'express longing', they also and at the same time *plead*, to give just a few examples. They are also *sound acts*.

To summarize:

Rhythmic phrases provide frames for sound acts. These sound acts themselves are realized by a configuration of choices from all the sound resources available in the given context. Melody often plays a key role, but not always and never only. Thus the sound 'caress' may be realized by a certain choice of melodic means (voice at high pitch level; narrow pitch range; slightly descending and undulating melody); but also and at the same time by certain rhythmic choices (for example a medium tempo); by a choice of 'social distance' (soft, hence close); and by certain choices of voice quality or instrumental timbre (slightly nasal, labialized) and so on. Change any of these, and the sound act will also change – change the voice quality of the aural 'caress' to nasal, tense and loud, and the melody might be better described as sounding like a whining complaint. .

Continuity

The *end* of a melodic phrase either sounds open-ended ('as if there is more to come'), or final ('as if there is no more to come'. In the case of *finality* the end of the melody falls to a low pitch, and, in Western music, to the tonic, the note in the key of which the piece of music is scripted and which therefore provides a sense of ending, a sense of resolution and conclusion. Continuity can be realized in a number of ways: by what is sometimes called a 'non-terminal fall', that is a falling pitch which does not fall deep enough to suggest finality; by a level pitch; by a rising pitch; and/or, in the case of music, by any note which is *not* the tonic.

The role of the tonic as a means for providing closure in music is specific to Western music. It was developed in the same period as central perspective in painting and had the same kind of unifying function. In the medieval modes, based as they were on the pentatonic, any note of the scale could provide the sense of an ending, and act as a 'key centre'. In the Renaissance a strict hierarchy became established between the fundamentals, so that any melody, whatever the harmonic progressions it traversed, had to return, ultimately, to the same predetermined note, the tonic. In this music there could be only one centre, one outcome, one conclusion. John Shepherd (Shepherd *et al.*, 1977; Shepherd, 1991) links these changes to contemporaneous changes in social organization. Where the intervallic relations of medieval music reflected a social system that could be characterized as 'a vast system of personal relationships whose intersecting threads ran from one level of the social structure to another' (Bloch, quoted in Shepherd *et al.*, 1977: 91), the intervallic relations in the new music gave expression to the more centralized and absolutist systems of social organization which had replaced the earlier ones:

> The architectonism of the tonal structure articulates the world sense of industrial man, for it is a structure having one central viewpoint (that of the key-note) that is the focus of a single, unified sound-sense involving a high degree of distancing (Shepherd *et al.*, 1977: 105).

As far as final and non-final pitch curves are concerned, many linguists see intonational finality as a redundant signal of grammatical completeness and continuity as a redundant signal of grammatical incompleteness (cf. the literature review in Van Leeuwen, 1982: 69–71), and often that is exactly what it is. Studying the intonation patterns of actual speech, however, shows that continuity indicators may also come at the end, and finality indicators in the middle of a sentence (as defined grammatically). In conversational speech almost every phrase ends with a continuity intonation. Speakers will only provide the sense of an ending when they have come to the end of what they want to say. And even then they may use a continuity intonation, to invite the other partner(s) in the conversation to take over and complete what they were saying. It is for this reason that many questions have a rising intonation: they invite a completion of the incomplete statement which every question is (the question 'Who did it?', for instance, can be seen as a statement lacking the 'doer' of the action, the question 'What did you do?' as a statement lacking the deed, the question 'Where was it?' as a statement lacking the place and so on). But not only questions, also statements can end on a rising intonation. What this means will depend on the context, and on how people value finality and open-endedness. Some people may see open-endedness as tentative and hesitant – they are likely to have a preference for 'report talk', to use Deborah Tannen's term, for being assertive and sure of yourself. Others will see it as interactive, cooperative and supportive, as leaving space for others to add their contribution. They are more likely to be 'rapport talk' oriented people.

Here is, again, the dialogue from *The Big Sleep* already quoted in Chapter 3, now with an acute accent indicating continuity intonation and a grave accent finality intonation. Carmen uses continuity intonation to 'hold the floor', to signal that her turn has not yet come to an end, but she does not use it at the end of her turns. This makes her lines sound like challenges, moves in a conversational ping-pong game, assertive and meant to be final, impossible to reply to. Marlowe, on the other hand, does use a continuity intonation at the end of his turn, and this makes him sound uncertain, in need of a bit of support for his ego. He is initially getting this ('Not bad looking'), but it is closely followed by the next challenge of the conversational contest ('Though you probably know it'):

    CARMEN: [You're not very táll//] [are yoù//]
    MARLOWE: [Yeah well I ér//] [I try to bé//]
    CARMEN: [Not bad looking//] [though you probably know ìt//]

In speech which cannot (or may not) be interrupted, there is often a dramatic increase in the amount of finality intonations. Radio and television newsreaders, for instance, often use finality intonations in the middle of sentences, which not only makes the phrases on which it occurs into self-sufficient morsels of information, unconnected to the rest of the sentence, but also lends a sense of overall authority to the news: the falling pitch is assertive, the tone of definite statements and commands, and if it is not accompanied by an actual 'conclusion', it becomes 'conclusiveness' for its own sake, a deliberate foregrounding of the fact that the speaker always has the final word. The example is from Radio 2GB, a commercial radio station which, at the time of recording, specialized in news.

    [A twenty-one year old màn//] [is in intensive cáre//] [in Sydney's Mona Vale Hospitàl//] [after breaking his báck//] [in an accident at a beachside swimming pòol//]

The same idea can be applied to music. The jingles quoted in the previous chapter for example differ in the way they use continuity. In the Southern Comfort jingle, the first line, sung by the man ('So listen to me baby'), ends in finality, and so does the chorus ('Take a shot of Comfort') – both descend in pitch and end on the tonic. This injects a touch of adversariality in the musical dialogue, a sense that each party wants to have the last word. In the Kidco commercial on the other hand ('Toys from Kidco go and go/Kidco/Kidco') the melodic phrases all end on a note of continuity. Here the 'rapport' of the group of children is emphasized and the musical dialogue is interactive and cooperative rather than adversarial – or so at least it has been portrayed by the makers of the jingle.

This is not restricted to musical dialogue. In the structure of songs, too, every line can be a self-contained and conclusive musical statement, or an open-ended one, reaching out to the next line for its continuation or completion. Many of the Dutch psalms and hymns I learnt in my youth are of the former kind, with most lines ending on a note of finality. On the other hand, in a Broadway song such as 'My Favourite Things', every line opens out to the next. Not even the verses end on a note of finality.

To summarize,

1. The end of a melodic phrase either displays continuity, open-endedness, or finality, closure. This is realized by the direction of the pitch movement at the end of the phrase, which may fall to a low level (finality), or stay at a relatively high level, or rise (continuity), and, in the case of music, by whether or not the phrase ends on the tonic. Finality and continuity therefore form a *textual* aspect of the melodic phrase, a way of connecting melodic phrases to each other – or disconnecting them from each other.

2. Intonational finality and continuity are independent meaning systems. They can be used to mark whether a spoken or musical utterance has or has not yet concluded, but also present or represent interactive attitudes, for instance assertiveness or tentativeness, an authoritative or a collaborative approach. In speech and song intonationally and verbally expressed attitudes can contrast with each other. What is verbally formulated as a definite statement can sound like a tentative query. What is verbally formulated as a question can sound like a curt command.

Melodic patterns

Many linguists and musicologists have analysed and classified the melodic phrase (also referred to as 'tone group', 'tone unit' and 'tune'). Halliday (1967), for instance, analysed it into a 'pretonic' and a 'tonic', and Crystal (1969) analysed it into a 'pre-head', a 'head', a 'nucleus' and a 'tail'. The latter analysis derives from the pioneering work of Armstrong and Ward (1926) and is in fact an analysis of the rhythmic structure of the phrase: the 'pre-head' is the anacrusis, the 'head' stretches from the first pulse to the main pulse, the 'nucleus' is the main pulse, and the tail anything that follows the main pulse. In musicology, Asaf'ev (1977) has described melodic phrases as consisting of an *initium*, an initial impetus, a *movere*, the main move, and a *terminus*, a stabilizing end configuration, along the lines, perhaps, of the acoustic structure of individual sounds, which have an 'attack', a 'body' and a 'decay' phase, and with a strong emphasis on the 'process'-like nature of musical sounds, on melodic phrases as 'gestures', 'moves'.

The classification of melodic phrases has usually been based on the direction of the pitch movement. Many linguists have linked *falling* speech melodies to statements and *rising* speech melodies to questions. Further types of speech melody may then be linked to other types of speech act. Brazil *et al.* (1980), for instance, distinguish two kinds of 'fall', the *falling tone*, typically used for 'proclaiming' information, information assumed to be new to the listener, and the *fall–rise*, typically used for 'referring' information, for establishing common ground with the listener. For Halliday (1967) the *fall* ('tone 1') is the melody of statements, WH-questions and commands, the *rise* ('tone 2') the melody of the 'yes–no' question, the *level tone* ('tone 3') the melody of the tentative or 'non-committal' statement, while the *fall–rise* ('tone 4') expresses a movement 'from the known to the unknown', a sense of reservation, and the *rise–fall* ('tone 5') a movement 'from the unknown to the known', a sense of definiteness and assertion. These glosses focus on the kinds of meaning I have associated with finality and continuity in the preceding section. When 'key'(pitch range) is also considered (cf. Halliday, 1970), emotive meaning is added to the description. If the sentence 'It's just starting to rain' carries a fall from mid level ('tone 1'), it will sound like an 'unemotional statement'. If it carries a fall from high level (tone 1+) it will sound 'excited', adding the unspoken message, 'Hurry up and come inside.' If it carries a fall from a low level (tone 1–), it will sound 'calm', adding the unspoken message 'I know it would'. In short, for Halliday:

> The intonation contour expresses the 'key', the particular tone of assertion, query, hesitation, doubt, reservation, forcefulness, wonderment or whatever it is, with which the speaker tags the proposition (Halliday, 1979: 66).

For other linguists, for example Fonagy and Magdics, emotive meaning is more central, and the same applies to musicological work. Cooke (1959), for instance, distinguishes 'ascending', 'descending', and 'arched' melodies. *Ascending* melodies express 'outgoing', 'active' emotions, *descending* melodies 'incoming', 'passive' emotions, and *arched* melodies combine the two. Further types again derive from 'key', which, in the case of tonal music, becomes a matter of precise intervals. Thus a pattern which descends from the fifth, via the minor third, to the tonic, is 'a phrase which has been much used to express an "incoming" painful emotion, in a context of finality: acceptance of, or yielding to grief; discouragement and depression; passive suffering; and the despair connected to death' (Cooke, 1959: 133).

My discussion below is based on the following assumptions:

1. Melodic phrases are configurations of different features (pitch movement, pitch range, pitch level and so on) which may combine in a number of different ways and each contribute elements of meaning to the sound act constituted by the melodic phrase as a whole. From the meaning potential of these component features we can derive the meaning potential of the whole melodic phrase.
2. Continuity and finality intonations (the end configurations of melodic phrases) are treated as separate from the sound acts formed by the whole phrases. This makes it possible to have, for instance, a 'tentative complaint' and an 'assertive complaint', or a final and irrevocable 'admission of defeat' and one which reaches out for comfort or reassurance.
3. In speech and song the words and the melody may either express similar or different meanings. Melodies are not just 'prosodic'. They are not just some colour for the verbally expressed meanings. They can also stand on their own.

Pitch movement

Melodies can be *ascending*, rising in pitch, or *descending*, falling in pitch – or any combination of these. Cooke (1959: 102ff.) has argued that ascending melodies are more 'active', more 'outgoing' and 'dynamic' than descending melodies. He links this to a physiological concomitant of singing: ascending in pitch requires an increase in vocal effort, descending in pitch allows the singer to decrease the effort. Again, the meaning potential of pitch movement is experiential, relates to what we *do* when we produce it with our voice.

The sound act value of melodic patterns derives from this. Rising pitch can energize, rally listeners together for the sake of some joint activity or cause. Falling pitch can relax and soothe listeners, make them turn inward and focus on their thoughts and feelings. The disc jockey of the top 40 radio station, for instance, must sound 'up' ('your sound has got to be a "hey let's get it happening" sort of approach...', cf. Van Leeuwen, 1992: 238) – to achieve this, he uses a rising intonation (Figure 5.5). The disc jockey of the 'Beautiful Music' station, on the other hand, must have a 'relaxed manner' and 'sound like a warm, friendly adult' (cf. Van Leeuwen 1992: 237–8) – to achieve this, he uses a falling intonation (Figure 5.6). Again, the 'heroic', missionary church hymn may use an ascending melody (Figure 5.5), the more pious and inward-looking hymn a descending melody (Figure 5.6) – also note the 'finality' intonation at the end of the 'heroic' hymn in Figure 5.5.

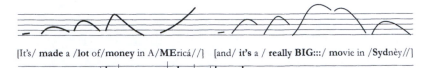

[It's/ **made** a /lot of/**money** in A/**ME**ricá//] [and/ **it's** a / really **BIG:::**/ movie in /**Sydnèy**//]

Soldiers of Christ a- rise and put your arm-our on

Figure 5.5   Ascending intonation in the speech of a Top 40 disc jockey and ascending hymn melody (Australian Hymn Book no. 481)

[and/**Watch** What/ **HAPP**èns//] [**TOO** fròm//] [Lucio/ **A**gos/ **TI**ni//]

Take my life and let it be con-se-cra-ted Lord to Thee

Figure 5.6   Descending intonation in the speech of a 'Beautiful Music' disc jockey and descending hymn melody (Australian Hymn Book no. 520)

Pitch movement can also be used to depict the movements of people, places and things. In Figure 5.5 the pitch rises on the word 'arise', as it does in countless other nationalistic and religious hymns and anthems (for example 'The Internationale'). Already towards the end of the twelfth century composers were beginning to portray the sense of words in this way, as in 'Redit Aetas Aurea', a song composed for the coronation of King Richard the Lion-heart in 1189 (cf. Harman and Mellers, 1962: 100). The melody descends on the words 'Now are rich men trodden down' and ascends on the words 'Poor men raised with singing'. There also is a regularized 'trodding' rhythm in the line 'Now are rich men trodden down', and the music suddenly takes flight on the word 'singing'. In the Renaissance it became standard practice to use ascending and descending melodies whenever the text mentioned rising and falling (Harman and Mellers, 1962: 203). But such word painting is not restricted to music. It occurs also when speech is used expressively, whether in everyday conversation or by specialists such as disc jockeys. The disc jockey quoted in Figure 5.5, for instance, uses pitch, loudness and timing to make the word 'big' as big as possible.

To quote a 'sound effect' example, it is not surprising that the take off of space ships, UFOs and so on is represented by rising melodies and their landing by falling melodies (think of Dr Who's Tardis, for instance). But other science fiction sounds may also use rising melodies. A background track called 'Evil Rises Up', created by Malcolm Clarke for the BBC Radiophonic Workshop, uses a complex overlay of low, fluctuating rumbles, metallic twinkles, distorted voices, intermittent zings and so on. Several of them gradually rise in pitch, creating suspense by increasing the listener's pent-up energy and nervous tension.

More complex patterns can easily be derived from the fall and the rise. A melody of anger, for instance, might use repeated brief outbursts of energy: to be brief yet energetic is exactly what characterizes any kind of 'outburst'. A harsh and tense voice quality can then make the outburst angry, and repetition will turn the angry phrase into something like a furious cascading of punches rather than a single blow.

Pitch range

Whether ascending or descending, melodies can move in large or small intervals, large strides and energetic leaps, or restrained measured steps. The melody in Figure 5.5, for instance, moves up by large jumps, like many other heroic hymns, national anthems and so on. The melody in Figure 5.6 moves down in small steps, like many other meditative and inward-looking melodies.

The semiotic force of this again rests on what it is we *do* when we increase or decrease the pitch range. When we increase it we are 'letting more energy out', when we decrease it we are 'holding more energy in', either because we do not have any left, or because we restrain and repress it. This can be coloured in in many different ways. We saw that for Halliday (1970) the fall from a high point is 'excited', the fall from a low point 'calm'. For Brazil *et al.* (1980: 23) the wide pitch range conveys 'excitement', 'surprise', 'anger', the narrow pitch range 'boredom', 'misery'. Without taking other factors into account, there is no way of knowing which term 'translates' the meaning of pitch range best. All we can say is that the wide pitch range allows us to give vent to strong feelings, whether of excitement or shock, of grief or joy, and that the narrow pitch range *constrains* the expression of strong feelings, whether as the result of a 'stiff upperlip' attitude, or because of modesty or tiredness, or because we are paralysed with fear, to mention just some of the possibilities. Only when we consider pitch range together with other factors can a choice be made from these possibilities – the tired voice, for instance, will not sound the same as the frightened voice, even when the same pitch range is used.

In music the same kinds of things may be expressed by varying the pitch range:

> Medieval and early Renaissance music tended to move in stepwise progres-
> sion at a normal medium pitch, befitting man's humble subjection to the
> deity; but with the growth of human self-realization, music drama, in the
> hands of Monteverdi and others, began to introduce more and more
> liberty of pitch movement to express the rhetoric of human passion; until,
> by the end of the nineteenth century, violent emotional unrest beat against
> the natural limits of audible pitch (Cooke, 1959: 109).

The example shows that pitch range not only characterizes the emotional temperature of individual sound acts, but also the emotional style of different eras, cultures, social groups or individuals. American English uses a narrower pitch range than British English for example and, according to Brazil *et al.* (1980: 23) 'Finnish speaking males, unlike females, have no "intonation", apparently because the pitch movement occurs within a very narrow range.' This difference is not restricted to Finnish speakers. McConnell-Ginet (1977) says that women use a broader pitch range and more rapid and frequent changes of pitch than men. In Anglo-American cultures women (and children) are given more licence to show their emotions than men, and this has an impact on vocal style: 'Part of women's being emotional in our culture derives from our *sounding* emotional' (McConnell-Ginet, 1977: 77).

The same applies to music. From his survey of singing styles across the world, Lomax concludes that a wide pitch range characterizes the singing in many 'extractor societies', that is societies whose survival mostly depends on hunting and gathering and/or fishing, and he links this to physical and social 'confinement':

> The use of wide intervals in the songs of most extractor groups may symbolize a less confining, freer, more wide-ranging approach to the use of space (social and/or ecological) for the individual who lives in a society where access to land, food, privilege, sex, status and other life resources is open to all members of the community on more or less equal terms... Prominence of very narrow intervals turns up in cultures whose members are confined spatially or restricted by a system of rigid status differentiation in their free use of productive and social resources (Lomax, 1968: 136).

Discussing the narrow pitch range in Bob Dylan's singing style, he comments:

> In our own society, made up of technicians, office workers, scientists, arbitrators, and supposedly reasonable people in every walk of life, audiences are often deeply moved by performers who address them with restraint and moderation (Lomax, 1968: 134).

Finally, pitch range can also be used for vocal and musical depiction. The melody heard behind the vocals in an Air New Zealand commercial I recorded, for instance, was a high whistle which ascended right into the musical stratosphere.

Pitch level

Speakers rarely use the complete pitch span their voices are capable of, and adopt different base pitch levels for different sound acts. Like the other aspects of pitch, pitch level relates to vocal effort. The higher the pitch level, the greater the effort needed, the more the voice is, literally and figuratively, 'keyed up'. The lower the voice, the more relaxed, and, literally and figuratively, 'low key', it will sound. This can again be a matter of the way we adjust our pitch level for particular sound acts, for example for the expression of joy or excitement. But it can also be a matter of general speech style, related to status for instance. Male news readers and other announcers speak at a higher pitch level when they are on air than in ordinary 'low key' speech. The Germans have a saying '*Wer hoch ist, spricht hoch*' ('High people speak high'). A high pitch level characterizes many different kinds of male singing style, too. I have already mentioned Philip Tagg's description of the typical voice of the male 'hard rock' singer:

> Even though microphones, which bring the singer nearer to our ears, have been in use since before the advent of rock, the male rock singer will nevertheless raise his voice to an average pitch at least an octave above what he uses for normal speech, while the loudness and grain of his voice will also bear greater resemblance to shouting, screaming or (at least) calling than to talking. Whether the vocal expression be one of despair, celebration or anger, the dominant character of vocal delivery in rock is one of effort and urgency (Tagg, 1990: 112).

But relatively high-pitched male voices are favoured in other styles of music also. Perhaps this has something to do with the fact that the high voice stands out more and that raising the voice usually increases both loudness and pitch. When music expresses dominance, it is often the highest voice which 'leads' by carrying the melody, although lower voices and instruments may compensate by using their higher registers and increasing loudness. In polyphonic music, on the other hand, the main melody may be carried by a lower voice. Think of the hymn melodies in Bach's *Choralbearbeitungen* for organ, which are played by the pedals, on the lowest register.

In all these cases the high-pitched voice also tends to be loud, assertive and 'public'. When high-pitched voices are softer and more intimate, another factor comes to the fore. Our experience also tells us that high-pitched sounds tend to be produced by small people, small animals, small musical instruments, small engines and so on, and low-pitched sounds by large people, large animals, large musical instruments, large engines and so on. Hence low voices are often seen as threatening and dangerous. In operas the tenor is the hero, the bass or baritone the villain. Very low, rumbling sound effects can be particularly ominous. High voices on the other hand can be used to make ourselves small, for instance in the speech melody of 'tenderness', as described by Fonagy and Magdics, or in the speech style many people adopt when addressing children. In the movies, women stereotyped as the 'innocent, vulnerable girl next door' seduce us with a high, childish voice (Marilyn Monroe), women stereotyped as dark and dangerous temptresses seduce us with a sensuous, low voice (Lauren Bacall), in their speech as well as in their singing. Clearly there are significant differences in the way high-pitched and low-pitched singing and speaking styles are gendered. Where men raise their voice to a higher pitch, women may do the reverse – for instance in newsreading. Poynton (1996: 8) recalls that:

> In 1970s Tasmania the same person who represented herself as 'Patricia Hughes' using a dark voice (the voice of authority) in reading the news on the Tasmanian 'highbrow' station 7ZL became 'Patti, your Thursday bird' using a lighter, hyper-feminized voice to introduce herself on the 'popular' station 7ZR.

Finally, musical instruments and other sound-producing objects can go outside the range of the human voice, which immediately gives them a 'not human' quality. This can then take on more precise coloration according to context, for instance as 'cold and technical', or as 'extra-terrestrial', or as 'sacred':

> The instruments we call warm and lyrical (cello, viola, horn, clarinet) most closely approach the range of the human voice... If composers wish to suggest a sublime or superhuman event or sensation they make consider-able use of those instruments which lie far outside the human vocal range. This is the most evident in church music, where the extremely high and low notes of the pipe organ can be used to suggest the voices of God and the celestial beings (Schafer, 1986: 122).

Electronic science fiction and 'techno' sounds also make great use of pitch levels above and below the reach of the human voice.

The articulation of the melodic phrase

Finally, the syllables, notes or other sounds of the melodic phrase may be articulated as short separate stabs, or connected together in a smooth, long line. The difference between 'staccato' and 'legato' in music is one manifestation of this. To the first kind of articulation I will refer as *disjunctive*, to the second as *connective*. Clearly it costs more energy to perform a series of separate attacks than to perform one long, connected motion, and so disjunctive sound production can come to stand for anything that includes the idea of a lively and energetic approach, or a bold and forceful attack, whatever precise words might be most relevant to describe its semiotic effect in a given context. Connective sound production, by contrast, can come to stand for anything that includes the idea of a smoother, more relaxed or sensual approach (unless of course most other features point in a different direction). Cooke (1959:101) gives some examples:

> One need only think of the impact which *staccato* gives to the opening theme of Beethoven's *Egmont* Overture: without it, the music would still be music, but would lose most of its force. Or consider how entirely the grave, reflective character of the opening theme of Schubert's Unfinished Symphony depends on legato: played *non-legato*, it would still make sense, but would lose its brooding, withdrawn character.

Not surprisingly, 'Beautiful Music' disc jockeys use connective articulation in lines like

> '... and the beautiful "Story of O", from Django and Bonnie'

And excited Top 40 disc jockeys use disjunctive articulation in lines like

> '2SM, with the Carpenters now, "Calling Occupants of Interplanetary Craft", the international anthem of World Contact Day!'

Articulation can also be used for word-painting, as when a radio announcer, in describing Massenet's *Scènes Dramatiques*, articulated the line 'the other is a staccato arpeggio motif' in a disjunctive, 'spiky' way and the line 'Desdemona's Slumber, a slow soft reverie' in a smooth, connective way. And it characterizes significant differences between the sounds in our environment, too – think of the difference between the scratching of a fountain pen and the tapping of the typewriter keys, or of the differences between the horse's hooves and the tyres' rumble, or the hand saw and the electric saw.

To summarize:

1. Pitch movement, pitch range, pitch level and melodic articulation combine in different ways to make their contribution to the realiza-

tion of sound acts. Pitch range, pitch level and melodic articulation can also form overall characteristics of the styles of speech, music and/or other sound production of a particular era, culture, social group, social context or individual.

2. Pitch movement may be level, falling or rising, or any combination of these. Its meaning derives from our experience of the way vocal effort must be increased to raise the voice and decreased to lower the voice. It could be described as realizing *activation*: the more the pitch rises the more active and interactive the participants involved in its production and reception will be; the more the pitch falls, the more the participants will be deactivated, brought into some state of non-activity – relaxation, contemplation and so on.

3. Pitch range realizes the *emotional extension* of sound acts, or of the style of speech, music and/or other sound production that may characterize an era, a culture, a social group, a social context or an individual. The more the pitch range increases, the more there is room for the expression of feelings and attitudes, the more it decreases, the more the expression of feelings and attitudes will be confined, whether because emotional energy is lacking, or because of its habitual or deliberate containment.

4. A high pitch level combined with 'formal distance' (loudness), realizes the *dominance*, the 'high' status, of a given sound act or sound style. When combined with 'intimate' or 'personal' distance (softness) it realizes *diminution*, small size, as in the intonation of 'tenderness' described by Fonagy and Magdics. However, pitch level is strongly gendered and the values reverse where female voices and instruments considered to be female are concerned: here, a low voice combined with loudness will realize assertiveness and dominance. Combined with 'intimate' or 'personal' distance (softness) it will seem 'dark' and 'dangerous'.

5. A *disjunctive* articulation makes every one of the sounds in a melodic phrase separate and emphatic. Connective articulation makes the sounds in a melodic phrase flow into each other in a smooth and sensuous way.

6. The meaning of all these aspects of the melodic phrase may be influenced by, or even be wholly derived from, *provenance*, that is,

from our ideas about and attitudes towards the era, culture, social group or social context with which we associate a certain way of using pitch movement, pitch range, pitch level and/or melodic articulation.

7. Pitch movement, pitch range, pitch level and melodic articulation are also frequently used for the *depiction* of the actions and qualities of people, places and things.

Gesture and texture

The pitch features that characterize sound *acts* (sound 'gestures') can also characterize sound *settings* (sound 'textures'). Think of the first three notes of any melody, then rhythmically repeat them, over and over: a melody which used to have an individual shape and an individual 'message' suddenly becomes accompaniment, setting, 'aural wallpaper' (McLuhan, 1966). It no longer 'speaks to us' and we no longer listen to it with any kind of focused attention.

By the sheer force of repetition any sound act can become part of a sound setting. And conversely, by the sheer force of being 'singled out', any of the 'anonymous' parts of a sound pattern can become an individual sound act. In visual art this effect has been exploited by 'pop art' artists like Andy Warhol. In music it is used, for instance, by the excellent jazz-rap group US 3 in tracks like 'Eleven Long Years'. They take short riffs and snippets of solos from the recordings of great jazz musicians like Horace Silver and Herbie Hancock, rhythmically repeat them, over and over, disengaging them from the chord 'progression' they belong to, and then turn these soloistic gestures into a (cultural) background for their message.

It should be pointed out, incidentally, that 'action' and 'setting' are not identical to 'Figure' and 'Ground'. Although the sound act, the melody, is usually also the 'Figure', and the accompaniment, the setting, usually also the 'Ground', modern dance music (hip hop, drum 'n' bass and so on) reverses this, foregrounding the setting, the environment, and backgrounding soloistic gestures.

In Chapter 3, we discussed a 1985 television news signature tune from the ABC, the Australian Broadcasting Commission. There was a clear melodic progression in this tune. The instrumental call and response phrases and the contrasting melodic fragments in the middle section all stood out as distinct, individual sound 'gestures'. By contrast, the news signature tune of Sydney commercial radio station 2UE had, in that same year, two simultaneous voices, one a rhythmic pattern of electronic clicks (another version of the busy teletypewriter cliché, perhaps) and the other, somewhat out of phase with the pattern of clicks, a cheap, squeaky electronic sound, repeating a brief melodic pattern over and over. Still, if something had been done with this melodic pattern, if it had been transposed in a 'parallel' key, inverted and so on, in short, if the kind of musical interactions described in the previous chapter (and used in the ABC news signature tune) had been applied to it, it would have become a distinct ongoing sound event with a beginning, a middle and an end, with a sense of linear *progression* rather than repetition and *cyclicity*, a sense of 'development' and 'progress', rather than a sense of 'eternal return'. It is of some interest, then, that the Australian Broadcasting Commission, the public radio and television station, used its news signature tune to musically represent a 'leader' (the newsreader) addressing a 'chorus' (the viewers), while the commercial station uses its tune to represent cyclicity: in the commercial station representation had already made place for repetition (Attali, 1985). Radio was no longer a public medium, but an accompaniment to action. The news was no longer a set of unique reports about unique events, but an hourly burst of information.

I have already discussed the close connection between repetitive sound patterns and the repetitive patterns of human actions such as walking, marching, running, jumping, performing various kinds of dance step, and also working – hammering, chiselling, grinding, stirring, weaving and so on. This function of sound returns as we walk with a walkman, drive with the radio on, work with music in our ears, and generally use music as a setting for our activities rather than as a message to listen to with concentrated attention. Music is now not only *about* setting ('ambience'), it becomes itself 'setting' for our everyday life.

Two more points need to be made about 'settings'. First, when repeated melodic phrases act as setting, they may either be totally identical, as is common in the popular music of the machine age, or vary slightly from time to time, with minute changes in pitch or shifts in accent or timbre. This kind of variation has been called *microvariativity* (cf. Middleton, 1990). It is not only the rule in nature, where many things are on the one hand cyclical, yet on the other hand never quite the same, but also in most of the world's musics.

Second, the kinds of setting we have so far discussed occupy a middle ground between 'setting' and 'action'. They are like sound 'gestures' in their melodic and rhythmic structure, and in their affinity to human body movement, but like sound 'textures' in having lost their individual identity and having become subjugated to the principle of repetition. Other sounds are always 'textural', the ongoing drone, for instance, which might waver in pitch or swell and recede at regular or irregular intervals, or the lofi 'wall of sound'. Such sounds do not display the rhythmic and melodic structure of human activity, and either belong to the slower time frame of evolving or revolving natural events (for example the wind), or to the faster time of the machine in which cyclicity can no longer be heard and transforms into a constant tone (for example electric hums).

Here is an example of 'setting' and 'action' at work in the music of the film *The Piano*, composed by Michael Nyman. Ada (Holly Hunter) plays (among other things) two kinds of melody in this film. The first is a romantic melody, using many of the conventions of sentimental nineteenth-century *salon* music: a slow, minor melody, descending pitch movement, confined pitch range; triple time, fluid arpeggios rather than chords and so on. The second is a fast, angular rhythmic pattern which repeats itself over and over with minor variations. Early on in the film, when Ada is reunited with her piano on the beach, she plays the first melody, a melody which expresses romantic yearnings. The orchestra, the 'community of instruments', backs her up in this. At the end of the film, after she has lost a finger and her piano, married her lover and moved from an environment of awesome yet threatening natural beauty into a provincial town, we hear her play the second theme. She is no longer a soloist. Her music is no longer self-expression, an individuated sound act. She has now become part of the musical group, and uses her piano to provide rhythmic texture for the melody played in unison by the 'community of strings'. She must now 'keep in step with the others', 'fit into the whole', accustom herself to 'repetitive work'. That is the story of the *music*: the film's resolution is perhaps more ambiguous and less pessimistic, because there the loss of the piano, now in its ocean grave, may yet be the gain of Ada's voice, however tentative her first attempts at speaking.

To summarize:

1. The same pitch features can characterize sound acts and sound settings. Sound acts are the individual moves in the ongoing, linear progression of a sound event with a beginning, a middle and an end. Sound settings are more static and either consist of short melodic patterns repeating themselves endlessly, or of more

amorphously vibrating or oscillating ongoing sound textures. The former can be related to human activities, and will be called '*social*' settings. The latter evoke non-human environmental states and processes, and will be called '*environmental*' settings.

2. The pitch patterns in environmental and social settings can repeat themselves identically (which will often carry a connotation of 'mechanicalness', or of other ways of being 'not natural'), or display *micro-variativity*.

3. Settings and actions can occur by themselves or in combination. When they occur in combination, either one may be perspectivally foregrounded or backgrounded.

The sonata form

In her book *Feminine Endings* (1991), Susan McClary discusses gender in relation to the discourse of musicology and in relation to the discourse of music itself. She shows how the 'technical' language of musicology is shot through with gender metaphors. For instance, a cadence or ending may be called 'masculine' if the final chord of a phrase or section falls on the 'strong' beat (pulsed moment) and 'feminine' if it is postponed to fall on a 'weak' beat (non-pulsed moment). Musicologists then come to the rescue of male composers who use 'feminine' patterns, as in this discussion of Chopin by E.T. Cone:

> Even in the case of movements that seem to remain incorrigibly feminine, some differentiation can still be made. In the case of Chopin's Polonaise in A Major, for example, a clever emphasis on one of the concealed cross-rhythms at the cadence can make the last chord sound, if not precisely masculine, at least like a strong tonic postponed by a suspension of the entire dominant (McClary, 1991: 10).

As for the discourse of music itself, European art music has long depicted men and women in different ways, in a tradition which was worked out in the music of operas, many of which had stories involving dangerous seductresses who led men astray and then either caused their downfall or were successfully subdued by them. The famous 'Habanera' theme of Carmen in Bizet's opera of the same name, is an example. McClary says that it depicts Carmen as 'slippery, unpredictable, and maddening'. The theme contains a 'setting', the 'instrumental vamp' McClary refers to, which can be related to the way Carmen moves:

> Before she even begins to sing, her instrumental vamp sets a pattern that engages the lower body, demanding hip swings in response. The rhythm is so contagious that it makes Jose – and the listener – aware both of her body and also (worse yet) of their own bodies. She arouses desire; and because she apparently has the power to deliver or withhold gratification of the desires she instils, she is immediately marked as a potential victimizer (McClary, 1991: 57).

The melody of the song describes the way she speaks:

> Her melody lines tease and taunt. Her erratic means of descending through the tetrachord (and, subsequently, the remainder of the scale – sometimes granting the tonic, but often withholding it sadistically at the last instant before implied gratification) reveals her as a 'master' of seductive rhetoric (McClary, 1991: 57–8).

The most important gendered pattern in the European music tradition is the sonata form. It occurs in the first movements of not only sonatas, but also symphonies, and it forms a kind of narrative pattern. There always are two themes, two basic sound acts, each in a different key, each in its own tonal territory, so to speak. The first is the 'masculine' theme, introducing the protagonist, the second the 'feminine' theme, introducing the antagonist. Incidentally, for those who find it difficult to disentangle the complexities of abstract music of this kind, try to imagine the kind of body movement that would go with these themes, try to imagine the themes as characters that enter the stage and display what they are like through the way they move. Or, better still, try to move to the music, to 'read' with your body, and then remember what you discovered in this way about the meaning of the music.

The 'masculine' theme typically uses some or all of the following: ascending melodies with dotted rhythms (see Chapter 3), a wide pitch range, disjunctive articulation, a high degree of loudness, and brass and percussion instruments. In other words, it seeks to sound assertive, energetic, active, forceful, even 'thrusting' – such are the adjectives that come to mind. The 'feminine theme' typically uses descending melodies with a narrow pitch range, suspension (delayed notes), a soft, connective articulation, and softer instruments such as strings and woodwind. In other words, it seeks to sound 'delicate', 'gentle', 'passive', 'inward-looking' and so on.

In the course of the musical piece, the story develops ('development' is the actual musicological term). Just as in a dramatic plot, the two 'characters' become involved in a conflict: the themes get transposed, transformed, inverted, intertwined, and it will be now the one, now the other, who will be 'on top'. In the end (and like the endings of dramatic plots, the endings in sonatas and symphonies are often 'climactic'), the masculine theme wins: the sonata form requires that the feminine theme is restated in the key of the masculine theme, so that the masculine theme subjugates the feminine theme, as it were, by drawing it in its tonal territory.

With this basic framework, McClary explains, many different stories can be told:

> The specific content of each composition casts many possible shades on this paradigm. Some are gleefully affirmative, demonstrating quite straightforwardly the triumph of the masculine over the feminine principle. Many of Beethoven's symphonies exhibit considerable anxiety with respect to feminine moments and respond to them with extraordinary violence. Other pieces, such as many by Mozart and Schubert, tend to invest their second themes with extraordinary sympathy, and this leads one to regret the inevitable return to the tonic and the original materials. For example in the Unfinished Symphony it is the lovely 'feminine' tune with which we are encouraged to identify and which is brutally, tragically quashed in accordance with the destiny predetermined by the disinterested conventions of the form (McClary, 1991: 69).

An example she analyses at length is the first movement of Tchaikovsky's Fourth Symphony. The first theme is an introduction played by the whole orchestra, the 'community of instruments'. It is a heavy, militaristic theme, representing a heavy, militaristic society. The theme descends step by step, increasingly deactivating and confining, indeed, paralysing the listener. Tchaikovsky himself said this about it:

> The introduction is fate, the fateful force, which prevents the impulse to happiness from attaining its goal, and which hangs above your head like the sword of Damocles. It is invincible and you will never overcome it (quoted in McClary, 1991: 71).

The second theme is the masculine theme. But it lacks many of the crucial characteristics of masculine themes and sounds more like a 'feminine' theme. The melody, played by strings and horn, goes downwards in small steps, expressing 'yearning and fear, a vulnerable, sensitive, indecisive masculinity' (1991: 71). The feminine theme, on the other hand, reminds us of the 'Habanera', and portrays an assertive, hence 'seductive' and 'dangerous' femininity. It is 'sultry, seductive and slinky', 'irrational with respect to its unexpected twists and turns' (1991: 71).

When the 'exposition' is over and the characters have been introduced, the 'development', the story proper, begins. The 'masculine' theme now reappears 'inside' the 'feminine' theme, trapped by it, caught within it 'like a fly trapped in a spider's web'. The hero eventually pulls himself out of this, but only to be overpowered by the introductory theme. After a struggle, he emerges victoriously, but exhausted. However, now the feminine theme appears again, and starts toying with the masculine theme once more. This too the hero overcomes, but only to see the introductory theme reappear and finish him off:

> At the end of the movement the first theme is presented in all its anguish, its plaintive appoggiaturas still unhealed, its complicity with violent closure as bitter as don Jose's [in *Carmen*] (McClary, 1991: 75).

McClary notes that Tchaikovsky was a homosexual in a world of patriarchically enforced heterosexuality. The year in which he wrote the symphony was a crisis year. He finally gave in to social pressure, married, and eventually attempted suicide in distress over this marriage and over the difficulties of his clandestine homosexuality. The story has the same basic components as many other musical stories (for example the duet from *Porgy and Bess*, discussed in the previous chapter, or the music of *The Piano*), but it uses them in a specific way: the 'community of instruments' here represents an oppressively patriarchal society, the first, 'masculine' theme a vulnerable and anguished protagonist, and the second 'feminine' theme an assertive and 'manipulative' antagonist.

Example: a film soundtrack

Below, the main distinctions presented in the chapter are summarized in the form of a system network (Figure 5.7), and used in an analysis of a section from a film soundtrack.

The example that follows is taken from the soundtrack of *The Piano*. It represents a scene which takes place towards the end of the film. Ada (Holly Hunter), Flora (Anna Paquin) and Baines (Harvey

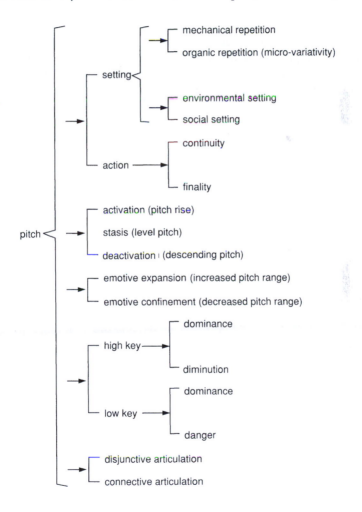

Figure 5.7   A system network for describing melodies

Keitel) leave the beach in a large canoe paddled by Maoris. The piano is tied to the canoe with a rope. After a while Ada signs that she wants the piano to be thrown overboard. Baines tries to dissuade her. She starts to loosen the ropes. The boat begins to heave over. Baines gives in and tells the Maoris to throw the piano overboard. As it sinks, the rope it was fastened with uncoils and loops around Ada's foot, dragging her into the water (or maybe she deliberately stepped into the loop).

The sound first contrasts a human ('social') and a natural ('environmental') setting: the canoe and the ocean. On the one hand there is the paddling of the canoe of the Maoris, a *regular* splashing, punctuated by the shouts of one of the Maori men (a repetitive speech pattern, a speech 'setting'). On the other hand there are the sounds of the ocean, very varied, with all kinds of wooshes and bubblings and rumblings and almost human sighs. The mix plays up the contrast. When Ada drags her hand through the water, the sound of the paddling almost completely disappears, even though the camera is still 'in the boat'. There are repeated underwater shots (the viewpoint of the ocean) and in these shots, too, the sounds of human activity completely disappear.

What does not disappear is the sound of the piano, low creaking and groaning of the wood, a rumble of the low strings. And these sounds mix in so well with the sounds of the ocean that it is hard to tell whether it is the water or the piano which rumbles. Here the soundtrack suggests harmony and affinity between the ocean and the piano.

Third, there is the dialogue. The brief extract does not show that it includes subtitled dialogue in the language of the Maoris and the signing of Ada. Here a contrast is made between the speech styles of Baines and Ada. Although Baines speaks 'up' when he tries to restrain Ada, for the most part his speech is 'down', confined, drawn into itself, and not reaching out. Flora's speech, on the other hand, reproduces the emotive expansiveness, the strength of feeling of Ada's signing.

Finally, there is the way the music starts as Ada is drowning, in the underwater shot, harmonizing and mixing in with the sounds of the ocean, as if both join to represent the submerged depths of Ada's unconscious.

Clearly this soundtrack has been composed with unusual attention to detail. Every strand in its texture resonates with subtle variations on the themes of the film.

1.	The regular splashing of the canoe	setting	social organic deactivating expansion mid level
	PLUS		disjunctive
2.	The groaning of the timber of the boat	setting	environmental organic stasis mid range danger
	PLUS		connective
3.	Regular shout of the leader '*Oyou*'	setting	social organic activating expansion dominance
	PLUS		connective
4.	Dialogue between Baines and Ada, with Ada's daughter Flora as translator of Ada's sign language '*Please Ada*'	action	activating expansion dominance disjunctive continuity
	'*You will regret it. It's your piano. I want you to have it*'	action	deactivating confinement mid range connective finality (except on 'piano')
	'*She doesn't want it*'	action	activating expansion dominance disjunctive continuity
	'*Sit down*'	action	deactivating expansion dominance disjunctive finality

5.	1 and 2 continue as we hear a loud groaning of timber while seeing the boat from below (underwater shot)	setting	environmental organic stasis mid range danger connective
6.	1 and 2 continue as dialogue picks up again '*Pull it over*'	action	activating expansion dominance disjunctive finality
	'*Alright. We'll pull it over.*'	action	deactivating confinement dominance connective finality
7.	Sound of the water as Ada slides her hand through it	setting	environmental organic stasis confinement mid level connective
8.	Return to (1) PLUS (2) with heavy groan from piano as boat lists	action	deactivating confinement danger connective continuity
9.	The men shout as they push the piano overboard '*Aoaah! Aah!*'	action	activating expansion *dominance connective finality*
10.	Rumble of low piano strings and loud splash as piano enters the water	action	deactivating expansion danger connective finality

11.	Woosh and sighs of water (underwater shot)	setting	environmental organic activating confinement dominance connective
	PLUS		continuity
12.	Rapid uncoiling of rope	action	activating confinement dominance connective continuity
13.	Shout of Ada as the rope catches her foot and drags her into the water *'Aaah!'*	action	deactivating confinement dominance connective continuity
14.	Low rumble and bubbling of water as the weight of the piano drags Ada deeper into the water (underwater shot)	setting	environmental organic stasis confinement dominance
	PLUS		connective
15.	Music phrase enters (soft strings)	action	deactivating confinement dominance connective continuity

Exercises and discussion points

1. Can you think of sounds (not speech or music) which convey happiness, tenderness and anguish (for instance a door opening happily)? How would they use the melodic features described in this chapter? What could these sound effects be used for?

2. Record a natural and an urban soundscape. Transcribe short sections from your recordings as a 'sound script'. What kinds of settings and actions occur in them?

3. Study the sound effects in television commercials for cars. What kind of emotional qualities do they convey, and how do they do it?

4. Find examples of music which have mechanical and examples which have organic repetition in their accompaniment. Why does repetition take the form it does in your examples?

5. Return to your recording of a nursery class (Chapter 4). Transcribe short sections from the speech of the teacher and the speech of one or more of the children. Analyse how the pitch features described in this chapter are used in each. What are the main differences and how would you explain them?

6. Write pitch contours for the lines of the following poem from William Blake's *Songs of Innocence and Experience* (1990: 32). Then read the poem, following the contours you have written. You might also like to try your hand at thinking up a melody.

> Little fly
> Thy summer's play
> My thoughtless hand
> Has brushed away
>
> Am not I
> A fly like thee?
> Or art thou not
> A man like me?
>
> For I dance
> And drink and sing,
> Till some blind hand
> Shall brush my wing
>
> If thought is life
> And strength and breath,
> And the want
> Of thought is death,
>
> Then am I
> A happy fly,
> If I live,
> Or if I die

Reflect on why you wrote the contours the way you did.

Chapter 6

Voice quality and timbre

The materiality of sound

In the Western semiotic tradition, the materials of which things are made have generally been regarded as not-yet-meaningful, as the 'tohu-wabohu', the unformed matter about which we read in the book of Genesis: 'In the beginning the earth was without form.' In order to create order out of this chaos and to be able to conceive of the nature of actual recognizable material objects (including signs), an immaterial abstract principle had to be conjured up, form. Form was the 'design' that could bring objects (including, again, signs) into being and define their nature. Or that is at least one (and for our present purposes the most relevant) conception of form, because there are others. For Aristotle, for example, form (*eidos*) was appearance, 'that what changes' about an object as time goes by; form and matter together (*hyle*) made up the actual object; and substance (*ousia*) was the invisible and unchanging essence of the object.

In the formative period of linguistics and structuralist semiotics, this opposition became a key principle. Von Humboldt already wrote that 'language consists partly in sounds, partly in unformed thoughts, the sounds being formed by the 'Lautform', the thoughts by the 'Ideenform' or 'Innere Form' of language (cf. Nöth, 1995: 68). The same idea is found in Saussure's *Course in General Linguistics* (1974: 112), where he comments on the material aspect of speech, the 'phonic substance' and says that 'phonic substance is neither more fixed, nor more rigid than thought; it is not a mould in which thought must necessarily fit, but a plastic substance', 'a vague plane of sounds'. In other words, the mould is *language*, and language is separate from the substance in which it manifests itself: 'Language is a form and not a substance' (1974: 122).

Hjelmslev's conception of 'substance' (1959, 1961) combines three elements: *expression form*, the abstract formative principle, the underlying 'design'; *expression substance*, matter-as-formed-by-form, the physically existing sign; and *expression purport*, the pre-semiotic matter, the unformed 'clay'. However, only expression form and what is signified by it, the expression content, make up, in their combination, the actual realm of semiotics, of the sign. Although a sign 'has' substance, this substance plays no role in the production of meaning, and is outside language. To talk about language is to talk about the shape of the mould, not about the stuff that is being moulded by it.

This attitude towards materiality has manifested itself in semiotic theory as well as in semiotic practice. It has brought about a linguistic science in which the difference between writing and speech is by and large ignored, and in which speech and writing are regarded as modelled by the same underlying design, the same grammar and the same vocabulary. With very few exceptions (for example Graddol, in Graddol and Boyd-Barrett 1994, Goodman and Graddol, 1997), it has ignored the graphic substance of writing, so that typography has, overall, remained a craft-oriented knowledge, primarily concerned with clarity and readability, rather than with typography as an independent semiotic system. Graphology, the study of handwriting, similarly remained little more than a somewhat suspect form of pop psychology and a branch of forensic science. As for the phonic substance of speech, the linguistic study of speech sound (phonology) carefully defined itself as concerned only with the form of speech sound, and as quite separate from the study of their materiality. This became the subject of a separate branch of knowledge, phonetics – and phonetics steered clear of studying sound as a semiotic system, concentrating on studying the physiology of sound production, the psychology of speech perception and the acoustics of sound.

As far as semiotic practice is concerned, schools have long emphasized 'neat', 'correct' and, above all, *uniform* modes of handwriting. Printed and typewritten pages also became increasingly uniform, to a point where differences in the size, shape and colour of letters were almost entirely eliminated, so that lettering could no longer function as an independent source of meaning. Today this clearly is changing. Aided by the rich typographical resources of the word processor, people are now everywhere (re)discovering the semiotics of typography – already pioneered for them by avant-garde designers of the 1920s and 1930s, graffiti artists, advertisers and others. The same applies to sound. Correct and clear 'diction', not expressivity and difference, were the aims of the dominant forms of 'educated' and 'professional' speech propagated by the key institutions of the nation state, the education system and broadcasting. This, too, is now changing. A much greater variety of voices can be heard on air. The many varieties of English speech become available again as a semiotic resource. The tide is turning. Studying to become a church minister in the 1930s, my father had to unlearn his local dialect and take elocution lessons to learn to speak 'properly'. Today, local dialects are reintroduced in the church he served, as part of a 'postmodern' celebration of cultural diversity and regionality.

In music, too, all attention traditionally focused on musical form – on those aspects of music which could be written down in (Western) musical notation. These happen to be the 'immaterial' aspects of music, the aspects which remain invariant when the music is performed on different instruments and/or by different players or singers. As in the case of speech, a single ideal of articulatory beauty was developed for the sound of the singing voice and the various musical instruments belonging to the tradition. Individual singers and musicians might differ in the degree to which they were able to achieve this ideal, but could not develop their own idiosyncratic styles. Vocal and instrumental styles had to be 'impersonal'. As Shepherd has put it, (1991: 65) the 'spiritual and the personal' have been 'squeezed out' in favour of 'bureaucratic rationality'.

In contemporary popular music sound matters more. Key singers and instrumentalists develop their own, immediately recognizable styles of singing and playing, and, thanks to recording, these can now become part of the language of music and be imitated and transformed by countless others. Saxophones can be soft and mellow, or tense and strident, sound like a hoarse whisper or a foghorn in the mist. Voices can be soft, smooth and well oiled, or rough, raspy and cracked. And singers as well as instrumentalists use a large repertoire of howls, wails, groans and other vocalizations. Williams-Jones (1975: 377) compared the singing styles of James Cleveland, an Afro-American gospel singer, and George Beverly Shea, an Anglo-American gospel singer. The former, in 'quasi-sermon fashion' 'utilizes the vast arsenal of vocal devices of his tradition: moans, grunts, wails, shouts, gliding pitches, and song speech'. The latter focuses on 'clear enunciation of words, clear, clean phrasing, and incorporates few glides or slides to and from pitches'.

As for the sounds in our environment, mass production has undoubtedly brought greater uniformity. There was much room for diversity in church bells, post horns and the cries of street vendors. There is less room for diversity in cheap electric doorbells, telephone dialling tones and car horns. Yet, here too choice and diversity may be increasing as designers begin to actually design the sounds of car doors and telephone dialling tones rather than treating them as mechanical and non-semiotic by-products of action.

Something similar is happening with film and television soundtracks. Until recently most film-makers paid little attention to sound, concentrating mainly on 'clean' dialogue and 'sync' effects. Sound effects were 'slaved' to the picture, just as sound effects in the urban environment are 'slaved' to the mechanical processes that cause them. The extract from *The Piano* we discussed in the previous chapter uses a different approach. Here complex, 'blended' sound effects do not just provide a sense of 'presence', but are carefully produced and put together for their expressive and emotive qualities. Sound effects of the creaking and groaning of timber and of the soft sighing and deep mysterious rumbling of the ocean can thus become as telling and emotionally affective as music.

Poststructuralist writing by Kristeva, Barthes and others has re-introduced the materiality of the sign. In his celebrated article 'The Grain of the Voice' Barthes (1977: 179ff.) opposes 'the features which belong to the structure of the language being sung, the rules of the genre, the coded form of the composers' idiolect, the style of the interpretation: in short everything in the performance which is in the service of communication, representation, expression', to the 'grain of the voice', 'the 'materiality of the body speaking its mother tongue', 'something which is directly brought to your ears in one and the same movement from deep down in the cavities, the muscles, the membranes, the cartilages'. The 'grain of the voice', he argues, affects the listener in a completely personal, even quasi-erotic way, providing pleasure and escaping the semiotic and the social. Barthes' and Kristeva's reinstatement of the affective dimensions of language and music was important and timely. However, perhaps it only reversed the polarities and placed on a pedestal what earlier had been marginalized as 'mere' performance. Sound never just 'expresses' or 'represents', it always also, and at the same time, affects us. The two cannot and should not be separated and opposed to each other, especially not in the case of sound. There is always both the social and the personal, both meaning and pleasure – or displeasure. The difference lies in how we *value* the social and the personal, or meaning and pleasure, and in the degree to which we acknowledge their unavoidable interconnections.

Dimensions of voice quality and timbre

In this section I will survey some key dimensions of voice quality and timbre, concentrating on features common to speech, music and other sounds. Three things should be kept in mind:

1. As always in semiotics, the same signifier may be used at different levels. It may, for instance, realize a particular 'move' – a speech act, an image act, a sound act, or constitute a habitual or prescribed characteristic of the style of an individual or group.

   To give an example, at the level of the 'move', the colour red may realize the act of 'warning', as in a traffic sign. High pitch might do the same, in a siren, for instance. But the colour red may also act as an overall characteristic of a given social situation or social group. It may be the colour of a daring party dress, for instance, or the uniform of an airline cabin crew (in which case the airline perhaps attempts to convey an image of pleasure, rather than, say, efficiency). High pitch, similarly, can be the pitch of the 'little girl voice' which a woman may adopt in a flirtatious conversation at the party, or the pitch of the part she sings in a choir. In many cultures the high-pitched voice is used for 'honorific' purposes (cf. for example Brown and Levinson, 1978), to, literally, make the voice, and thereby in a sense the whole person, small when greeting a higher status person.

   These examples show that some situations provide more choice than others. Neither the red dress, nor the little girl voice are original creations. They are recognizable interactional clichés. But no one is compelled to use them. They will be seen as personal taste and liked or disliked accordingly (which may of course have consequences for the person's standing in the social group). Still, the uniform of the cabin crew and the pitch of the soprano part in the piece of choral music are different matters – deviate from them, and you might be fired. Not using the honorific voice, similarly, would be a breach of politeness conventions and might well have undesirable social consequences.

2. Every sound quality is a mixture of different features. A voice is never only high or low, or only soft or loud, or only tense or lax. The impression it makes derives from the way such features are combined, from the voice being soft *and* low *and* lax *and* breathy, for instance – and of course also from the context in which this voice quality is used – from who uses it, to whom, for what purpose

and so on. This is so with all sounds. The car horn can be used to warn another driver, greet a friend, aim cat-calls at female passers-by, express youthful exuberance, and more. In addition the sound qualities are not pairs of binary opposites but *graded* phenomena. Sounds are not either tense or lax, either high or low and so on, they occupy a position on a scale that runs from maximally tense to maximally lax, from maximally high to maximally low and so on – and the meanings of these sound qualities are also graded.

3. Finally, there is the problem of how to talk about these meanings. This is usually done by means of adjectives – and the problem is that the same component of sound quality may attract many different adjectives. The 'tense' voice, for instance, has been called 'metallic', 'brassy', 'bright', 'clear', 'keen', 'piercing', 'ringing', 'sharp', 'strident', the lax voice 'muffled', 'dull', 'guttural', 'mellow', 'obscure', 'soft', ' thick' and so on (Laver, 1980: 141). Also, in these adjectives the descriptive and the evaluative mix. It is evidently 'good' for a voice to be 'bright' and 'clear', and 'bad' for it to be 'piercing' and 'strident'. Again, which of these labels apply will depend on the context. Imagine a relatively formal business meeting with minimally ten people present, men as well as women, the latter probably in the minority. It is likely that the men (and perhaps some of the women also) will think women should sound 'soft and sweet' and call tense and loud female voices 'shrill' and 'strident' (as a child I was taught to consider such voices vulgar, it was how 'fishwives' spoke). They will probably also think that men should *not* sound soft and sweet, but assertive and energetic, and they might call soft, low and lax male voices 'thick and muffled', and lacking in 'clarity'. All this is of course a crucial aspect of the social semiotics of sound quality, but to appreciate it, we need to go beyond the adjectives, and consider what the sounds actually are, or rather, how they are actually materially produced, and with what range of meanings and values they can therefore potentially become associated.

Tense/lax

What happens when you tense the muscles of your throat is an experience we all have in common. The voice becomes higher (lower overtones are reduced, higher overtones increased), sharper, brighter, and, above all, more tense, because in their tensed state the walls of the throat cavity dampen the sound less than they would in relaxed state. When you open your throat and relax your voice, the opposite happens. The voice becomes more relaxed and mellow. Other sounds with the characteristics of tense voices can then also partake of these meanings – compare the ambulance's shrieking siren to the ship's low and booming foghorn, or the frenetic wail of John Coltrane's tenor saxophone in, say, 'Africa', to the mellow sound of Stan Getz in 'Misty'.

The sound that results from tensing not only *is* tense, it also *means* 'tense' – and *makes* tense. This can then be further coloured in by the context in which the sound is used, to become 'aggression', 'repression', 'excitement' and a host of other meanings which can be said to include the idea of 'tension'. As we have seen, Fonagy and Magdics (1972: 286ff.) list vocal tension as a feature of sound acts expressing emotions such as 'fright', 'anguish', 'scorn' and 'sarcasm'. This could be extended to the more habitual tense voice 'settings' we might interpret as symptoms of nervous dispositions, anxious personalities or ingrained cynical attitudes. But tension not only characterizes specific emotions of this kind. A certain amount of it is needed whenever we are in a public or formal situation; whenever we cannot afford to relax, but must 'speak up', project ourselves, display some energy; whenever we cannot take it easy, but must stay alert, attentive; whenever we cannot say or do whatever comes to mind, but must control and restrain ourselves; in short, whenever things are not casual, laid back and informal.

As for the tenseness or laxness of other sounds, the crucial factor is the *rigidity* of the objects that cause the sound and/or the rigidity of the resonating environment. Compare the same drum hit with hard drum sticks or soft mallets, or think of the way drummers sometimes put a pillow inside the bass drum to take away the higher overtones. Public life in the city is full of tense sounds – high heels on marble stairs; the clatter of forks, knives and plates in the restaurant kitchen; the metal doors of cars and trains slamming shut. Compare them to soft shoes on grass, the dull thud of the rubber-lined fridge door, the muffle of heavily carpeted and cushioned rooms, and immediately tension will fall away.

Rough/smooth

A rough voice is one in which we can hear other things besides the tone of the voice itself – friction sounds, hoarseness, harshness, rasp. The opposite of the rough sound is the clean, smooth, 'well-oiled' sound in which all noisiness is eliminated. Much of the effect of 'roughness' comes from the aperiodic vibration of the vocal chords which causes noise in the spectrum (Laver, 1980: 128). As this is more audible in the lower pitches, it is more easily heard in male voices or the lower register of musical instruments. This accords with Lomax's observation (1968: 192) that the rough voice is, worldwide, more common in male speech and singing and also strongly correlated with the degree to which boys are trained for assertivity, which tends to occur more often in hunting societies and less often in agricultural societies.

Again, the meaning of roughness lies in what it is: rough. The rough voice (think of Louis Armstrong) is the vocal equivalent of the weatherbeaten face, the roughly plastered wall, the faded jeans, the battered leather jacket. The smooth voice is the vocal equivalent of unblemished young skin, polished surfaces, designer plastic, immaculate tuxedos. How this is valued depends on the context. In Western classical music perfection and polish are highly valued. In the Afro-American tradition, on the other hand, roughness is highly valued:

> In most traditional singing there is no apparent striving for the 'smooth' and 'sweet' qualities that are so highly regarded in the Western tradition. Some outstanding blues, gospel and jazz singers have voices that may be described as foggy, hoarse, rough or sandy. Not only is this kind of voice not derogated, it often seems to be valued. Sermons preached in this type of voice appear to create a special emotional tension. Examination of African singing traditions indicates that there, too, 'sweetness' of voice is not a primary objective, and that other considerations are regarded as more relevant to good singing (Courlander, quoted in Williams-Jones, 1975: 377).

Throughout the industrial age, the sounds that have characterized the urban environment have been rough. Doors and floorboards creak, typewriters rattle, trams rumble and grate in their cast-iron rails. A world in which all this noise is eliminated, in which doors hum softly as they open, and in which cars murmur melodiously as they float along without the slightest sound of friction, such a world, often invoked in car advertisements and science fiction films, is an almost womb-like (or boudoir-like) world of pleasurably cushioned aural sensations. We have already made a step towards it as the computer has replaced the manual typewriter, the video recorder the film projector and so on, although the combustion engine is still with us, and, for the time being, continues to keep us in touch with the gritty realities of the industrial age, in which sounds were rough and noisy (although it is eliminated or replaced by music in most car commercials).

Breathiness

In the breathy voice too, an extraneous sound mixes in with the tone of the voice itself – breath. But the effect is quite different. Hear it for yourself. Breathe in deeply, then breathe out, speaking softly at the same time. There is the breathy voice, always also soft, and frequently associated with intimacy. Advertisers use it to give their message a sensual, even erotic appeal, and singers and instrumentalists use it for the same reason – for instance Archie Shepp in the intimate saxophone and piano duos he has recorded with Abdullah Ibrahim.

Sound effects can be breathy as well – think of the sound of the ocean as created for *The Piano*, or the sound of 'Spectres in the Wind' in a 'suspense effects' CD produced by the BBC Radiophonic Workshop – both use as one of their components the sound of a softly sighing breathiness that almost touches listeners, almost engulfs them with the overwhelming closeness of its presence.

Soft/loud

In Chapter 2 we discussed softness and loudness, so here we need to repeat only the essentials. Soft and loud are most crucially associated with distance. Distance, in turn, is most crucially associated with social distance (though it can of course also be used to portray physical distance). The loud voice carries furthest and claims most territory. The soft voice, on the other hand, excludes all but a few others, and can therefore become associated with intimacy and confidentiality.

The power of loudness is not restricted to the human voice. The more powerful people or institutions are, the more noise they are allowed to make. The loudest noises, Schafer has argued, are always 'sacred noises': 'Thunder, the voice of God, migrated first to the cathedral, then to the factory and the rockband' (Schafer, 1977: 179). Schafer also recounts how a group of Hara Krishnas in Vancouver were fined for causing excessive noise with their chanting, which they had been doing next to a building site whose noises exceeded 90 decibels (1977: 201). Needless to say, the builders were not fined.

High/low

Register, the scale from the very low 'in the chest' voice to the very high voice (falsetto for men) we already discussed in the previous chapter. Because men's voices are on average lower than those of women and children, the meanings of high and low relate to gender (and age) in complex ways. Men use the higher regions of their pitch range to assert themselves and to dominate – only the very highest regions (for example counter-tenor) can become ambiguous in gender terms. A man who speaks low is usually trying not to be dominant, trying to make himself vocally small by mumbling a bit – the booming bass is the exception, and, at least in the Anglo-American context, usually considered a little too overbearing.

Women, on the other hand, use the lower end of their pitch range to be assertive. It is difficult however to do so while at the same time being loud (this creates the special 'booming' quality already mentioned) and so women are faced with a dilemma. Either they speak low (which is assertive) and soft (which is intimate), which can invoke the 'dangerous woman' stereotype, or they speak high (thus 'belittling' themselves) and loud (thus being assertive) which can invoke the 'shrill and strident fishwife' stereotype. In either case the dominant norms of the public, assertive (and 'masculine') voice will be at odds with the dominant norms of the private, intimate (and 'feminine') voice.

Pitch level relates to size and social importance also in the case of the sounds in our environment. Large vehicles (boats, trains) are given deeper-sounding horns than cars, and scooters have high-pitched horns, even though arguably they do not differ much in terms of the distance from which they would need to be heard.

Vibrato/plain

Sounds are either plain and unwavering, or have some kind of 'grain', some kind of regular or irregular wavering, warbling, vibrating, pulsating, throbbing, rumbling and so on – a more detailed account of the subtle differences between all these possibilities will have to wait for another occasion. Clearly this applies not only to the human voice, but also to other musical and non-musical sounds.

Vibrato again 'means what it is'. The vibrating sound literally and figuratively *trembles*. What makes us tremble? Emotions. Love, for instance. Strings are particularly good at producing vibrato sounds and hence universally used to 'pull the heartstrings', to present and represent love and romance. But also other emotions, for instance fear: one of the tracks from the BBC suspense effects CD quoted earlier is titled 'Uncanny Expectations' and has a drone which pulsates at about the speed of slow footsteps.

Not trembling, sounding plain and 'unmoved' can also acquire a variety of contextually specific meanings – think of the plain sound of the boys' choir in Bach's *St Matthew Passion*, and the way in which its quality of 'not wavering' can come to mean, perhaps, 'unwavering' faith, or 'rock steady' innocence.

There is yet another side to vibrato, unconnected with, indeed far removed from, the world of human emotions. The natural world, physics has taught us, is full of vibrations, many of them oscillating at a speed beyond the capacity of human sensory perception. The technical world, too, has accelerated vibration to a point at which it can no longer be heard as such: beyond 20 cycles per second any vibration becomes a constant pitch, turns into one of the hums, whirrs, buzz tones and engine whines that dominate our 'lofi' urban environment. This kind of impersonal, dehumanized vibrato is often represented electronically, by rapid warblings or metallic shimmerings of what sound like thousands of high-pitched pinpoint sounds. Adam Birdsall, a student of mine at the London College of Printing, drew my attention to a particularly good example, a 'techno' track called 'Alien Tekno' which began by overlaying many of these kinds of sounds: shimmering zings, rapidly warbling electronic whistles, low rumbles, slow organ tremolos, fast bass ostinatos and more.

Nasality

More has been written about nasality than about almost any other aspect of voice quality, partly because it has been difficult to define, and partly because nasality judgements have usually been value judgements: the languages, dialects and singing styles and so on which people call 'nasal' are the languages, dialects and singing styles they do not like.

The usual phonetic definition of nasality says that it is sound produced with the soft palate lowered and the mouth unblocked, so that air escapes both via the nose and via the mouth. Paradoxically, however, you can produce a 'nasal' sound by holding your nose closed – if you then unblock your nose again and produce the same type of sound with your nose unblocked, you will notice that you have to tense your voice a little. When you reduce the overall muscle tension, the nasality will disappear. This suggests that the impression of 'nasality' results from the combination of two factors: vocal tension and what has been called a 'cul-de-sac resonator' (West *et al.*, 1957), that is, a resonating chamber which opens off from the passageway through which the sound escapes to the air, but is itself closed off. The nasal cavity is not the only possible cul-de-sac resonator – tensing of the faucal pillars (the muscular arches visible in the back of the mouth on each side of the soft palate) can have the same effect.

Nasality is thus closely related to tension, which explains why 'pinched and nasal tones pervade many of the sounds of pain, deprivation and sorrow' (Lomax, 1968: 193), and why we hear nasality in moaning and wailing and screaming. But perhaps these are just some of the reasons why we might produce a tense voice. Less dramatically, nasality may occur whenever there is inhibition and repression, whenever we find ourselves in a stressful situation, whenever we must control or restrain ourselves. It occurs, for instance, when 'an individual of lower social or economic status addresses one of higher rank', or 'with a woman being polite to her husband, or a man asking a favour' (Crystal, 1970: 191). And Lomax, in his overview of singing styles across the world, has shown that it correlates, among other things, with degrees of sexual repression. In cultures which place few restrictions on women, singing tends to be relaxed and without nasality. Cultures which have a certain degree of permissiveness, yet strongly condemn pregnancy outside of approved relations tend to have female singing styles with greater nasality. Where women are very much repressed (very early marriages, clitoridectomy, very severe sanctions for adulterous women and so on) singing tends to be both very tense and very nasal:

> It is as if one of the assignments of the favoured singer is to act out the level of sexual tension which the customs of the society establish as normal. The content of this message may be painful and anxiety-producing, but the effect upon the culture member may be stimulating, erotic and pleasurable, since the song reminds him of familiar sexual emotions and experiences (Lomax, 1968: 194).

Another factor which female singing style is correlated with is the division of labour between the sexes:

Vocal tension (narrow, nasal vocalizing) is far higher in non-complementary societies, where men perform all or most of the main subsistence tasks. On the other hand, wide, relaxed voices seem to be the norm in complementary societies (Lomax, 1968: 200).

The 'wide, clear, relaxed voice' thus indicates both a 'non-aggressive, non-dominant, security-building attitude towards feminine sexuality' (1968: 198) and the importance of the role of women in basic subsistence.

Shepherd (1991) has discussed the voices of different kinds of rock singers. 'Hard rock' voices are rough, loud and high. Their timbre resembles shouting or even screaming. Resonance is produced almost entirely in the throat and the mouth: the singer is 'all mouth'. According to Shepherd, this 'reproduces tension and experiential repression as males engage with the public world' (1991: 167). As we saw, Tagg linked the same style to the soundscape of the city: to make yourself understood, valid as an individual, you have to shout above the din of the city' (1990: 108).

In a female rock singing style which Shepherd describes as the style of 'woman as emotional nurturer' the voice is soft and warm, with an open throat, and relatively low. It uses the resonating chambers of the chest, says Shepherd, so that the voice comes from the region of the heart or the breast. Softer male singers such as Paul McCartney tend to use the head as resonator and therefore sound 'lighter and thinner'.

> The typical sound of woman-as-sex-object involves a similar comparison. The softer, warmer, hollower tones of the woman singer as emotional nurturer become closed off with a certain edge, a certain vocal sheen that is quite different from the male-appropriated, hard core of timbre typical of 'cock' rock. Tones such as those produced by Shirley Bassey in 'Big Spender', for instance, are essentially head tones, and it could in this sense be argued that the transition from woman the nurturer to woman the sex object represents a shift, physiologically coded, from the 'feminine heart' to the 'masculine head' (Shepherd, 1991: 167–8).

Our understanding of the sound qualities I have discussed so far rests mostly on our knowledge of what it is we do when we produce them with our voice, or, in the case of wind instruments, with our lungs, our tongue, our lips and so on. But we not only produce sounds with our vocal apparatus, we also produce sounds with our *hands*, as we pluck, stroke, tap, beat and bang material objects, either with our bare hands or with instruments (hammers, chisels, sandpaper, or, in music, bows, sticks, mallets, brushes and so on), in our everyday life and work as well as in music. We can even produce sounds with our feet, when we walk or dance the flamenco, for instance, or when we play the bass drum or the pedals of an organ.

At least two things need to be said here. First, all the dimensions of sound we have so far discussed also apply to these sounds. The sounds we produce with our hands and our feet can also be tense or lax, for instance, whether because of the tensing of our muscles or because of the rigidity or lack of rigidity of the objects we use – think of high heels hitting a hard road, joggers jogging on grass, chinese slippers shuffling on carpet. In the same way sounds produced by the hands and/or feet can be high or low, soft or loud, rough or smooth, and vibrating or non-vibrating.

Second, the meaning of these sounds lies not only in the sound qualities so far discussed, but also in what we are doing when we produce them, whether we are gently caressing the objects involved or aggressively attacking them, for instance. Schafer (1977: 109) has given an excellent example of the broader cultural significance of these physical modes of sound production and their relation to everyday physical action:

> The substitution of the punched string piano for the plucked string harpsichord typifies the greater aggressiveness of a time in which objects were punched and beaten into existence by means of industrial processes where once they had been stroked, carved and kneaded into shape.

One key mode of action of the post-industrial age, in the office as much as in the musical group, is the gentle tapping of keyboards with keys that offer hardly any resistance to the touch – transferring to such keyboards from more old-fashioned ones which still required some force, was initially difficult. It required inhibiting the body, learning to control the movement of the hands as delicately as people bidding in an auction must control their facial expressions – even the tiniest twitches matter.

In this area, too, electronic sound presents a challenge, partly because it often becomes very much a 'mind event' rather than a body event, difficult to relate to physical, bodily experiences and physical, material objects, and partly because the kinds of actions we have to perform to produce them often bear little connection to the sounds themselves, as when a vibrato is produced by touching a button rather than by vibrating one's finger on the string, or the sound of a Spanish guitar by tapping the keys of a piano rather than by plucking strings. Sounds lose their materiality, their link with the actions that produce them, and as a result their meaning might increasingly come to be seen as conventional rather than motivated. If we are to keep mind and body together, and not reduce all semiotic action to moving a mouse on a mouse pad or tapping keys, we urgently need to develop new, subjectively meaningful 'interfaces' between physical actions and the sounds they produce.

Finally, I have discussed the semiotics of voice quality and timbre mostly from the point of view of 'experiential meaning potential'. But clearly 'provenance' plays a role as well: when a sound travels, its meaning is associated with the place it comes from and/or the people who originated it, or rather, with the ideas held about that place or those people in the place to which the sound has travelled. In late-eighteenth-century France, for instance, the hurdy-gurdy, until then a rural instrument, was imported into the court orchestra, because there was among the aristocracy of the period a nostalgic longing for the 'simple country life'. The sound of the hurdy-gurdy thus came to represent that 'simple country life', as conceived of at the court, and was able to powerfully affect listeners with nostalgia (cf. Winternitz, 1979, Ch. 4). In the 1960s, the Beatles and other groups introduced the sitar into their music, to express a certain way of valuing the East, then current in 'psychedelic' youth culture. The principle is very often used in advertising music, and in mass media music generally. Nattiez (1975: 22) has linked it to the idea of 'connotation', and said that its 'decoding' involved three phases, (i) recognizing the sound as a 'foreign body' in the music, (ii) being able to identify its origin, and (iii) being able to link it to the relevant 'mental associations' or bundle of cultural references. All this is not necessarily done consciously, especially not in the case of mass media. As Berger has said, connotations are 'merely reminiscent of cultural lessons half-learnt' (1972: 140).

Connotation is not restricted to music. Speech accents, too, can carry connotations deriving from ideas held about the people whose accents they are. Among Dutch intellectuals and artists in the 1960s it was fashionable to adopt a smattering of broad Amsterdam accent, whether or not they originally came from Amsterdam. Amsterdam was the 'red' city, centre of political movements such as the Provos and the Kabouters. Returning to Holland after a long absence in the mid 1980s I was surprised to find that many of the more publicly visible intellectuals and artists affected a touch of Rotterdam accent, again, whether or not they hailed from that city. Perhaps I should not have been surprised. Rotterdam is the city of commerce and business. It is only apt that its accent should have risen in value at the peak of the 'yuppie' era.

Sound effects can also travel – for example from the everyday environment into music. Musical timbres can remind of motorbikes and powerdrills, police sirens and car alarms. Tagg heard 'the hell of B52 bombers over Vietnam as played on a Fender guitar by Jimi Hendrix' (1990: 108).

To summarize:

1. Sound quality is multidimensional, a combination of different features which all help define what the sound quality presents or represents.

2. The significations these features contribute to the sound quality can be derived from an experiential meaning potential, that is, from what we *do* when we produce the sounds, either vocally or with our hands and/or feet, and from our ability to turn action into knowledge, to extend our practical experience metaphorically, and to grasp similar extensions made by others (cf. Lakoff and Johnson, 1980).

   Key sound quality features include (i) *tension*; (ii) *roughness*; (iii) *breathiness*; (iv) *loudness*; (v) *pitch register*; (vi) *vibrato* and (vii) *nasality*.

   Tension can relate to increased alertness, self-control, stress and so on, in short, to every situation in which it is not desirable or possible to relax or act without constraint. It is a graded feature: sounds can range from maximally tense to maximally lax.

   Roughness, again, 'means what it is' – and can be metaphorically extended to other sense modalities and other experiences of friction and irregularity. Roughness, too, is a graded feature: sounds can range from maximally rough to maximally smooth.

   Breathiness derives its meaning from our knowledge of the kinds of situation in which it can occur – when we are out of breath, or unable to control 'heavy breathing' due to excitement. It is most often associated with intimacy, and also admits of degrees.

   Loudness relates most strongly to the need to cover distance. This often causes it to be associated with dominance and power. The opposite then applies to softness. Sounds can range from maximally loud to maximally soft.

   Pitch register is on the one hand associated with size (small things make high noises, large things low noises) and on the other hand with the fact that the louder voice also tends to rise in pitch, so that 'high', too, can have many metaphoric extensions related to power and status. Power and status are then considered 'high', and 'rising' is associated with increased power or status. A third variable is the experience that women's voices are, on average, higher than men's voices. These factors interact in complex ways that can only be disambiguated in the specific contexts in which the registers are used. Register is, again, a graded feature.

Vibrato relates to increased emotionality or loss of control (inability to keep the voice 'steady'). Plain unwavering tones can come to signify anything that can be interpreted as 'steady', 'unwavering', 'firm' and so on, or, conversely, as 'dull', 'bland', 'expressionless' and so on, depending on how emotionality is valued in the context. Different degrees and kinds of vibrato are possible.

Nasality is a concomitant of tension which carries strong negative value judgements.

The meaning of sounds can be related in similar ways to the hand (or foot) actions that produce the sounds. Jazz drummers caress the cymbals with wire brushes when they play slow, soft and soulful ballads, and hit them with sticks when they play more tense and energetic rhythms.

When sounds *cannot* be related to human action, their meaning is based on the very fact of their being 'not human'. Depending on the context this can be related, for instance, to the world of science and technology, or to sacred, supernatural or extra-terrestrial worlds.

3. The meaning of a sound quality can also rest on *connotation*, that is, on the listeners' attitudes to the place where that sound quality comes from and to the people with whom its 'origin' is associated. As such attitudes are usually based on second-hand experience they may be strongly mediated by education and the mass media (for example Hollywood films). Simon Frith has a telling example (1984: 84):

> The 'reality' of film musical settings actually refers to historical and geographical myths (themselves constructed, in part, by previous musics in previous films set in these places and times). Thus the music for *Zorba the Greek* became so powerfully connotative of 'Greece' that Greek restaurants (even those in Greece itself) have to use the music to convince customers of their 'Greekness'.

The sounds of speech

So far we have only touched the surface of what can be done with the human vocal apparatus. We can, for instance, speak with closed or open jaw – the latter is a key contributor to the distinctive timbre of Indian and Pakistani English. We can speak with retracted, 'pursed' lips or with protruding, 'pouted' lips – a feature of 'little girl speech'. And so on. And then we are not even touching on the actual speech sounds, the vowels and consonants. The vocal apparatus is in fact an extraordinary instrument which easily beats the synthesizer in the amount of distinct sound qualities it can produce. It is an instrument of which we can change the size and shape at will and instantaneously. We can lengthen it or shorten it, widen it or narrow it, increase or decrease the size of its air outlets, change the shape of its resonating chamber by changing the shape and position of the tongue and so on.

But what is the semiotic value of all these different sound qualities? For most twentieth-century linguists the answer to this question has been: none. For them, 'phonemes', speech sounds, have no intrinsic, but only distinctive value. They only serve to tell words apart from each other. If a language has both a [p] and a [b] then the different qualities of these two consonants serve to tell apart word pairs like [pet] and [bet] or [pail] and [bail], which otherwise would sound identical. An analogous theory of images would treat colour as serving only to distinguish objects from each other, not to depict the colours they have, or to create an emotive impact. Colour *can* be used in this way, for instance in railway maps, where one line is green, another red, another blue and so on, even though they may all use grey carriages. But it can also be used in other ways. Linguists do of course realize that onomatopoeia (speech sounds imitating sounds in the environment) and sound symbolism exist, but they consider them relatively marginal phenomena. And in any case, the argument usually goes, onomatopoeic words differ strongly from language to language, while in the case of sound symbolism you can always find exceptions. Thus the dog goes *bow-wow* in English, *arf-arf* in American English, *gnaf-gnaf* in French, *guau-guau* in Spanish, *how-how* in Arabic, *gau-gau* in Vietnamese and *won-won* in Japanese. As for sound symbolism, while it is true that many words whose meaning includes the idea of 'little' contain the vowel [ɪ] (for example *little, mini, piccolo, itty-bitty*), there are also words with an [ɪ] which mean the opposite (for example *big, immense*).

Still, it cannot be denied that there are series of words which correspond in meaning as well as in sound: *flap, flee, flex, flick, flinch, flow, fly* (there are many more) all have a sense of a sudden movement away from the speaker; *slam, slash, slice, slit* all convey that an action is performed somewhat aggressively; *slide, slip, slither, slop* all include a sense of losing control over an action. Sometimes a vowel change in the middle of a word can change its meaning into the opposite, as with *gleam* and *gloom*, or into something 'heavier', as with French *siffler* ('whistle') and *souffler* ('blow') (cf. Ullman, 1962: 84ff. for more examples). People's ability to use sound for making meanings, not only in art, but also in everyday conversation, in jokes, in advertising, in newspaper headlines and so on, and people's ability to respond to such meanings, in short, people's knowledge of the 'poetic function' of language and its realizations (Jakobson, 1962), form an important part of their linguistic competence, even if it is not recognized as such by many linguists or taught as a key aspect of literacy in schools. Language as studied by many linguists and taught in the education system has neglected the emotive side of language, the music of language, or, at best, banished it to the margins. But the music of language has not gone away. In the words of Konrad Bühler, it continued to grow like grass between the stones of an old courtyard, ineradicable.

Romantic poets stressed the expression of emotions and consequently were also interested in the emotive power of sound. These lines from Byron betray some doubt as to the possibility of direct affective communication through language:

Oh that my words were colours! But their tint
May serve perhaps as outlines or slight hints
            (*Don Juan Canto VI*, stanza cix).

But Rimbaud had no such doubts:

I have invented the colour of the vowels! – A black, E white, I red, O blue, U green – I have ordered the form and the movement of each consonant, and with instinctive rhythms I have flattered myself that I have invented a poetic verb, accessible one day or another to every sense (*Les Plus Belles Œuvres*, Vol. 3: 141).

And later avant-garde artists would dispense with language altogether and work directly with sound. This poem by the Dada poet Hugo Ball dates from 1916:

Gadji beri bimba
glandridi aluli loinni cadori
gadjama bim beri glassala
glandridid glassala tuffm i zimbrabim
blassa glassa guffm i zimbrabim

Such ideas and practices formed the beginning of a long and still continuing revival of interest in *synaesthesia*, the exploration of correspondences between qualities perceived by the different senses, for example between vowels and colours, or between musical sounds and colours. It is clear that such correspondences are an important semiotic resource. The very words we use to denote the qualities of colours, sounds, textures and so on, happily cross from mode to mode. We can speak of smooth textures as well as smooth sounds, soft noises as well as soft colours or soft materials, clear lines as well as clear voices and so on. At the same time, such sensory qualities can often be related to other ones in more than one way, which perhaps accounts for the many differences between the various synaesthetic 'tables of correspondence' that have been constructed by artists and psychologists, and also in different cultures. Plain unmodulated colour, for instance, can be likened to 'unwavering' (non-vibrato) sound, but also to 'smooth' (non-rough) sound. Light colour can be likened to high-pitched sound (on the basis of high energy) or to tense sound. This flexibility and these multiple possibilities are precisely what makes synaesthesia such a rich semiotic resource.

Maybe it is best to start again with the question of what exactly is it we *do* when we produce a particular speech sound. Schafer's descriptions in *When Words Sing* (reprinted in Schafer, 1986) are based on this principle, even if he does not always explicitly formulate the links between the way a sound is articulated and what it can mean:

B   Has bite, Combustive. Aggressive. The lips bang over it.
I   Highest vowel. Thin, bright, pinched sound, leaving the smallest cavity in the mouth. Hence useful in words describing smallness: *piccolo, petit, tiny, wee.*
L   Watery, luscious, languid. Needs juice in the mouth to be spoken properly. Feel it drip around the tongue. Feel the saliva in 'lascivious lecher.'
M   In the Phoenician alphabet 'mem' originally stood for calm sea, the sea then being the fundamental tone in all maritime soundscapes. Today it might mean calm motor, the motor being the fundamental in all

contemporary soundscapes. But consider also the murmur of the bees in Tennyson's 'The Princess':

> The moan of doves in immemorial elms
> And murmuring of innumerable bees

O   The second most frequent vowel in English. It suggests roundness and perfection. Consider the sound of children's voices singing in the dome of a cathedral as heard by Verlaine: 'O ces voix d'enfants chantant dans le coupole.'

P   Pip, pop, pout. Combustive, comical. Listen to the soft popping of the pipesmoker (Schafer, 1986: 180–1).

Introducing this 'alphabet', Schafer says that he is 'not interested in phonetic dogma, but in colourful metaphors that unlock secrets' (1986: 180). So am I, but even though the science of articulatory phonetics has traditionally steered clear from semiotic considerations (with exceptions, for example Fonagy), it can still be a most useful tool for carefully thinking through these issues. Two things should be remembered. First, as mentioned already, every sound is a *bundle* of different qualities. The [ɪ] for instance, is not only 'little' (because of 'leaving the smallest cavity in the mouth') it is also 'frontal', requiring the tongue to move to the front of the mouth, and 'high', requiring the tongue to move up. Second, speech sounds, as opposed to many non-speech vocalizations like *mmmm* or *ssssh*, come in syllables. So the word *big* is not only characterized by the [ɪ], it also has the [b] and the [g], and it is the combination of these three which must be interpreted, just as, in the case of colour, it is the particular mixture of colour which matters. The word [bɪg], for example, has both the 'combustive' bang of the [b] and the frontality of the [ɪ]. In other words, the 'bigness' of *big* is both 'explosive' and 'upfront' – quite different from the 'bigness' of *large*, which is more distant and slowly moving. Critics who dismiss sound symbolism because not all words with an [ɪ] denote something small, assume a 'code book' approach to meaning, in which every individual item has a fixed meaning. Some meanings are indeed like this. But fixed meanings are fixed by people, and as argued above, sound symbolism has escaped the kind of close fixing that has gone on in the spelling and grammar and lexicography of written language. Its meanings have never been fixed to the same degree, and therefore worked, by and large, not on the basis of rules and code books, but on the basis of generative semiotic principles. At most there may be the formative (but not formally taught) influence of culturally significant language designers (for example poets and song writers) and genres (for example advertising) on people's semiotic practices and preferences.

In discussing what the different speech sounds can *mean*, the obvious starting point is the distinction between vowels and consonants. Essentially, this is the difference between 'open' and 'closed', between a relatively free flow of energy and various forms of constraint, or even blockage of the airflow (cf. Jakobson, 1968). In all its abstraction this may seem a rather bland statement, but have you ever wondered why some languages (for example Hawaian) are very open, full of a's and o's and i's flowing into each other, while others (for example Czech) are full of wellnigh unpronounceable consonant clusters? What caused the need for such constraint in the one case, and what prevented it from developing in the other? The answer to such questions might now lie too far back in history to be retrieved, but in other cases it may be open to investigation. Hodge and Kress (1988: 92) asked why in many languages informality is expressed by eliminating consonants (for example *gonna* instead of *going to*, *give 'em* instead of *give them*), and concluded that formality involves 'high constraint, control and culture', and informality a comparative lack of constraint and repression, a comparative free flow of energy. This fits in with the approach of Elias (1978), who saw increased restraint and 'affect control' as a fundamental characteristic, perhaps *the* fundamental characteristic, of the 'civilization process' that has taken place in Europe over the last five centuries.

Vowels are multidimensionally determined, in a way which is based on the position and movement of the tongue during their articulation. You can easily check this out for yourself. If, for instance, you touch the tip of your tongue while saying [ɪ] as in *bid*, and then move to saying the [a] of *part*, you can feel your tongue moving backward, away from your finger: the [ɪ] is a frontal, the [a] a back vowel. Here is an overview of the relevant dimensions:

Frontality

This is the dimension of front (for example [i] as in *heed*) vs back (for example [a] as in *hard*). It can give rise to metaphorical extensions related to the idea of distance. Many words whose meanings include a sense of 'close' or 'far' use the contrast. In Dutch *dit* ('this') is frontal, *dat* ('that') back, *hier* ('here') frontal, *daar* ('there') back and so on. In English the [ɪə] of 'near' is frontal and the [a] of *far* pronounced far back in the mouth. The French have *ici* and *là-bas*, the Germans *hier* and *dort* and so on.

Height

This is the dimension of high (for example [ɪə] as in *here*) vs low (for example [æ] as in *that*). It can give rise to sound symbolism and metaphorical extension in the same way as frontality – think of the higher [ʌ] in *up* and the lower [aʊ] in *down*, or of the higher [aɪ] and the lower [oʊ] in the words *high* and *low* themselves.

Aperture

This is the difference between vowels pronounced with the mouth comparatively closed and the oral cavity consequently comparatively small (for example [i] as in *heed* and [u] as in *hood*) or with the mouth comparatively open and the oral cavity therefore much larger (for example [a] as in *hard*). The metaphorical extensions of openness and closedness are frequently discussed in the literature, as when the [a], [u] and [ɔ] (*large, book, paw*) are called large, and the [i] and [ɛ] (*beed, bed*) small (Sapir, 1929) or the [a] and [ɔ] 'heavy, big and round', or the [i] 'small, light and pointed' (Brown and Hildum, 1956).

As for the consonants, without giving a complete overview of all factors involved, some of the semiotically most fertile dimensions now follow.

Voicing

This is the difference between, on the one hand, consonants which have 'tone', so that they can be 'sung' and achieve a certain loudness (for example [l], [m], [n], [v]), and, on the other hand, consonants which do not have 'tone', and must therefore always be quiet, near-silent releases of air (for example [h], [f], [s]). Put your finger on your larynx and you can feel it vibrating as you say *mmmmm* and stop vibrating as you move to *sssssh*. Words for 'silence' and 'stillness' (and for all manner of silent and still people, places, and things) start with the unvoiced [s] or [ʃ] (as in *ship*) in many languages. Here is the sound

of an arrow whistling past, from the comic strip *Phoebe-Zeitgeist*:
SSSSSSSST!

Plosives

Some consonants involve *blocking* the airstream and then suddenly
releasing it, in a small explosion of sound. They are the voiced [b], [d]
and [g] and the unvoiced [p], [t] and [k]. Put a thin piece of paper in
front of your mouth, then say 'p', and you will see the effect of the
sudden release of air. As a result plosives are apt for expressing things
that are sudden, unexpected, explosive and so on, whether on a loud
scale (voiced plosives): *boom, bomb, bang, burst* and so on, or on a small
scale (unvoiced plosives) as in Schafer's pipe noises or the 'pitter-patter'
of the rain. Different plosives are articulated in different positions, the
[p] and the [b] frontally, the [k] and the [g] in the back, and the [t] and
the [d] in the middle. This can make sounds come closer or move away,
as in this explosion from *Phoebe-Zeitgeist*: KA-BLAAM!

Fricatives

Fricatives involve *constricting* the airstream, making a very narrow
passage for it, and thereby creating the turbulence we hear. They are
the unvoiced [f], [θ] (as in *thigh*), [s] and [ʃ], and the voiced [v], [ð] (as
in *thy*) [z] and [ʒ] (as in *measure*), and they are particularly good at
expressing anything to do with friction, whether literally or figuratively – the *fluent flow* of air, the *swelling* and *swirling* of water, the
scraping and *scratching* of surfaces, not to mention such human actions
as *huffing* and *puffing*, *sniffing* and *snuffling* and so on. Think of the
arrow's whistle cited above, or this lash of the whip, from the same
source: THAAWAAT!

Closely related to the fricatives are the [l] and the [r]. Both involve
a degree of constriction. In the [l] the tongue does block the mouth,
but leaves passageways open on either side, and these are wide enough
not to create turbulence, so that the [l] is the most *gliding, fluent* and
flowing of fricatives, *lax* and *lazy* compared to the others. The [r] is
difficult to classify. In some words it is more like a 'semi-vowel' (see
below), for instance in *red* and *road*. In other cases, for example *train*,
or *scrape*, it creates a particular kind of *grating* friction.

Nasals

Then there are the nasals, the [m], the [n] and the [ŋ] (as in *sing*) – all voiced. With the vowels they have in common that they are resonant, albeit more weakly so. There is no fundamental obstruction involved, as the air can flow through the nose. With the consonants they have in common that there is no mouth aperture. The sound is 'kept inside', as it were, not actually uttered. It remains a *hum*, a *murmur*, a *mumble*. *Mmmm* can be the most non-committal of reactions, neither 'yes' nor 'no', the act of explicitly keeping your thoughts inside. Or, if it is a long undulating *mmmmmmm*, it can be a reaction of delight or pain which is at once expressed and not expressed.

Semi-vowels

Finally there are the 'semi-vowels', the [j] (as in *yacht*) and the [w], both voiced, and, like vowels, releasing the airflow freely. The reason why they are classified as consonants is distributional. Every syllable must have a vowel, but that vowel can never be a [j] or a [w]. These 'semi-vowels' must act as transitional sounds. It follows that words (or languages) which make a lot of use of semi-vowels as their consonants are among the least 'constrained' – whatever precise complexion this might take on in the given context.

Here are two words to think of. First the word *womb* – the unconstrained [w], then the [u], as far back, as deep down in the mouth as possible, and using only a small mouth aperture, and finally the [m], a calm murmur 'kept inside'. Then think of the word *crypt*, blocked off on both sides by plosives, with a small, short vowel in between – a cramped space, thoroughly guarded by obstructions and constrictions. Pronounce these words. Taste them on the tongue to 'unlock the metaphors', as Schafer put it, to explore the rich semiotic potential of speech sound. Of course, there are many sounds that cannot, or not so easily, be analysed in this way, perhaps because we no longer know their original referents or literal meanings, or perhaps because they are used in a purely distictive way in the given context, just as colours can be used in a purely distinctive way in certain contexts. But that does not mean that speech sound is not a rich semiotic resource which has been much underused and undervalued in the age of print:

How do we break language out of its print sarcophagus? How do we smash the grey coffins of muttering and let words howl off the page like spirits possessed? (Schafer, 1986: 199).

To summarize:

1. Speech sounds can derive their significance from provenance, from the associations that come with certain 'accents' for instance (for example Australian or American vowels). But their greatest semiotic potential derive from the way they are articulated – from the vowels' dimensions of frontality, height and aperture, and from the consonants' degrees and modes of blocking, constricting and restricting the airstream.

2. Although vocalizations and onomatopoeic words (including the verbal sound effects of comic strips) may consist of a single sound, speech sounds usually come in syllables, to form larger semiotic gestures whose meaning and effect derive from the way they are combined, as demonstrated by the analysis of the words *womb* and *crypt* above.

An example: the singing voice

Here are the main distinctions introduced in this chapter, in the form of two system networks, one for 'sound quality' (Figure 6.1(a)) and one for 'speech sounds' (Figure 6.1(b)).

Note that the 'smooth' fricative is the [l]. In the standard phonetic interpretation the [l] would never be classified as a fricative, but placed in a class of its own, as a 'lateral' – the name derives from the fact that the airstream escapes via passageways each side of the tongue. Here it is seen as the 'frictionless fricative', in which the air glides over a surface rather than that it meets with friction and scrapes, grates, hisses and so on.

As a final example, we look at extracts from two songs by Madonna, concentrating on the sound quality of the voices and instruments. Madonna uses her voice quite differently in the two songs. The electronic timbres of the instrumental sounds, on the other hand, are rather similar.

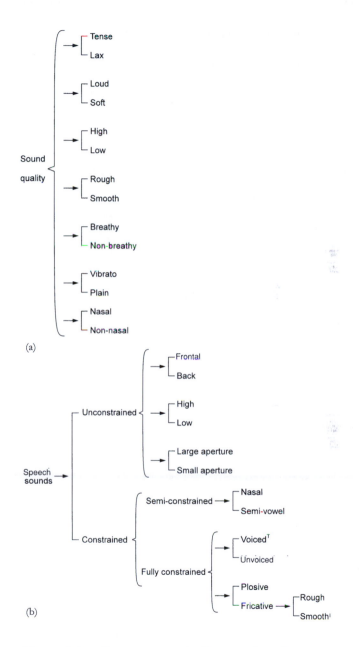

(a)

(b)

Figure 6.1   System networks for sound quality

'Like a Virgin'

1. Bass pattern	tense; mid loudness; mid pitch; smooth; vibrato (metallic shimmer); non-breathy; nasal (metallic)
2. As (1) continues, fade in drums	tense; mid loudness; mid pitch; rough (cymbal hiss); plain; non-breathy; non-nasal
3. As (1) and (2) continue, fade in rhythmic pattern of repeated brassy chords on synthesizer	tense; mid loudness; mid pitch; smooth; plain; non-breathy; nasal
4. As (1), (2) and (3) continue, enter *I made it through the wilderness* *Somehow I made it through* *Didn't know how lost I was* *Until I found you.* *I was beat, incomplete* *I've been had, I was sad and blue*	tense, loud, high, smooth, occasional vibrato; non-breathy; somewhat nasal
5. As (1) and (2) continue, (3) changes to sustained chords: *But you made me feel* *Yeah you made me feel* *Shiny and new* *Like a virgin*	

'Live to Tell'

1. Long synthesizer drone	tense; mid loudness; mid pitch; smooth; vibrato (wavering); non-breathy; non-nasal
2. As (1) continues, fade in pattern of rotating fifths on keyboard	tense; mid loudness; mid pitch smooth; vibrato (metallic shimmering); non-breathy; nasal
3. As (1) and (2) continue, fade in drums (bassdrum and cymbal)	lax; loud; low; rough (hiss of cymbal); plain; non-breathy; non-nasal

PLUS:

4. Bass pattern	lax; mid loudness; low; smooth; plain; non-breathy; nasal (muffled quality)

5. Fade out (2) and fade down (1) which now changes pitch at irregular and widely spaced intervals; enter:
I tell the tale to tell
Sometimes it gets so hard to hide
    it well
I was not ready for the fall
Too blind to see the writing on
    the wall
	lax; soft; low; smooth; plain; breathy; non-nasal

6. Add plucked 'harpsichord' sounds	tense; soft; high; smooth; plain; breathy; nasal
and synthesizer voice doubling the melody:	tense; mid loudness; mid pitch; smooth; plain; non-breathy; nasal
A man can tell a thousand lies *I've learnt my lesson well* *Hope I live to tell* *The secret I have learnt* *Till then it will burn inside of me*	increased tension, loudness and pitch; smooth; vibrato on some key words; non-breathy; non-nasal

The instrumental accompaniment, the 'environment', in which Madonna sings these songs is dominated by cold, unresonant, unresponsive electronic sounds – dark, muffled and dry bass sounds; cold, bleak chords with a metallic twang; pinched and nasal drones, overlaid with metallic shimmers.

In this environment Madonna sings two rather different songs. In 'Like a Virgin' she addresses a 'you' who saved her from perdition and made her feel 'new and shiny', 'like a virgin touched for the very first time'. She addresses this 'you' in a high, 'feminine' voice. But she combines this 'little girl' voice pitch with a more hardened sound, quite tense and strident, bearing the scars of abuse and betrayal.

In 'Live to Tell' the lyrics tell of a lesson learnt the hard way. Here Madonna's voice is less high and less tense, lower, more relaxed, more sure of itself as well as softer, breathier and warmer. Only after a while do an occasional vibrato and increased tension add the strength of relived emotion to some of the key moments. At this point two other (instrumental) voices join in, as though representing two other women with the same or similar experiences – a tense, high voice, playing around the melody in staccato notes, and a more strident and sustained voice, doubling the melody.

We saw that Lomax relates tension and nasality in female singing to the amount of sexual repression in the culture whose favoured singing style it is. In contemporary Western culture many women must live a profoundly contradictory sexuality – on the one hand they seem to be given a great deal of sexual licence, on the other hand there is continued sexual abuse, enslavement and subtle repression, which often cannot be acknowledged because it is supposed to no longer be there. It is these kinds of contradiction which Madonna so poignantly registers and expresses in her voice.

Exercises and discussion points

1. Record at least three distinctly different male and female voices from radio and television commercials and analyse them according to the dimensions introduced in this chapter. How is the meaning potential of these voice qualities 'coloured in' by the given context?
   Now do the same with singing voices.

2. Make a collection of 'sound effects' from comic strips. What is it about the speech sounds that makes them apt signifiers for representing the sounds they represent? In what ways does the typography help represent the sounds?

3. Conduct an experiment. Ask four people what they think the *slithy toves*, the *mimsy borogoves* and the *mome raths* from Lewis Carroll's famous 'Jabberwocky' (1994: 15) might look like (and/or sound like!). Ask specific questions, based on the meaning potentials discussed in this chapter (for example 'How large is it?', 'Is it rough or smooth' and so on). You can of course add further questions, for instance, if you are interested in synaesthesia, 'What colour is it?'

   > 'Twas brillig, and the slithy toves
   > Did gyre and gimble in the wabe;
   > All mimsy were the borogoves,
   > And the mome raths outgrabe.

   How similar are the answers?

4. Make a collection of different laughs (*chi chi chi, hohoho* and so on) as actually used by people you know. Attempt an interpretation of why these particular people laugh in this particular way, on the basis of the meaning potentials of the sounds, as described in this chapter.

5. You are designing a audio 'logo' for yourself, for use in your computer, on your answerphone and so on. Choose appropriate values from the meaning potentials discussed in this chapter. How would you like to come across? As 'energetic' or 'relaxed', rough or smooth and so on? What kind of sound(s) might meet the specification?

5. Design footsteps for the characters in a fairy tale of your choice (for example *Hansel and Gretel,* or *Little Red Riding Hood*). Choose appropriate values from the meaning potentials discussed in this chapter. How should the footsteps come across? As heavy or light, tense or lax and so on?

Chapter 7

Modality

The idea of modality

Linguists have pointed out that the linguistic representation of a given state of affairs always also involves assigning a degree of truth to that representation. The previous sentence, for example, was assigned a high degree of truth (because of the word *always*), but I could also have said 'that the linguistic representation of some state of affairs *often* involves...' or 'the linguistic representation of some state of affairs *may* involve...', and that would have assigned a lower degree of truth to my assertion. The term 'modality' refers to the linguistic resources for expression such *degrees of truth*, for instance such resources as the modal auxiliaries *may, will, must* and so on, modal adverbs like *perhaps, probably, certainly* and so on, modal adjectives and nouns (for example, *probable* and *probability*) and so on.

For logicians modality is about the likelihood of propositions being true or false, the probability that what a proposition asserts actually corresponds to something that exists in the real world, but for social semioticians (for example, Hodge and Tripp, 1986; Hodge and Kress, 1988) modality expresses not so much the actual objective truth, but the truth as seen by the speaker: speakers or writers assign modality to their assertions to express *as how true* they would like these representations to be taken. High modality can be assigned equally to things which do and to things which do not exist in the real world. People use the modality resources of language to *negotiate* (or renegotiate) the truth of representations, or to impose truths on those over whom they have power, and they do so in order to arrive at a shared view of what the world is like, a common conception of reality, which can then be used as 'a basis for judgment and action' (Hodge and Kress, 1988: 147).

156

In an earlier publication (Kress and Van Leeuwen, 1996) Kress and I used the following text as an example. It is taken from a chapter about Australian Aborigines in an Australian social studies textbook for primary schools called *Our Society and Others*:

> Governor Phillip, the settlers, and the convicts could find no churches or cathedrals or works of art like those of Britain. Perhaps this made them think that Aboriginal people had no religion. In fact, the Aborigines had very complicated religious beliefs. These had been passed down from one generation to the next through Dreamtime stories for thousands of years. For the Aborigines the whole land was a cathedral. Their art was joined to their religion. Much of their art had been kept safely for thousands of years (Oakley *et al.*, 1985: 142).

This text contains three voices, three representations of the same subject matter, by three different people. First there is the way in which 'Governor Phillip, the settlers and the convicts' represented Aboriginal religion. This voice is given low modality ('they *thought*', not, for instance 'they *concluded*', or 'they *discovered*'); the children addressed by this text, it is implied, should no longer think that way, because '*in fact* the Aborigines had very complicated religious beliefs'. Then, however deeply buried in generalities and abstractions, there is also the voice of the Aborigines themselves, the voice of *their* truth, *their* way of representing the world. In the text this truth is called 'belief', rather than, for instance, 'knowledge'. In the dominant discourses of 'our society', 'belief' has lower modality than 'knowledge', 'dream' lower modality than 'reality', and 'religion' lower modality than 'science'. This, too, Australian primary schoolchildren must learn: the truths of the Aborigines can be admired as beautiful *stories*, as *dreams*, but they are not the kind of factual truth 'we' learn at school, for instance through textbooks such as *Our Society and Others*. Finally there is the voice of the textbook writers who present these different truths and who assign different modalities to them, in order to align their young readers with the truth that has highest modality, the truth that is to become 'our' truth', the truth of 'our society'(as taught in the education system), rather than that of the 'others' of the title of the book.

As described by Halliday (1985), the modality resources of language not only allow assigning different *degrees* of truth to a representation, they also allow a choice between different *kinds* of truth. Think for instance of the difference between 'objective' modality (for example, *It is likely that* this will involve...') and 'subjective' modality (for example, *I believe that* this will involve…'), or between 'probability' modality ('This *probably* involves…') and 'frequency' modality ('This *often* involves…'). All these types of modality at the same time allow for degrees of truth, such as the difference between *I believe* that this will involve…'; and *I know* that this will involve'. Which degree and which kind of truth will be assigned to a given proposition, and as how valid a given 'kind of truth' will be seen, then depends on the values of the social group in which the modality judgements are made. '*Belief*', for instance, will rate higher in church than in the science lab, and for any true believer some beliefs (one's own) will have more truth value than others (those of others).

Social semioticians have extended the linguistic concept of modality beyond language, pointing to the importance of non-verbal communication in expressing modality (for example, Kress and Hodge, 1979; Hodge and Tripp, 1986), and theorizing the modality of images (Hodge and Kress, 1988; Kress and Van Leeuwen, 1990; 1996). The idea is that the question of truth plays a role in every kind of communication, even in such semiotic modes as the semiotics of food or dress, and that modality judgements are always related to the values of the social group in which they are made. The truth of food, for instance, may be related to notions like 'natural', 'organic' versus 'artificial', 'synthetic', and that truth is not only expressed in the language we speak about these foods, but also through the 'food signs' themselves, or visually, through the packaging. 'True' bread, for instance, must be brown, chunky, with visible grains in the crust. Its packaging will probably use brown and yellow colours and feature tasteful pen drawings of sheaves of wheat.

In this view, modality is of course no longer only associated with representation, and it could be argued that the word 'true' is therefore inappropriate, since 'true' must always be 'true *to* something'. On the other hand, it could also be argued that in everyday language we *do* use words like 'real' and 'true' in relation to food, and that 'truth' is, in the end, 'true to the values held by the group whose truth it is', rather than 'true to some kind of objective reality'. Far from being a descent into total relativism, this brings values back where they belong, in the forefront of the discussion, where we can negotiate whether or not they can give us a sound basis for judgement and action.

Before applying the idea of modality to sound, I will need to sketch the way Gunther Kress and I have applied it to visual communication (Kress and Van Leeuwen, 1996), since I will draw heavily on this work in the remainder of the chapter. The key concepts in our theory are *modality configuration and coding orientation* (the latter term derives from the work of Basil Bernstein, for example, 1981). To start with the former, we argued that visual modality is expressed by configurations of the *degrees* to which specific image parameters are articulated:

- Degrees of the *articulation of detail* form a scale which ranges from the simplest line drawing to the sharpest and most finely grained photograph or artwork.
- Degrees of the *articulation of the background* form a scale which ranges from zero articulation, as when something is shown against a white or black background, via lightly sketched in backgrounds, to backgrounds shown in maximally sharp detail – with many degrees of background articulation in between.
- Degrees of *colour saturation* range from the absence of saturation (black and white) to the use of maximally saturated colours.
- Degrees of *colour modulation* range from the use of flat, unmodulated colour to the representation of all the fine nuances and modulations of any given colour.
- Degrees of *colour differentiation* range from monochrome to the use of a full palette of different colours.
- Degrees of *depth articulation* range from the absence of any representation of depth to maximally deep ('fish eye') perspective, with other options, such as simple overlapping or isometric perspective (perspective without vanishing points) in between.
- Degrees of the *articulation of light and shade* range from zero to the articulation of the maximum number of degrees of 'depth' of shade, with options such as simple hatching in between.
- Degrees of the *articulation of tone* range from the absence of any tonal gradation to just two shades of tonal gradation, black and white (or two shades of grey).

In all these cases, we argued, articulation can be amplified or reduced. Different image parameters may be amplified or reduced to different degrees, resulting in many possible *modality configurations*. These configurations will cue people's modality judgements, people's judgements of 'as how real' images are meant to be taken. Newspaper cartoons, for example, tend to have reduced articulation of detail, background, depth and light and shade, and no articulation of colour and tonal gradation. By comparison the articulation of these same parameters in news photographs is much amplified. This corresponds to their modality value: cartoons are taken as visual 'opinions' and hence as less factual than news photographs. Magazine advertisements almost always depict the products they advertise with great sharpness, colour saturation and differentiation, but reduce articulation in the photos (drawings, gouaches and so on) that show the 'promise' of the product (how glamorous you will become or how much success you will have if you use the product), for instance through soft focus and reduced colour differentiation (an overall golden glow or blue haze, or a sepia monochrome, for instance). In this way they depict the product as real (it is what you can actually buy) and the 'promise' of the product as fantasy, hence lower in modality.

It is not the case, however, that modality always decreases as articulation is reduced. If this were so, simple line diagrams would always have low modality and be judged as 'not real'. But despite their greatly reduced articulation, scientific line diagrams are clearly to be read as images with high truth value, and not as fictions or fantasies. This complicates matters. It means that there is no fixed correspondence between modality judgements and points on the scales of articulation I described above. Instead, the modality value of a given modality configuration depends on the *kind* of modality which is preferred in the given context, and the choice of a particular kind of modality, in turn, derives from the *coding orientation* of that context, the values which underlie semiotic choice in that context. In our work on images, Kress and I discussed four such contexts.

In many contexts the *naturalistic coding orientation* remains dominant. Its view of visual truth is as follows: the more an image of some object resembles the way we would see that object if we saw it in reality, from a specific vantage point and under specific lighting conditions, the higher its modality. This, at least, is the theory, for in reality naturalistic modality judgement depends very much on the way in which the currently dominant naturalistic imaging technology records the visual world: it is probably no exaggeration to say that Kodak has set the standards for 'standard average 35 mm colour photography', and hence for naturalistic modality. When images show a colour saturation, a sharpness, a depth and so on, which exceeds these standards, people will judge them as 'more than real' – and such images are likely to be found in fantasy genres: children's books, animation films, advertisements, tourist brochures and so on. It follows that the cues we use to judge naturalistic modality change over time. At the moment most people probably see holographic images as 'more than real', a touch uncanny. But if they were to replace flat images in the most common media of naturalistic representation (television, amateur photography and so on) they would probably lose that 'more than real' quality.

In the *technological coding orientation*, visual truth is based on the practical usefulness of the image. The more an image can be used as a blueprint or aid for action, the higher its modality. Maps are of this kind, patterns for making clothes, architectural drawings, the assembly instructions of a 'do it yourself' kit. The corresponding modality configurations will tend towards reduced articulation. Perspective, for instance, may be reduced to zero, as foreshortening would make it difficult to take measurements from the image. Colour will often be absent, regarded as non-essential, except when used for 'separating', for telling apart what would otherwise look too similar, as, for instance, in the colour codes of the London Underground map.

In the *abstract coding orientation*, common in scientific visuals and modern art, visual truth is an abstract truth: the more an image represents the deeper 'essence' of what it depicts, the more it represents the general pattern underlying many superficially different specific instances, the higher its (abstract) modality. This is expressed by reduced articulation. Specifics of illumination, nuances of colour, the details that create individual differences are all irrelevant from the point of view of the essential or general truth. This is most clearly seen when naturalistic and abstract visuals are combined. Children's books about dinosaurs, for instance, will have detailed naturalistic pictures of dinosaurs in primeval landscapes to excite the children's imagination – and simple line drawings to help them recognize the essential characteristics of different kinds of dinosaur. The same contrast is found in advertisements which use science (or pseudo-science). But abstract modality also plays an important role in modern art. A Picasso painting of a woman represents the 'essence' of woman (according to Picasso), not the detail of a specific woman in a specific place, seen from a specific angle under specific lighting conditions: 'The common pursuit of artists and scientists has always been, and will always be, to probe a reality beyond appearances' (Miller, 1995: 185).

In the *sensory coding orientation*, visual truth is based on affect, on the effect of pleasure or displeasure created by visuals, and it is realized by a degree of articulation which is amplified beyond the point of naturalism, so that sharpness, colour, depth, the play of light and shade and so on, are, from the point of view of a naturalistic coding orientation 'more than real'. Colour, for instance, is now used, not as a more or less arbitrary 'colour code' intended to provide clear 'separation' between different represented elements, as in technological modality, nor for its resemblance to reality, as in naturalistic modality, but for its emotive impact, its soothing or stirring or unsettling *effect* (a whole psychology of colour has evolved to elaborate this). Sensory modality is common, for instance, in food photography, where high detail and intense colour are meant to arouse the appetite, or in advertisements for perfume, where images must evoke the sensory pleasures of smell – in Western culture it is for the most part in the realm of the *sensory* that we locate synaesthesia, hence the interest of the Romantics in synaes-thesia. The sensory coding orientation with its heightened use of image parameters and its 'more than real' qualities, is also used in the work of surrealist painters like Dali and Delvaux, who create dream-like, intensified viewing experiences, or in the paintings of Franco Magnani, an artist with total visual recall of the Italian village which he grew up in and then never visited again for thirty years:

> Stones… are portrayed with the utmost accuracy – every shade, every colour, every convexity or crack, lovingly dwelt on and delineated. There is an extraordinary tactile or kinaesthetic quality in Franco's stones (Sacks, 1994: 171).

Different criteria are used in different contexts. We do not expect scientific images to provide sensory pleasure, nor do we normally use art works as blueprints for constructing the objects they may depict – although both can be and have been done. Today, however, the conventions for using visual modality resources are changing. Annual company reports display their graphs in three dimensions, in full colour, and against the background of virgin landscapes of green, undulating hills, in which the three-dimensional bar graphs emerge like so many featureless skyscrapers – in other words, they drop naturalism and mix the sensory with the abstract. Newspapers increas-ingly use drawings where formerly photographs were used, and in Hollywood feature films cartoon characters begin to mix with live actors – again, abstraction enters where naturalism used to hold sway. Something is changing in the modality of images, and it is therefore likely that something is also changing in the way people judge the modality of images.

Against this background, we now turn to the modality of sound. I will begin by asking whether it is true that in the case of sound, too, naturalism has been the dominant coding orientation. I will then attempt to describe the cues we use for judging the modality of sound, and assess whether the interpretation of the modality of sound is also linked to coding orientations of the kind I have just described. Finally I will ask whether the changes that are occurring in visual modality also apply to the modality of sound.

Naturalism and abstraction in music and film soundtracks

From the sixteenth century onwards, music increasingly developed means for musical *representation*, for the *imitatio naturae* (Attali, 1985; Dahlhaus, 1985). A sixteenth-century *Fantasia* by John Mundy (d.1630) already depicts lightning (jagged melody fragments), thunder (rushing scales in the left hand), and 'faire wether' (a calmer, slower melody). In the eighteenth century not only painters but also composers liked to explore the representation of landscapes and pastoral themes. One of the most enduring examples is of course Vivaldi's *Four Seasons*, although today not everyone listening to this music while waiting to be connected to a telephone operator will perhaps follow the story and hear the dog bark in 'Spring' or the teeth chatter at the end of 'Winter'. In the nineteenth century heroic battle scenes became a popular subject, for painters as well as composers. Concert patrons received programme notes to help them follow the story of complex works like Louis Jullien's *The Fall of Sebastopol* (1854), which began softly, with distant drums and trumpets, to represent the advance of the English, the French and the Turks, and ended with the 'deafening noise of exploding mines, the roar of cannons, the whistling of bullets, the hurtling of shells, the rattling of drums, the shrill sound of trumpets, the ships blown into the air, the cries of the fugitives, and the shouts of the victors' (Orrey, 1975: 122). Snippets of relevant national anthems were worked in to help the audience tell the opposing sides apart.

The tradition continued in the twentieth century. In the 1920s and 30s, painters (Léger) as well as composers began to use machine motifs in their work (Honegger's *Pacific 231*, Antheil's *Ballet Mécanique*, Prokoviev's *Dance of Steel*). Musical landscape painting also continued. We have already discussed the work of Charles Ives and the importance of perspective in his musical evocations of landscapes and events. Another example is Vaughan Williams' *Sinfonia Antarctica*, which evokes the silence and desolation of the Antarctic landscape through a wordless soprano, a female chorus and a wind machine, the ice formations through xylophones and glockenspiels, and the cracks in the ice cap through massive organ chords.

The tradition was continued by Hollywood. Early film music was played live by pianists, or, in larger cinemas, by orchestras or on Wurlitzer organs (which included bells, whistles and other sound effects among their stops). More often than not they used existing naturalistic music by nineteenth-century composers, with titles like 'Morning Mood', 'Spring Feeling' and so on. After 1929, Hollywood imported classically trained composers, students of Honegger and Schoenberg (cf. Tagg, 1983). It is through this music, and its continued existence in media 'mood music' catalogues that the language of depictive music is still very much alive, known by everyone who is at all exposed to Hollywood films, television commercials and so on, even though they do not always know what it is they know. What composer George Antheil said about the movies in 1945, is, I think, still equally valid today with respect to television:

> Hollywood music is very nearly a public communication, like radio. If you are a movie fan (and who isn't?) you may sit in a movie theatre three times a week listening to the symphonic background scores which Hollywood composers concoct. What happens? Your musical tastes become molded by these scores, heard without knowing it. You *see* love, and you *hear* it. Simultaneously. It makes sense. Music suddenly becomes a language for you, without your knowing it (quoted in Frith, 1984: 82).

But while in painting the quest for ever greater naturalism was never questioned, in music naturalistic representation met with mixed feelings. Beethoven gave the movements of his Pastoral Symphony titles like 'Scene by the Brook', 'Happy Gathering of Villagers', 'Thunderstorm', yet felt he had to defend the work as 'more the expression of feeling than painting' (quoted in Dahlhaus, 1985: 21). The same sentiment can be felt in the sleeve notes of a 1985 recording of Honegger's *Rugby* and *Pacific 231* (Erato 2292-45242-2). Apparently the impression must be avoided that this is 'just' *Tonmalerei*, painting with sound.

> '*Rugby*' (1928) is not programme-music, despite its title. Honegger made clear that his aim was to express, in his language as a musician, 'the attacks and counters of the game, the rhythm and colour of a match at Colombes stadium.' '*Rugby*', in fact, is a sort of very free rondo, in two episodes. '*Pacific 231*' is no more descriptive. 'What I was looking for in "*Pacific*"', declared Honegger in 1924, 'was not so much to imitate the sounds of the locomotive, but to translate visual impressions and physical enjoyment

with a musical construction.' He was later to insist on the importance he attached to a purely musical idea: 'I have composed a sort of great, varied chorale...'

There are two kinds of argument against musical naturalism. The most 'hardline' view is that music is not, and cannot be, representational at all, that it is a pure play of forms, a kind of abstract, tonal mathematics. This view has been held by music semioticians like Ruwet (1967) and Nattiez (who said that 'music, by itself, signifies nothing', 1971: 8), by music sociologists like Adorno (1976) for whom 'structural hearing' was the highest form of music appreciation, and by composers, for instance Stravinsky (1936: 91):

> I consider that music is, by its very nature, powerless to express anything at all, whether a feeling, an attitude of mind, a psychological mood, a phenomenon of nature. If, as is nearly always the case, music appears to express something, this is only an illusion and not a reality.

It should be clear from everything I have said about music in this book that I find it more rewarding and enriching to listen to music as socially meaningful, in a variety of ways – cognitively as well as emotively, representationally as well as interactionally, concretely as well as abstractly.

The other, less 'hardline' view is that musical representation is necessarily rather abstract and therefore should not aim at the naturalistic, 'faithful' representation of all the detail of a specific sound at a specific time and in a specific place, but represent the essential characteristics and the emotive temperature (the 'mood') of a *type* of sound or action (the 'busy hum', 'the peaceful stream'). In other words, the truth of the musical representation of a sound should not lie in maximum fidelity to what you would have heard if you had heard the sound in reality, but be judged by a combination of emotive–interpretive and abstract–generalized criteria. This, incidentally, is exactly what contemporary film sound designers do. They move away from naturalistic recording and seek to combine relatively abstract representation, representation of essential qualities, with emotive effect:

> When conceiving a sound effect, Serafine will first analyse the physical nature of its source: is it delicate, is it awkward, does it fly? Next, he will attempt to pinpoint its affects: can it frighten, is it calming, must it astonish you? (Mancini, 1985: 362).

The same applies to using the voice for naturalistic sound representation. In many hunters' societies people are expert at imitating animal sounds, but in the West such naturalistic vocalization remains a gimmick, a party-trick rather than an art. Non-musical instruments for producing naturalistic sound effects have also remained marginal, whether in the theatre (gongs, thundersheets and so on) or elsewhere. They are used for creating incidental 'effects' rather than be allowed to develop the capacity for creating integrated soundtracks, 'noise works' of the kind envisaged by the Futurist artist Russolo. In all these ways, then, there was a definite impulse towards using sound as representation, but on the condition that it should be a relatively abstract and emotionally charged form of representation, rather than one that strived for greater and greater naturalism, as did the visual arts, at least until the mid-nineteenth century.

To some extent this changed once sound recording entered the picture. Here, high fidelity, high faithfulness to an 'original' became the key objective. In photography and film there were opposing tendencies towards a naturalistic, 'documentary' approach and a more abstract 'artistic' approach, but sound recording would, for a long time, remain dedicated to just that, recording live events. Film pioneers in the 1920s had envisaged non-naturalistic roles for sound. Pudovkin, for example, thought that film images should relate the exterior dramatic events and film sound the characters' subjective inner experience of these events, and René Clair thought that sound should be 'interpretative' rather than 'imitative' (cf. Weis and Belton, 1985: 86–96). Despite this, film sound remained for the most part 'slaved' to the image, reproducing the speech of the actors and adding a naturalistic sense of presence and continuity through synchronous sound effects, continuous atmosphere tracks and perspectivalistic mixing. In the case of music, similarly, it would be a long time before works would be written only to be recorded, and not also or in the first place to be performed live, as is the normal practice in the case of film, where very few films are recordings of live theatre performances. Although it was recognized that recording could transform the sound of music, for instance through close miking, the aim, especially in the recording of classical music, was high fidelity. 'I want to make records which will sound in the public's home exactly like what they would hear in the best seat in an acoustically perfect hall', said EMI producer Walter Legge (quoted in Chanan, 1995: 133).

As in the case of images, judgments of high naturalistic modality depend on the currently dominant recording technologies. When mono was the norm, stereo was experienced as 'more than real'. People marvelled at demonstrations in which the sound of trains and cars seemed to move from one end of the room to the other, and at the way the space craft in *Star Wars*, the first stereo optical film, roared across the wide screen. But once stereo became ubiquitous, other innovations were needed to create the 'more than real' effect, Dolby sound, for instance, which increases the frequency response by as much as two and a half octaves, or 'Sensurround'. As Michael Cimino, who pioneered the use of Dolby in *The Deer Hunter*, said:

> What Dolby does is to give you the ability to create a density of detail of sound, a richness so you can demolish the wall separating the viewer from the film (quoted in Schreger, 1985: 351).

And 'density of detail', amplification of the degree to which detail is articulated, is of course one of the cues of 'sensory modality', 'gut impact', as discussed in the first section of this chapter.

More recently, all this has changed. Recording music is no longer just a matter of reproducing live performances, and in many contexts recording technicians have become artists in their own right, 'musical creators of a new kind' (Chanan, 1995: 147). Recording tools such as the mixing panel are now treated as musical instruments, able to create aural perspectives which have no counterpart in the real world. Parameters like reverb are used, not just to create 'the acoustically perfect hall', but as independent signifiers, sound quality variables in their own right, alongside tenseness, roughness and all the other sound qualities we discussed in the previous chapter. Hence reverb can be used, for instance, to make some sounds appear subjective and 'interior', almost as though heard from inside the body, and others as more objective and 'exterior', as suggested in my discussion of a 'drum 'n' bass' track in Chapter 2. Technology has been drawn into the realm of semiotics.

As a result the ideas of people like Pudovkin and Clair have become newly relevant. Sound is no longer recorded, it is *designed*. It is no longer 'slaved' to what we see, but can play an independent role, just as many of the sounds in our everyday environment are no longer 'indexical', mechanically caused by whatever they are the sound of, but designed: if I switch on my computer, I hear, not a mechanical click, but a musical chord. As I open a door, I may hear, not the clicking of the lock, but an electronic buzz. The green light of the pedestrian crossing produces a frenetic beep. Muzak replaces the waiting tone of the telephone. As scientists contemplate the use of speech synthesizers in cars to tell drivers that they are running out of petrol and so on, they wonder what kind of voice a Ford or a Toyota should have. We should therefore focus on the as yet little known history of sound design, rather than repeat the more familiar history of sound technology as a movement towards ever greater naturalistic 'fidelity'.

One area in which sounds were already 'designed' long before new technologies of sampling and mixing began to move sound design into the mainstream, was the animated cartoon. In animated cartoons sound is primary. While in most films music and sound effects are added after the image track has been edited, in animated cartoons the soundtrack is designed before the images are produced, something which has been derogatorily referred to as 'mickey-mousing', but in fact means that the whole film is written as a musical score in which

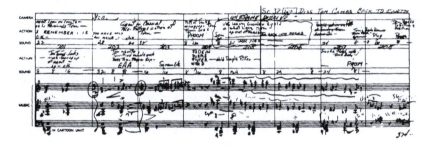

Figure 7.1   A page from the 'dope sheet' of the MGM cartoon
Heavenly Puss

the characters' movements and the sounds are treated as instruments, cf. Figure 7.1.

In this context, many of the sound effects were designed, rather than recorded. Walt Disney's sound effects man Jimmy MacDonald used both his voice and all kinds of self-made contraptions to produce his sound effects. 'If a film needed a bear growl, then Macdonald would roar through the top of a hurricane lamp. If a snake hiss was sought, then Macdonald would flutter his tongue to produce the best hisses ever heard' (Mancini, 1985: 364). As for sound effect props:

> To walk onto the Burbank stage where his gadgets are stored is to enter a
> sorcerer's den. There are many traditional devices, such as gongs, mallets,
> and small-hinged doors, which trace their ancestry to radio, burlesque,

legitimate theatre, and, most likely, campfire raconteuring. Others, though, are one-of-a-kind relics: a giant round vat used to create the cauldron bubbles in *Snow White*; a rotating valve device that produced the chugs of *Dumbo*'s locomotive; a series of truck brake drums that, when struck, produced the sounds of giant bells in countless Disney films (Mancini, 1985: 364).

Still more significantly, these films often erased the boundaries between sound effects and speech (Dumbo's locomotive not only chugs, but also and at the same time pants 'I-think-I-can-I-think-I-can' as it chugs uphill), and between sound effects and music (the locomotive sound also provides percussion for the music track). In Disney's *Three Orphan Kittens* (1937), one of the kittens chases a fly which lands on a jam tart. As it hits out at the jam tart with its paw, trying to catch the fly, small fountains of jam erupt with sounds that blends naturalistic squirts and musical whistles, and form a infectious musical rhythm. The chase of a feather over the keys of a grand piano, later in the film, takes things a step further still, and even involves 'prepared piano' sounds as one of the kittens walks over the strings and gets caught up between the hammers.

Today's sound designers use sampling to achieve this fusion between sound effects, speech and music. I remember my exhilaration when I first experimented with these new tools and sampled a sound effect of a dog barking, to then 'play dog bark' on the keyboard, creating low growls by playing ascending melodic figures with my left hand in the lower register, and choirs of yelping puppies by playing several melodic snippets at once in the higher register. To be able to play, on the keyboard, 73 kettle drums simultaneously was, at first, an equally astonishing experience. Mixing, similarly, is now used, not to regulate levels for the sake of obtaining a naturalistically convincing perspective, but for *blending* different sounds in order to create entirely new sounds, as already discussed in relation to the sound of the ocean in *The Piano* and as also exemplified by the combined chugging, panting, talking and percussion playing of Dumbo's locomotive:

> Serafine's work for *Tron*, the first feature film to be entirely computer-animated is illustrative. Every non-living thing seen in Tron's artificial world has no direct counterpart in the real world. Serafine was therefore obliged to anchor the film's alternate reality to everyday experience through blended sound effects. A bulky vehicle drones with the propellor noises of an old aircraft bomber (for menace) and the Goodyear blimp (for

bulk). The whoosh of a disc-weapon combines the scream of an angry monkey with the crack of a whip, creating a device that sounds aerodynamically swift and distressingly aggressive (Mancini, 1985: 363).

The point is, such practices break the connection between what we hear in a soundtrack and what we would hear 'in reality'. Sound has finally become what film pioneers like Pudovkin and Clair dreamt of, a semiotic mode in its own right, operating, like music, on the basis of an *abstract-sensory* coding orientation.

The modality of sound

The modality of sound can be approached along the same lines as the modality of images. Here too, modality judgments are 'cued' by the *degree* to which a number of different parameters are used in the articulation of the sounds, and here too, the context, and more specifically the *coding orientation* used in that context, determines the modality *value* of a particular sound – the *degree* and *kind* of truth we will assign to it.

Imagine four different 'locomotive' sounds. The first is purely musical. Perhaps it is the locomotive from Honegger's *Pacific 231*. In this piece, the whistle is played by strings abruptly sliding up, while brass, strings and timpani play the chugging of the engine, first low and slow, then gradually faster and higher as the machine gathers speed. Only conventional musical instruments and conventionally stylized patterns of tonality and rhythm are used. No 'sound effects' or 'non-musical' instruments are mixed in. It is both recognizably a locomotive and recognizably music, both representational and emotively affective.

The second would be a naturalistic recording, such as can be obtained from any sound effects record. Here too, we will recognize the whistle and the chugging, but there will be other noises as well, clicks, squeaks, hisses, the grinding of wheels and so on, and melody and rhythm will not be stylized according to musical conventions. This sound comes close to what you would hear if you could transport yourself back to the era of the great steam engines, although it can never of course represent the whole multidimensional and physical experience of 'being there'.

The third might be a scene from a film in which the sound of the locomotive must frighten the viewer. Perhaps a character is lying flat between the rails, unable to move as the train approaches. Now the sound will be exaggerated, overwhelming, as close to 'three-dimensional' as possible, a deafening roar, heightened reverb, ear-piercing grinding of wheels on rails, a shrill and screaming steam whistle. What matters here is not in the first place that we get a sense of 'being there', but that the sound *terrifies* us.

The fourth is the locomotive from Disney's *Dumbo*. Here the chugging sound is almost musical, a relatively abstract, 'essential' and typical chugging, just as the cartoon drawings of the locomotive represent an archetypal, typical locomotive. The sound quality of the music, similarly, is relatively flat. For all we can hear, the strings might as well come from a synthesizer. They lack the embodied physicality, the 'grain of the voice' that closely miked real strings, played 'with feeling', might give, and signify only the *idea* of strings. On the other hand, some aspects of the sound are exaggerated, amplified rather than reduced, for comic effect – again, in exactly the same way as happens in cartoon drawings, where naturalistic detail is much diminished by comparison with photographic representation, but where the features that *are* represented are exaggerated for comic effect.

Imagine now an instrument that would allow the transformation of these locomotive sounds into each other, an instrument with which you could, for instance, add 'texture' to Honegger's locomotive, line the musical sounds with the clacking of wheels on rails, the hissing of escaping steam and so on, or change the deafening roar of the 'fright-ening' locomotive into a more precisely pitched, musical sound, say the sound of six double basses, and change these basses, either into the 'pure' essential, stereotypical basses you might get from a synthesizer, or into closely miked basses that are bowed aggressively and without vibrato for a snarling and growling effect. Although such an instru-ment does not (yet?) exist, sound designers already do this kind of thing, and as a result they can manipulate the *genre* of sound we will hear, and create 'documentary realist' sound, 'humoristic' sound, 'heightened dramatic' sound, 'surreal' sound and so on. Such genres of sound, in turn, rest on different coding orientations and differ-ent kinds of truth. Documentary realism rests on the truth of 'resemblance', on what you would hear if you were there on the scene, and recording events as they happen, warts and all. Humoristic truth is the truth that cannot be said 'straight' and must therefore clothe itself in humour. Heightened dramatic truth is the truth of felt emotion. And so on. And it should be remembered that all these kinds of truth can apply equally to representing people, places and things that actually exist and those that do not. Documentary realism can be applied to locomotives as well as flying saucers, humoristic exaggeration to pianos as well as musical jam tarts.

I will now try to list the main sound modality cues, the articulatory parameters which my imaginary instrument would allow me to manipulate.

Pitch range

Degrees of the articulation of pitch range from monotone (the absence of any pitch variation) to a maximally wide pitch range, with, in between, stylized forms such as chanted calls and responses in church, or African drum languages, which have a limited number of 'set' pitch levels. In the case of recorded sound, the frequency response of the recording and replay equipment will obviously have a bearing on this parameter.

Maximally reduced pitch range negates human emotion. It is used, for instance, to present or represent the sacred in ritual chanting or drones, and in the presentation of machine speech – although it is not difficult to synthesize intonation, the stereotype of the monotone machine voice (cf. the Daleks in *Dr Who*) persists. Many functional sounds in our environment (telephone rings, doorbells and so on) have also become monotone, but there are signs that this is changing, and that we may return to something similar to the time in which such sounds were more musical (church bells, the postman's horn and so on).

For naturalistic representation and 'neutral', 'non-dramatic' everyday speech and music, a fairly wide pitch range is of course necessary. But beyond a certain point the extension of the range will become 'more than real' or be experienced as emotively heightened, for instance in emotionally charged speech, or in moments of high drama in an opera.

Durational variation

Degrees of the articulation of duration range from the completely uniform duration of all the sounds involved in a given sound event to the use of a maximally varied amount of different durations, with stylized forms in between, for instance the short–long of Morse code, or the very 'mechanical' reading of metrical verse.

Like the wide pitch range, the wide durational range can be tied to the expression of affect. In emotive speech we lengthen the keywords considerably ('Amaaaaazing!'), while rushing other words, stumbling over them in our excitement or anger. Speakers who restrain their emotions, on the other hand, speak in more 'measured' and even ways. Such measured rhythms are also distinctive of many formal or 'serious' occasions, such as the psalm singing in Dutch 'black stocking' churches, and in the representation of 'not-human' sounds such as machine voices. Naturalistic representation and 'neutral', everyday speech and music require a fairly wide variety of durations. But again, beyond a certain point the durational extremities will be heard as 'more than real' or exaggerated.

Dynamic range

Degrees of dynamic articulation range from a maximally wide range (a range from *pianissimo* to *fortissimo*) to the use of just one degree of loudness throughout a sound event.

In Chapter 2 I described the role of loudness in sound perspective and in the (re)presentation of social relations. But, as with everything in sound, there is the emotive dimension as well. It is not accidental that Romantic music, in which the expression of emotion became more foregrounded, began to use an increased dynamic range: although the musical use of pitch had been rationalized by a mathematically based system of precise pitch intervals, and the musical use of duration by equally precise metronomic schemata, dynamics had remained relatively 'free', represented only by *p*s and *f*s (or *ppp*s and *fff*s) in the musical score.

Instruments which do not allow ongoing dynamic variation are always a touch more abstract, lacking the most immediate traces of human articulation. Sacred instruments like the organ are of this kind, and so is the modern synthesizer – hence its use for the representation of abstract, alienating environments in songs like Madonna's *Live to Tell*, and generally in forms of modern music which represent an alienated 'techno' world.

The same applies to speech and non-musical sound. Speakers who seek to sway their listeners emotively will amplify their dynamic range. Speakers who seek to drily report facts will flatten it. Again, objects over which we have some form of manual control can be used 'emotively' (think of leather-clad motorbike *aficionados'* aggressive revving while waiting for the red light, or of doors being slammed in anger, or shut softly and carefully to avoid disturbing a loved one). But many modern machines are impervious to such forms of human control and will drone on at the same level of loudness whatever happens.

Perspectival depth

Degrees of perspectival depth range from the completely 'flat' sound event which has neither 'foreground' nor 'background', to maximum depth, maximum differentiation between foreground and background, and, where present, intermediate levels.

When the soundtrack of a factual TV programme or film carries just the voice of a commentator or anchorperson, recorded in a studio, without any audible background noise, the sound is a good deal more abstract and less naturalistic than when we hear a reporter speak 'on location', with the din of the traffic as a naturalistic aural *setting*. Making such settings extra loud, 'more than real', usually creates an emotive effect, and this is less likely to occur in factual programmes, at least until recently, because factual programmes such as *Crimewatch* now increasingly use dramatic amplification for emotive effect.

'Dream' and 'hallucination' sequences in naturalistic dramas may reduce some parameters, for instance by flattening the perspective or removing it altogether (just as, visually, dream sequences may be played out against a black background), and amplify others, for example reverb. Philip Ashley-Brown, a radio producer and one of the students in my 'Semiotics of Sound' seminar at Macquarie University, found a good example in the film *Rocky II*: 'The climax in *Rocky II*', he wrote, 'goes for 13 minutes. Synthesized music with heavy reverb represents the point of view of Rocky when he is almost knocked out. The continuous background sounds are faded out and replaced by the synthesized music to create a sense of unreality. Each blow he receives is represented by a prominent drum-like sound.'

Degrees of fluctuation

Degrees of the articulation of fluctuation range from the completely steady sound to the maximally deep and/or rapid 'vibrato'. In Chapter 6 I argued the close association of 'vibrato' and emotionality. The 'fluctuation range' is therefore again a scale which ranges from the restraint or ritualization of emotion, via a relatively neutral 'naturalism', to the increasingly strong *expression* of emotion.

The steady sound is associated with the 'non-emotional', for instance in 'serious' and 'formal' contexts. In my younger years I accompanied many church services, some of them on harmoniums with a 'vox humana' stop. The use of this stop was not favoured. It was seen as inappropriate for sacred music, too sentimental, even vulgar. When it comes to the strings behind Hollywood kisses, on the other hand, vibrato is essential, and so it is in relation to other kinds of emotion – fear for instance, as in the electronic hums and bubblings of 'Dr Jekyll's Lab' from the BBC *Essential Death and Horror Sound Effects* record, or the vibrating sonic chaos of the 'Sea of Mercury' in the BBC *Essential Science Fiction Sound Effects* record. Such tracks shiver and tremble to make *us* shiver and tremble.

Degrees of friction

The scale that runs from 'smooth' to 'rough' was discussed in the previous chapter. It not only opens up an important metaphoric meaning potential, but also plays a role in sound modality. A completely smooth, completely 'pure' sound, a sound completely free of what jazz musicians call 'dirt', is a highly idealized and abstract sound, suitable for expressing the abstract truth, but less in touch with the grit of the 'real world'.

Naturalistic representation requires a certain amount of 'grit', or 'noisiness'. Anne Skelly, another of my students at the Macquarie University 'Semiotics of Sound' seminar, analysed naturalistic sound effects in a period film: 'There is incredible "texture" in the sounds – "whistles", "whirrs" and "putts" of engines, the grinding of carriage wheels on cobblestones, the jiggling of the harness, the gurgling and churning of water at the mill.' Tony Meek, another student of the seminar, noted that in a television science fiction series, such texture was much reduced: 'The sound of the aircar has no friction, no "air" or "windtunnel" noise, even though we are travelling through air. The gunshots are highpitched and disappear abruptly rather than that they degrade into an echo.' The difference between these two approaches is of increasing significance. Visual as well as audio *recording* technologies, having developed in the service of naturalistic representation, are good at reproducing and producing 'grit'. The newer *synthesizing* image and sound technologies are not. From a naturalistic point of view, the point of view which still dominates most people's judgements of the modality of films and television programmes, they produce a uncannily abstract, clean and sterile world, however great their power of resolution.

As always, there is also the level beyond naturalism, the level of the 'more than real', where what matters most is the emotive effect. In a lemonade commercial the bubbles fizz and the ice cubes clink against the glass in crystal-clear and hyper-real fashion – to arouse thirst. In a perfume commercial the soft, deep, whispering and slightly hoarse voice almost breathes in our ear – to seduce us. In a horror film the wind howls, the doors creak and the footsteps crunch in the gravel with more than real loudness and texture – to instil fear and foreboding.

The same applies to the human voice and to musical instruments. The synthesized saxophone sound may have the right overall timbre and the right 'attack', but, like the 'aircar' in the science fiction film, it lacks friction. It is too clean, too pure, too idealized, too essential and too generalized a saxophone, at least from the point of view of the 'naturalistic' and the 'sensory' truth. The same applies to electronic voices which do not represent 'acoustic' instruments. In all these cases we have the abstract truth without the sensory element, because the traces of human articulation are not there – the taking of breath, the friction of the bow, the touch of roughness, harshness or hoarseness that betrays real emotion.

Absorption range

The degree of articulation of absorption ranges from the completely 'dry' to the maximally spacious, reverberating and resonating sound.

A naturalistic soundtrack will need a certain amount of reverb to come across as being located in a 'setting', whether it is the 'acoustically perfect hall' or some other setting. But, as we have already seen, beyond a certain point reverb will be associated not so much with the representation of space as with an effect of unreality or dread, as in the climax of *Rocky II*. This may have deep roots in the dread evoked by the enormous rooms in palaces, cathedrals and other institutions of power, and in the mysteries of labyrinths and crypts.

Degree of directionality

Sound is not as directional as vision. It bounces off walls and other surfaces and reaches us from all sides. Nevertheless, there are sounds which can be pinpointed to a specific source, and sounds which surround us, 'wrap-around' sounds. The human voice, the music played on a stage and the speakers behind the movie screen belong to the former category – sounds, in other words, which are often used in activities that are predominantly representational. The sound of the environment and the music coming from speakers in all corners of the room or the car belong to the latter category – sounds, in other words, which are often used in activities that are oriented towards participation and sensory impact.

I now turn to the second aspect of sound modality, to the question: how are these cues used in people's judgements of modality?

The abstract–sensory coding orientation

In the first section of this chapter I discussed the idea of 'abstract modality' as it applies to visual communication. The more the articulation of a representation is reduced, in all its aspects, the more abstract modality, abstract truth value, *increases*, because its truth criterion lies in the degree to which the representation can capture the underlying *essence* of what it depicts, or represent its subject in a *generalized* way. This truth criterion applies, for instance, to the scientific diagram, which dispenses with almost everything that is needed for naturalistic representation (colour, perspective, the play of light and shade and so on) and reduces the detail of the representation to a minimum (the diagrammatic representation of a person, for instance, leaves out the individual features of that person, and provides only the basic outline of a 'figure', a person-in-general).

It is rare for sound reproduction to be abstract in this sense. Our culture prefers the visual medium for its scientific diagramming, perhaps because it is difficult, indeed, almost impossible, to be completely dispassionate and unemotional in the medium of sound. The most abstract form of sound is music. But unlike scientific diagrams, music is always also sensory. This is possible because musical abstraction is largely due to the *rationalization* of the way in which music uses pitch and duration for the purposes of representation, from the way it stylizes and regularizes pitch intervals in accordance with a mathematically proportioned schema (the harmonic series of overtones), and from the way it regularizes durational intervals according to an equally rationally proportioned set of standard durations (whole note, half note, quarter note, sixteenth note and so on). Whatever the sounds or movements represented, the chugging of a locomotive or the slinky, hip-swinging walk of Carmen in Bizet's opera, they must be stylized and idealized to fit within these schemata. But musical rationalization does not necessarily mean that the pitch and/or duration *range* is reduced. Both may still be exceptionally wide, and hence exceptionally charged with emotion. It is this that makes it possible for music to be both abstract and sensory, and to aestheticize the sensory at the same time as it emotionalizes the abstract.

Further abstraction can then stem from other factors, for instance from the reduction of friction, or from the conventionalization of fluctuation (vibrato) in classical music – we already saw that classical music insists on a naturalistic approach to the articulation of absorption and directionality ('the best seat in an acoustically perfect hall'). Other kinds of music, on the other hand, may use 'sensory' roughness and a less conventionalized approach to fluctuation, as well as a less naturalistic approach to absorption and directionality. In other words, music may mix the abstract–sensory, 'aestheticized' approach with the more 'raw' sensory approach to different degrees and in different ways, allowing as many modality configurations as are also possible in the visual arts (cf. Kress and Van Leeuwen, 1996: 171ff.).

It is this which lies behind the modality judgement in the quote from the sleevenotes of Honegger's *Pacific 231*. The writer tries to rescue Honegger from the possible accusation that he has not been true to the *abstract–sensory* spirit of classical music and that he has indulged in naturalistic representation rather than in the 'musical idea', and the 'translation of visual impressions and physical enjoyment in a musical construction'. In doing so, he uses abstract and formal terms as well as emotive adjectives, to reinforce that the relevant truth criterion of modern 'art' music is both abstract *and* sensory.

Naturalistic coding orientation

The same people who uphold the abstract–sensory coding orientation when judging the modality of classical music, may uphold another when it comes, for instance, to the movies. Here, they might reject the abstract–sensory approach as 'mickey-mousing' and prefer a more naturalistic and imitative approach, an approach where the truth criterion is 'Would it have sounded like this if I had been present when this scene happened?'

In the case of presentation, the naturalistic approach lies in a certain neutrality in which articulation is neither reduced and ritualized, nor dramatized and emotionalized, but judged on the basis of what is considered 'normal' and 'everyday' – which, of course, is just as much bound up with cultural norms as naturalistic representation is bound up with representational technologies.

In both these cases, presentation and representation, high naturalistic modality requires a fairly wide range of all the parameters of articulation. If we think of each articulatory parameter as a fader on my imaginary sound transformation instrument, the faders should, perhaps, be three-quarters open. But not fully open. There must always be room for more, for amplified presentation and representation, for the 'more than real' and the 'more than ordinary'.

Sensory coding orientation

In the sensory coding orientation the representational and the presentational begin to mix. The aim of the seductive advertisement is not to represent seduction, but to seduce. The aim of the horror film is not to represent horror, but to horrify. What matters is emotive impact, the degree to which the sound event has an *effect* of pleasure or its opposite. And this is done by amplifying the articulatory parameters, by widening the pitch range, increasing the durational variation and so on.

A final point. I may so far have given the impression that all the articulatory parameters move *en bloc* in the direction of the abstract–sensory or the sensory. This need not be the case. In many *modality configurations* some of the articulatory parameters are reduced and others amplified. The humoristic sound of the animated cartoon is one example. It may be abstract–sensory in most respects, but it is sensory, 'more than real', in the way it exaggerates pitch movement for comic effect. 'It's a Wonderful World' sung by Louis Armstrong and accompanied by an orchestra, is another example. It is both sensory, because of the concrete roughness of Louis Armstrong's voice, and abstract–sensory because of the more stylized articulation of the orchestral voices. In Madonna's 'Live to Tell', the 'environment', as represented by the accompaniment, has reduced articulation, while Madonna, by comparison, has increased, amplified articulation. Thus the environment is depicted as a good deal more abstract, dehuman-ized and impersonal than Madonna and what she has to tell.

How all this is judged will depend on the truth criteria that are brought to bear on the judgement. If you go for sensory impact, you will like Louis Armstrong, but reject the 'artificiality' and 'stylization' of the accompaniment. You would probably have preferred a bluesy combo, because you like your emotion raw rather than cooked. If you apply an abstract–sensory criterion, you will like the orchestra, but feel, perhaps, that Armstrong 'can't sing', because you like your emotions less raw, more restrained, more conventionalized and aestheticized. But it is also possible to have a more multidimensional modality judgement and to perceive how these kinds of music *mix* genres and their truths to create different degrees and kinds of modality for the different elements they comprise, and new kinds of emotive impact.

To summarize:

1. The term 'modality' refers to the degree of truth assigned to a given sound event. The term 'truth' takes on a somewhat different meaning depending on whether it pertains to presentation or representation. In the case of representation, 'truth' means 'a true representation of the people, places and/or things represented', in the case of presentation it means 'true to the spirit of the genre, and the values which underpin it in its context'.

    The expression 'truth assigned to' indicates that modality is about 'as how true' something is (re)presented, and not about 'how true it really is'. The truth of a representation lies not in the question of whether or not the represented person, place, thing and so on really exists, but in the question of *as how true* it is represented (for example, in whether a factual or dramatized genre of sound is used), and the truth of an emotive statement lies not in whether the emotion is 'really felt that way', but in 'as how emotional' it is expressed.

2. Modality is judged on the basis of the degree to which the sound event makes use of the following articulatory parameters:

- *Pitch extent* is a scale running from monotone to a maximally wide pitch range
- *Durational variety* is a scale running from a single standard length of sound for all the sounds of a sound event to maximally varied range of durations
- *Dynamic range* is a scale running from a single level of loudness to a maximally wide loudness range
- *Perspectival depth* is a scale running from a 'flat' representation ('Figure' only, and no 'Ground' and/or 'Field') to maximum articulation of the 'setting' (that is 'Ground' and/or 'Field')
- *Fluctuation range* is a scale running from a completely steady sound to maximally deep and/or rapid fluctuation
- *Friction range* is a scale running from maximally smooth to maximally rough sound
- *Absorption range* is a scale running from maximally dry to maximally spacious, reverberating and resonant sound
- *Degree of directionality* is a scale running from the sounds whose sources are most easy to pinpoint to the sounds whose sources are least easy to pinpoint.

3. In the case of representation, *abstract–sensory* modality hinges on the simultaneous presence of abstract representation and emotive effect. The more a sound event fulfils this criterion, the higher its modality. The typical modality configuration is that of 'classical' music: rationalized wide pitch range, rationalized wide durational range, wide loudness range, reduced friction range, conventionalized fluctuation, and a naturalistic degree of absorption and directionality.

   In the case of presentation, abstract–sensory modality hinges on ritualized and emotionally restrained forms of interaction in which pitch range and durational range will be rationalized as well as reduced, while most of the other articulatory parameters will also be reduced, except for absorption and directionality, which may be amplified.

4. In the case of representation, *naturalistic* modality is based on a criterion of verisimilitude. The more a representation is felt to sound like 'what one might hear if present at the represented event', the higher its naturalistic modality.

In the case of presentation, naturalistic modality is based on a criterion of 'normality' and 'everydayness'. The more a sound event is felt to be neither ritualized and formalized, nor dramatized and infused with emotion, the higher its naturalistic modality.

Naturalistic modality requires a fair amount of amplification of the articulatory parameters, but must nevertheless leave room for the further amplification needed to express the 'more than real' and the 'extraordinary'.

5. In *sensory* modality presentation and representation merge, and the truth criterion lies in the degree to which a sound event is felt to have an emotive impact. The more this is the case, the higher the sensory modality. Sensory modality is expressed by amplification of the articulatory parameters.

6. In a given *modality configuration* some articulatory parameters may be amplified and others reduced. This will create a 'mixed' coding orientation. Mixed coding orientations are common in high art practices which question definitions of truth and reality.

7. It may also be that some elements of the (re)presentation have reduced modality, while others are amplified. This means that some elements are (re)presented as 'less true' than others – which these are will depend on the coding orientation underpinning the modality judgement.

Example: television drama

To conclude I will summarize the main ideas introduced in this chapter (Figure 7.2), and analyse the soundtrack of an excerpt from an episode of *The X-Files*.

The *X-Files* extract that follows is from an episode called 'Colony'. An abortion clinic doctor who will turn out to be one of three identical men, hence a possible alien clone, sees the rescue of a mysterious bounty hunter on television in the clinic's coffee room. He panics and runs into a long, tiled corridor. The bounty hunter lies in wait for him, grabs him, kills him and then sets fire to the building. The shots in this sequence are for the most part close up and taken from a low angle with a mobile camera. In the next scene Scully visits Mulder's office,

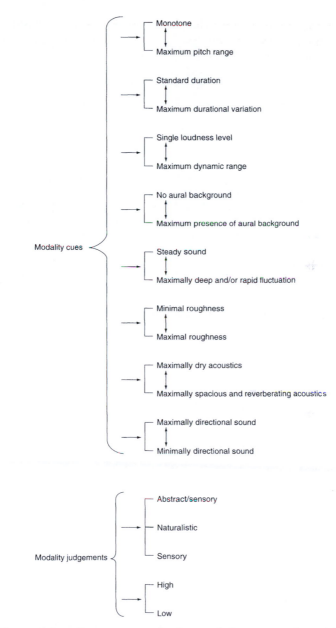

Figure 7.2   System networks for modality cues and modality judgements

and the investigation begins. Here the shots are eye-level, considerably wider, and more static.

1. As the doctor leaves the coffee room and runs through the hospital corridor, we hear a loud metallic clang, overlaid with electronic effervescence, followed by a raspy and wavering electronic drone	Abstract ('alien'): Reduced range; reduced friction Sensory ('anxiety') Amplified dynamics; amplified background (loud electronic music); amplified fluctuation; amplified reverb
PLUS	
2. The doctor's agitated breathing, loud, and miked close up	Sensory (amplified level and texture)
PLUS	
3. The doctor's footsteps, much softer	Abstract (reduced naturalistic setting)
4. As he opens a set of swinging doors, we hear the doors open	Abstract (reduced naturalistic setting)
5. Immediately the doctor is grabbed by the bounty hunter and we hear a loud intake of breath and a strained groaning	Sensory (amplified level and texture)
PLUS	
6. Hunter: *'Where is he?* Doctor: (a loud whisper) *'I don't know'*	Sensory (amplified level and texture)
PLUS	
7. The electronic drone changes to a low heartbeat	Sensory (amplified level)/ Abstract (it is a *stylized* electronic heartbeat)

8.	While the hunter throws the doctor down and kills him by inserting a long steel pin in his neck, we hear a loud swishing noise as the pin is drawn from its sheath with a spring mechanism	Sensory (amplified level and texture)
9.	As the heartbeat continues, we hear a hissing noise as a green fluid bubbles up from the wound	Sensory (amplified level and texture)
10.	As the heartbeat continues we hear a swishing noise as the pin is retracted into its sheath	Sensory (amplified level and texture)
11.	Sparks fly as the hunter rips the cover from an electricity panel. Two explosions follow and the room is ablaze almost immediately. We hear the loud crackle of the sparks and the two explosions	Sensory (amplified level and texture)
12.	As the hunter walks through the corridor with a menacing expression and flames behind him, the heartbeat sound continues and we also hear sustained electronic drones slowly rising	Abstract (reduced pitch, dynamics, duration, friction; stylized fluctuation)
	Alarm bell in background	Abstract (reduced naturalistic level)
13.	As Scully enters Mulder's office, the heartbeat sound and the electronic drone fade out and room atmosphere fades in	Increased naturalistic perspective
14.	As Mulder takes Scully to his desk to show her something on his computer,	
	Mulder: *I have been looking for you* Scully: *I was just down the street*	Naturalistic (increased pitch, duration and dynamic range in dialogue; less friction and fluctuation)
15.	As Mulder and Scully cross to the computer we hear footsteps and other sync effects	Naturalistic level

The interest of this excerpt lies in the contrast between the scene of the killing and the scene in which Mulder and Scully begin their investigation.

The first *reduces* naturalistic sound representation. We do *not* hear what we would have heard if we had been there, as ear-witnesses. The sound of the television in the coffee room cuts out. There are no machine hums. There is no sense of the presence of other people. Even the doctor's footsteps in the tiled corridor and the alarm bell (which normally would have been very loud) have been reduced to almost nothing. In this way everyday 'objective' reality recedes into the background, to make place for 'unreality', or, if you like, the subjective reality of fear, with its amplified and closely textured breathing and straining and groaning, and its hyper-real representation of the swishing of the sinister pin-blade stiletto. The insistently present electronic background track, similarly, is at once abstractly representational (the heartbeats, the representation of 'alienness', the subjectivized 'room atmosphere') and sensory (the increased loudness, the stylized fluctuation, the dense shimmers and effervescences). At the same time, reality does not disappear altogether. The footsteps and the alarmbell *can* be heard, however faintly. We cannot completely exclude the possibility that the event is 'objectively' true.

As soon as we enter Mulder's office, normality returns. Instead of a subjectivized electronic atmosphere track we now hear naturalistic room atmosphere. Instead of strained, groaning whispers, we now hear everyday conversational voices. The sounds of footsteps and the computer are neither softer nor louder than we feel they would have been if we had heard them in reality. From the naturalistic point of view, this scene of *rational investigation* has highest modality, the other scene shows us at best what *could* have happened. But from the sensory point of view, the killing scene has highest modality, because of its much greater emotive impact.

Modality patterns of this kind are increasingly common. In car advertisements, for instance, naturalistic sound is used more and more sparingly. Instead of engines, car doors, rubber wheels on asphalt, wind, we hear music – music which abstractly represents the sounds of the car and at the same time conveys the pleasures of driving it. Even factual programmes have begun to use abstract–sensory sound, in the increasingly common 'reconstructions' of crimes, accidents and so on. Such soundtracks at the same time *de-realize* the world and evoke a strong emotive response. They then contrast with the soundtracks of the programme sections that are recorded in the studio and remain naturalistic in tone – but set in an artificially created environment, rather than in the 'real world'. Perhaps all this will bring about a gradual shift in the modality criteria we apply to television, a shift from the naturalistic to the abstract–sensory. If so, it is all the more urgent to make the newly dominant truth criteria explicit and open to debate, because in everyday life we cannot, in the end, get by without some reliable criteria for deciding what is and what is not true.

Exercises and discussion points

1. Study the soundtrack of a dream sequence from a film. Write the 'sound script' and analyse the modality configurations of the sounds. What has been done to give the sound a 'dreamlike' modality?

   Alternatively you might like to look at the sound modality of a daydream sequence, a memory sequence, a hallucination sequence, or some other sequence 'seen through' a special 'mental state'.

2. Compare the modality of an excerpt of the soundtrack of (i) a fly on the wall documentary, (ii) a commercial for a luxury product (for example, beauty products, expensive cars), (iii) a Disney or similar cartoon.

   What is the modality of the dialogue, the music and the sound effects in each?

3. Choose a piece of music which depicts a person, place or thing. Which aspect(s) of that person, place or thing are depicted, and how? Why have these aspects been chosen rather than others?

4. Write a 'sound script' for this excerpt from Doris Lessing's *The Grass is Singing* (1988: 202–4). Include music as well (describe it in words). Indicate in a separate column what kind of modality the different sounds should have.

   > 'He's outside,' she remarked breathlessly to Dick, as if this was only to be expected.
   >   'Who is?'
   >   She did not reply. Dick went outside. She could hear him moving, and saw the swinging beams of light from the hurricane lamp he carried. 'There is nothing there, Mary,' he said, when he returned. She nodded, in affirmation, and went again to lock the back door...

'Aren't you getting undressed?' asked Dick at last, in that hopeless, patient voice.

Obediently she pulled off her clothes and got into bed, lying alertly awake, listening. She felt him put out a hand to touch her, and at once became inert. But he was a long way off, he did not matter to her: he was like a person on the other side of a thick glass wall.

'Mary?' he said.

She remained silent.

'Mary, listen to me. You are ill. You must let me take you to the doctor.' (...)

'Of course, I am ill,' she said confidingly, addressing the Englishman. 'I've always been ill, ever since I can remember. I am ill *here*. She pointed to her chest, sitting bolt upright in bed. But her hand dropped. She forgot the Englishman, Dick's voice sounded in her ears like the echo of a voice across a valley. She was listening to the night outside. And, slowly, the terror engulfed her which she had known must come. Once she lay down, and turned her face into the darkness of the pillows; but her eyes were alive with light, and against the light she saw a dark, waiting shape. She sat up again, shuddering. He was in the room, just beside her! But the room was empty. There was nothing. She heard a boom of thunder, and saw, as she had done so many times, the lightning flicker on a shadowed wall. Now it seemed as if the night were closing in on her, and the little house was bending over like a candle, melting in the heat. She heard the crack, crack; the restless moving of the iron above, and it seemed to her that a vast black body, like a human spider, was crawling over the roof, trying to get inside. She was alone. She was defenceless. She was shut in a small black box, the walls closing in on her, the roof pressing down. She was in a trap, cornered and helpless. But she would have to go out and meet him. Propelled by fear, but also by knowledge, she rose out of bed, not making a sound. Gradually, hardly moving, she let her legs down over the dark edge of the bed; and then, suddenly afraid of the dark gulfs of the floor, she ran to the centre of the room. There she paused.

Afterwards, reflect on the modality 'settings' you decided on.

Chapter 8

Afterword

Metafunctional configurations

When Gunther Kress and I were developing our approach to the semiotics of visual communication, one of our main tools was the linguistics of Michael Halliday, in particular his 'metafunctional hypothesis' (cf. Halliday 1978, 1985). According to this hypothesis, language simultaneously fulfils three broad functions, and linguistic resources are specialized with respect to these metafunctions, operating simultaneously in text, each playing its own part, like instruments in an orchestra. Kress and I broadened this hypothesis, and assumed that *every semiotic mode* will simultaneously fulfil these three metafunctions. Here is a brief gloss:

- *The ideational metafunction*
  One of the things that language enables us to do is construct representations of 'what goes on in the world'. The linguistic resources for doing this include lexis, which provides the terms that 'stand for' the 'participants', the people, places and things in the world, and the system of transitivity, which enables us to create different relations between these participants – if, for instance, you have the participants 'man' and 'tree', you can make 'man' the 'actor' of an action ('the man chops the tree down') or 'tree' ('the tree shades the man'), you might also have a 'reaction' instead of an 'action' ('the man loves the tree') and so on.

- *The interpersonal metafunction*
  The interpersonal metafunction is the function of constituting and enacting relations between the people involved in a communicative event, of using language to do things to, or for or with other people. The linguistic resources for doing this include the system of person,

with which you can create solidarity ('we'), or exclude others ('us' and 'them' language) and so on, and the system of mood, with which you can make statements (declarative), ask questions (interrogative), tell people to do things (imperative) and so on.

● *The textual metafunction*
  The textual metafunction is the function of marshalling the combined representations and interactions into the kind of wholes we call 'texts' or 'communicative events'. The linguistic resources for this include the 'given/new' system with which you can make new information flow from already shared information, and various resources for creating cohesion in text, for making text 'hang together'.

Kress and I used the metafunctions as our entry point for thinking about visual communication. We began with questions like: How do images relate the people, places and things they portray to each other, so as to form coherent representations? What kinds of 'interpersonal resources' do images use to create a relation between the image and the viewer? This method worked well for us, and for others who have used our work and built on it. So I naturally I attempted to use it again, especially as the tools had in the process become better adapted for use with 'non-linguistic' semiotic modes. But the method did not work as well with sound as it had with vision. The resources of sound simply did not seem as specialized as those of language and vision, and the mode of sound simply did not seem so clearly structured along metafunctional lines as language and visual communication. I always ended up feeling that a given sound resource (say pitch or dynamics) was used both ideationally *and* interpersonally, or both ideationally *and* textually and so on. So I decided on a different approach, and used the *material* aspects of sound as my entry point, rather than its communicative functions. In other words, I began by asking questions like: What can you do with *dynamics* in speech, music and other sound? What can you do with *pitch* in speech, music and other sound? And so on.

Looking back I would now say that different semiotic modes have different *metafunctional configurations*, and that these metafunctional configurations are neither universal, nor a function of the intrinsic nature of the medium, but cultural, a result of the uses to which the semiotic modes have been put and the values that have been attached to them. Visual communication, for instance, *does* have its interpersonal resources, but they can only be realized on the back of ideation, so to speak. If you want to say 'Hey you, come here' by means of an image, you have to do it by representing someone who makes a 'Hey you, come here' gesture. You cannot do it directly. With sound it is the other way around. Sound does have its ideational resources, but they have to be realized on the back of interpersonal resources. In the semiotics of sound you cannot represent 'disharmony' without actually having two 'voices' (human, instrumental or otherwise) clash with each other. Nor can you represent 'tenderness' without actually addressing your listener in a tender way. We have seen it throughout this book: the same resources are used for what, following Martinec (1996), I have called presentation and representation. And these resources were originally presentational: they grew out of interaction and were only later pressed into the service of representation. This, as it happens, is also how, according to Halliday (1978), children learn their mother tongue, and even how, perhaps, language itself has developed, in the distant past. The child begins by using language in the here and now, for immediate interactional purposes, and only later develops the means for using language to represent what is not present in the 'here and now'.

Mode, medium and the process of semiosis

The resources of language are not tied to a specific *medium* – I use the word here in the way artists use it when they speak of the medium of 'oil', or 'tempera on paper' or 'bronze mounted on marble base', that is, as referring to the *materials* we use and the *material processes* we are involved in when we articulate a message. Language can be realized graphically, as writing, or auditorily, as speech. Something similar applies to music. A given 'composition' can be played on a piano or by an orchestra, and, however different the sound, we still consider it the 'same' composition. Again, in the field of industrial design, a car can be the 'same' whether it is red or green, or a chair whether it is executed in chrome or plastic.

There is another common element between these cases. They all use *visual* communication, that is writing and/or drawing, to produce 'designs' which are not regarded as the actual or ultimate semiotic artefact or event, but as a 'plan' for it (a script, a score, a blueprint, a syllabus, an action plan and so on). This allows the functions of 'design' and 'execution' to become separate stages, perhaps even the responsibility of different people, with all the increased possibilities for the exercise of power and control which this entails. Should we reserve the term *mode* for semiotic modes that have reached such a level of elaboration and abstraction and allow such formal and 'dematerialized' organizing principles to be discussed, taught and written up or drawn for the purposes of design?

Now look at it from the other end, from the side of 'media', modes of expression which have not developed such formal and abstract 'grammars'. Here, as we have seen, meaning is constructed quite differently, on the basis either of an *experiential meaning potential,* hence grounded in the materiality of the medium and in our bodily experience of that materiality, and/or in *provenance,* hence grounded in intertextuality, in histories of semiotic border crossings. These ways of meaning-making are, by comparison, flexible, unsystematic, not yet formalized, not yet able to be captured in code books. Children's meaning-making works this way, as Kress has shown in his book *Before Writing* (1997), and so does meaning-making in other not or not yet strictly regulated contexts of semiosis, for instance in the creative arts.

Perhaps this is another reason why the semiotics of sound cannot be approached in quite the same way as the semiotics of language or of images. It is not, or not yet, a 'mode', and it has therefore not or not yet reached the levels of abstraction and functional structuration that (written) language and image have reached, as a result of their use in socially crucial 'design' processes. Sound is a 'medium' or perhaps part (already) 'mode', part (still) 'medium'. If that is true, I have to ask myself a question. What have I been doing in this book? Have I attempted to turn a 'medium' into a 'mode', by systematizing it and describing it on a more abstract level, and that at a time when the new profession of 'sound designer' makes its debut and when computer technology (for example, speech and music synthesis) allows a much greater separation between the design and the execution of sound than has hitherto been possible? Or have I reintroduced 'medium' more fully in semiotics?

Evidently there is a bit of both. If the status of sound is to be raised, sound will have to become more like a mode, debatable, teachable. On the other hand, if *sound* can be raised to that status, there is every chance that this can help change the concept of mode and the structure of grammars, and contribute to reconnecting the concrete and the abstract, the representational and the interactional, the cognitive and the emotive, as I have tried to do in this book.

One thing is clear. The movement is 'from the bottom up'. There has to be a 'medium' before there can be a 'mode'. And if semiotic articulation and interpretation are not to stagnate in eternal repetition, they have to be able, from time to time, to go back to the source, to reconnect with the meaning potentials that are opened up by our physical experience of materiality and our social experience of the 'otherness' of other times and other cultures.

Making meaning

I have said it a number of times in the course of this book: if there are fixed meanings, it is because people have fixed them, even if we cannot always trace the path back to the moment of fixing. If we can *objectify* signification, and say 'the sign x means y' (rather than 'in this particular instance so-and-so used the sign x to mean y'), it is because at some stage people have objectified and decontextualized the sign, and made it into the 'coin' with which de Saussure compares signs: two sides, sound and meaning, indissolubly welded together, and given an abstract exchange value.

Fixing meaning is making rules, imposing authority, the authority of the dictionary, for instance ('X means y, because the *OED* says so'), or the authority of convention ('That's what everybody says it means') or the authority of tradition ('That's what it has always meant') – linguistics traditionally held this view of meaning, arguing that meanings are arbitrary, decided upon by some process of arbitration, and from then on to be obeyed. Another source of authoritative meaning lies in *origin*: 'The sign x originally meant y and therefore y is and should forever remain its meaning.' This argument was used a great deal in the sermons I heard as a child: interpretations of biblical texts were grounded in the original Hebrew or Greek meaning of key-words, hence in a sense of a created order which had then, in the course of history, become corrupted. Yet another source of authority is the authority of the author: 'The sign x means what the author of the sign intended it to mean' – a whole industry of secondary authors must then attempt to fix just what these intentions might have been.

The picture of meaning I have given in this book is different. It is one in which sign producer and sign interpreter are involved in the same kind of activity, making meaning, and use the same semiotic principles to do so. Gunther Kress has formulated the principle (1993, 1997): sign producers use the semiotic resources available to them according to their interest at the moment of sign production. Exactly the same thing can be said of sign *interpreters*: they use the interpretative resources available to them according to their interest at the moment of sign interpretation.

You could ask: what kind of moment? A moment we experience as unique, without precedent, hence without other than material constraints on our interest and on the semiotic resources we may use? Or a moment experienced as a *recognizable* kind of moment, a moment to which therefore certain more or less institutionalized constraints apply (habits, traditions, conventions, explicit rules or even laws), with respect to our interests, as well as with respect to the semiotic resources we can or may use? There will probably be a bit of both, with perhaps sometimes a tendency towards the 'unique', at other times a tendency towards the 'typical' end of the spectrum. Moments are rarely completely unique, at least for adults who have become habituated to the world in which they live. But nor do events ever repeat themselves identically. Again, this applies also to interpretation. Is the sign entirely new, totally open to any interpretation? If not, how constrained are we as to the kinds of semiotic resources we may use (for example, the various theories and methodologies we could use to interpret music)?

So there are, with respect to any instance of sign production and/or sign interpretation two broad questions to consider: (1) 'What is the 'interest of the moment' and what, if any, are the social constraints on that interest?' and (2) 'What are the semiotic resources available at that 'moment' and what are the social constraints on their availability and use, if any'? When considering the social constraints themselves, we can look at the degree of freedom available (and on how we know there is that degree of freedom), and at the kinds of rules that apply and the kinds of sanctions there may be on transgressing them.

Sound confronts us with a relatively unexplored semiotic terrain. For most of us, it has been an unsemiotic by-product of mechanical action, an unsemiotic carrier of 'arbitrary' speech sounds, and, in the case of music, something about the meaning of which we do not have much more to say than that 'it means a lot to us'. So here is an area where not many constraints exist (as yet?), an area where we can unlock semiotics doors and open up new meanings, as I have tried to do in this book.

Students often ask me whether the meanings I suggest are 'the' meanings of sound, or my 'subjective interpretations'. I then say that I would like to put it somewhat differently. They are neither objective nor subjective, but *inter*-subjective. They offer ways of sharing subjectively experienced meanings, means for dialogue, even if the experience itself remains subjective. I have no interest in telling you what this or that sound means, I want to offer you some tools for making meanings. That is why this book is a '*do*'-book, a 'know-how' book, rather than an '*is*'-book, a 'know that' book, why, for instance, the exercises I have included aim not at the 'comprehension' but at the *use* of my ideas. You are welcome to interpret my terms quite differently from the way I interpret them myself, and if you want to invent other terms, good, go ahead. I would like my text to be read the way jazz musicians improvise on a tune, rather than the way classical musicians interpret a score. The latter must recreate authoritatively imposed meaning, and do so according to the intentions of an author. The former take ideas from everywhere, and then do something new with it, something uniquely their own, yet shared in dialogue with fellow musicians and audiences.

Immersion

It is often said that vision allows, even prefers, things to be held still, so that they can be scrutinized in detail, dissected. This can lead to praising vision as the most objective of the senses. 'Visual acuity exalts clarity and precision, lucidity and distinctiveness, all of which are moral qualities' (Parret, 1995: 335). Sound, by contrast, is seen as immaterial and evanescent: it is not, and can never be, an object which can be grasped and possessed. It can only be experienced and remembered, 'There is no way to stop sound and have sound. I can stop a moving picture and hold one frame fixed on the screen. If I stop the movement of sound, I have nothing, only silence, no sound at all' (Ong, 1982: 32). On the other hand, while vision concentrates on the permanent and unchanging, hearing is particularly good at grasping 'the dynamics of things coming into being over time' (Wulf, 1993: 10).

It is also said that vision creates a sharp division between its subject and its object. The object of vision is precisely that, an object, an inert 'thing' which we may scrutinize with detachment and in which we can then discover the permanent qualities and attributes that convey its unchanging character and essence. The subject of vision, the 'observer', on the other hand, possesses and controls this object, but remains outside of it (her, him) at a distance. 'To see is to gather knowledge and to be in power' (Parret, 1995: 335). This finds its extreme realization in 'panopticism' (Foucault, 1979: 195ff.), in which people are controlled by the constant surveillance of eyes they never themselves see: 'The

Panopticon is a machine for disassociating the see/being seen dyad: in the peripheral ring one is totally seen, without ever seeing; in the central tower, one sees everything, without ever being seen' (Foucault, 1979: 202). Sound, on the other hand, 'pours into the hearer' (Ong, 1982: 72). It connects, and it requires surrendering oneself to, and immersing oneself in, participatory experience. A society which values sound over vision would therefore also be a society which values lived experience over detached analysis, memories over possessions, and subjective immersion and surrender over objective scrutiny, control and power.

Another frequently mentioned characteristic of vision is its directionality. Vision is narrow beam, a searching torchlight on the environment that picks out the details one by one. It 'comes to a human being from one direction at a time; to look at a room or a landscape, I must move my eyes around from one part to another. Sound, on the other hand, comes to us from all sides. It envelops us and places us in the centre of a world, and it establishes us at a kind of core of sensation and existence' (Ong, 1982: 72). Referring more specifically to serial music, Eco makes a similar point. 'The listener must allow a centre to emerge from the sound continuum. Here are no privileged points of view, and all available perspectives are equally valid and rich in potential' (quoted in Chanan, 1994: 269). Sound *unifies*.

A further point is that vision cannot go beyond the surface of things. Hence there is always the suspicion that there must be something 'deeper', a hidden meaning, underneath the surface, and invisible. What is seen is never sufficient. It must always be interpreted, explained. Sound, on the other hand, can 'register interiority without violating it' (Ong, 1982: 71) and help us to directly perceive what is 'deep' and 'hidden' and below the surface. We can *hear* the hollowness of the wall, or the heart within. And indeed, our own body, rather than staying outside of what it perceives, itself resonates with what it hears, and hears itself, further diminishing the opposition between inside and outside, surface and depth. No wonder that sound has so often been associated with the mystical and the religious, while vision was associated with knowledge, especially scientific knowledge. Sound is also harder to shut out. It 'invades us' (Welsch, 1993: 95). As Murray Schafer has said, we have no ear-lids. As a result our will is less effectively imposed on hearing. We cannot look away and pretend not to have seen. We are willy-nilly involved in and connected with the world of sounds and resonating with it, rather than remaining observers, detached and in control.

Finally, vision is said to isolate and individuate. Observation is, after all, a solitary activity, while hearing incorporates and creates communion. When we say 'What are you looking at me for?' we express unease at being observed, scrutinized and thereby made into an object. It is different with listening. Listening is connection, communion. 'We must hear to perceive speech and to be able to speak ourselves. Hearing is connected with people, with our social existence' (Welsch, 1993: 95). 'It is above all through hearing that we live in communion with others' (de Buffon, 1971: 199).

The trend in communication is now towards immersion rather than detachment, towards the interactive and the participatory rather than towards solitary enjoyments, towards ever-changing dynamic experiences rather than towards the fixing of meanings as objects to be collected. Even though sound is at present still very much undervalued and underused in the new media, and often treated as little more than a kind of optional extra, there is every chance that it will have a much increased role to play in the very near future.

Appendix: System networks and sound scripts

System networks

1. To describe a particular resource (semiotic or otherwise) in the form of a system network, first inventorize the available choices. Say the resource you want to describe is 'doors'. For the the sake of a simple example let us say you come up with the following inventory:

   > Glass doors
   > Sliding doors
   > Modern front doors

   In reality the list will be longer and that can make the job complex. It can be simplified by restricting the domain you are looking at, for instance by deciding to look only at domestic doors in Eltham, or at the doors of late-nineteenth-century churches. This also makes it easier to do your inventory. You can walk around in Eltham and visit the local showrooms, or buy a book about late-nineteenth-century churches.

2. Now look at each item in the inventory and ask the following two questions:

   (a) What is the salient, defining characteristic of each kind of door and how can it best be generalized?' (There may be several salient characteristics, as in the case of the 'modern front door' – see below)

   (b) What is the opposite of this characteristic or what would be relevant alternatives to it? (Sometimes the opposites or alternatives are already included in your inventory.)

   The salient characteristic of glass doors is that they are made of glass, which can be generalized by saying that they are transparent.

The opposite of this clearly is 'non-transparent' or 'opaque' (if you find yourself at a loss for a word, consult a thesaurus).

The salient characteristic of sliding doors is the way they open. There are alternatives, for instance hinged doors.

The salient characteristic of modern front doors are (a) that they are exterior, (b) that they are *front* doors, and (c) that they are modern. There are opposites to all of these: interior doors, back doors, and old-fashioned doors.

3. What we have found so far can be written as a set of 'systems':

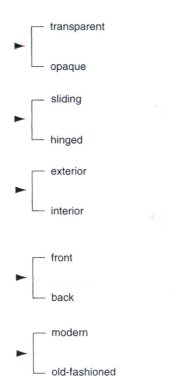

4. Now look at each of these systems and ask: is this choice an '*either–or*' choice or a *matter of degree*?

Arguably two of the systems admit degrees: transparency (you can have frosted glass doors, for instance) and 'modernity' (you can have super-modern or slightly old-fashioned doors).

This can be indicated by double-headed arrows as follows:

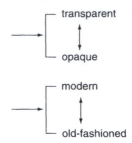

5. Now examine each of the systems in (3) above and ask whether any of them are really subsystems of one of the other systems.

   This is definitely the case with front doors and back doors: they are both exterior.

   So:

6. Finally work out to which degree the choice from the different systems can be *combined*. For example can you have old-fashioned transparent exterior sliding doors? And so on. If all choices can be combined, use a curly bracket to indicate this. If there are one or two restrictions, use I (for 'if') and T (for 'then') superscripts. For instance, while there might be sliding back doors, sliding front doors are not very common. So the superscripts indicate: 'if front, then hinged'.

7. Now the system network is complete. All the pieces of the puzzle are in place, and you can start using it to ask interesting questions, for example, 'Which doors are more often transparent, front doors or back doors, and why?

   Of course the network is only as good as your initial inventory and analysis of salient features.

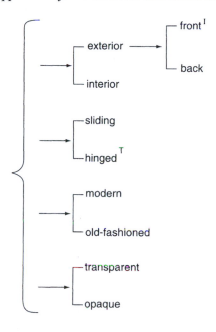

Sound scripts

The main purpose of doing a sound script is to itemize every individual component of the soundtrack, and to give each one a separate number, regardless of whether it stands alone or is heard together with other sounds. There are different ways of doing this and the one described here is not necessarily better than others. You can adapt it to suit your own needs, which may differ depending on the kind of sound event you are transcribing. You will in fact see minor variations in format between the scripts in this book. The main aim is to make them as easy to read as possible, despite the artifice of the numbering.

Let us say we have the following excerpt. First we hear the sound of a howling wind fade in. Then enter footsteps in crunching snow. Next we hear a snippet of dialogue. The wind continues during the whole of the segment, and the footsteps also continue during the dialogue. After the dialogue we hear only the footsteps and the wind, and then a newsreader's voice. When the voice starts, wind and footsteps cut out.

Here is one possibility:

---

1. Fade in howling wind
2. Enter footsteps in snow (as wind continues)
3.   John: *Are you allright?*
      Cathy: *I can't see very well*
4. Howling wind and footsteps continue
5.   Newsreader: *A severe snowstorm tonight claimed several lives*
                              (... etc.)

There is no need for much technicality. I find that indenting and italicizing the dialogue helps readability. I only use the following common technical terms: *fade in* (gradual increase of the sound level from zero), *fade out* (general decrease of the sound level to zero), *fade down* (decrease of the sound to a low background level), *fade up* (increase of the sound from low background level to full foreground level), and *cross-fade* (gradual mix from one sound or group of sounds to another). Sometimes I find it useful to indicate the speed of the fades, for example, *slow cross-fade to...* If I do not mention any form of fading the transition is a cut or a fade in or out which is so fast that it does not come across as 'gradual' and hence does not really count as a fade (from the point of view of the listener).

Glossary

Absorption Modality scale* running from maximally dry to maximally spacious, reverberating and resonant sound.

Abstract–sensory modality A criterion for judging the modality* of sound events* which rests both on the presence of abstract representation (representation concentrating on certain essential or generalized aspects of what is represented) and on emotive effect. The more a sound event fulfils these criteria, the higher its abstract–sensory modality. A musical representation of a steam train will have high abstract–sensory modality if it represents, for instance, only the rhythm and pitch contour of the locomotive, but not its 'mechanical' sound: the use of a musical instrument rather than a sound effect would achieve the 'sensory' dimension.

Action See sound act.*

Activation The semiotic potential of ascending* pitch and increased pitch range.* It derives from the increased effort required for increasing pitch and pitch range, and can therefore be used to rally people together in some common activity, to represent people, places and things as active, energetic and so on.

Adjacency pairs Adjacency pairs consist of two sequentially ordered and complementary moves* in the ongoing sound event,* for instance a call and a response, a doorbell and the buzzer that opens the door, a question and an answer. The first of the two moves is called the initiator move,* the second the reactor move.*

Aperture The degree to which the mouth and oral cavity are opened up for the articulation of different vowels. For example, the [i] of *heed* has a small, the [a] of *hard* a large aperture. The semiotic potential of aperture derives from the metaphorical extension of 'open' and 'closed'.

Ascending Melodies which have a rising pitch (which 'go up') are called ascending.

Articulation of melody See connective articulation* and disjunctive articulation.*

Blended A quality of unison* sound interaction in which the individual voices, instruments and/or other sounds can no longer be discerned and all blend together into one large sound. Also used for the blending of different sound effects in film soundtracks.

Breathy   Sound quality caused by simultaneous breathing and tone production. Derives its semiotic potential from the kinds of situation in which it occurs, for example, being out of breath, being unable to control our breathing due to excitement and so on.

Coding orientation   Coding orientations are systems of values underlying the way messages are 'encoded'. They provide criteria for judging the modality* of sound events.* In the case of sound the possible criteria are abstract–sensory,* naturalistic* and sensory.*

Connective articulation   The sounds that form a melodic phrase* are connected together in a long smooth line. The traditional musical term is *legato*.

Constrained   Speech sounds are constrained when their articulation involves blocking or restricting the release of air in some way, as is the case for most consonants. See also fully constrained,* semi-constrained* and unconstrained.*

Continuity   A sound act* has continuity when the end of it sounds as if there is more to come. This is often realized by level or rising pitch.

Continuous time   Continuous time is a form of unmeasured time* which either has no pitch variation at all or a drone in which the pitch wavers in slight and irregular ways.

Danger   A gender stereotype in which a low pitch register* combined with intimate distance* or personal distance* conveys a 'dark' and 'dangerous' femininity.

Deactivation   The semiotic potential of descending* pitch and a decreased pitch range.* It derives from the decrease in effort which goes with decreasing pitch and pitch range. Hence it can be used, for instance, to relax people, or to represent people, places and things as calm, quiet and so on.

Descending   Melodies which have a falling pitch (which 'go down') are called descending.

Dialogue   A form of sequential* sound interaction in which two voices (instruments, other sounds) and/or groups of voices (instruments, other sounds) take turns.

Diminution   A high pitch register* combined with intimate distance* or personal distance* (softness) can be used to present or represent people, places and things as small in size.

Directionality   Modality scale* running from the sounds whose sources are most easy to pinpoint to the sounds whose sources are least easy to pinpoint.

Disharmonious   A form of simultaneous* non-unison* sound interaction in which the voices, instruments and/or other sounds appear to conflict and clash with each other. The traditional musical term is *dissonance*.

Disjunctive articulation   The sounds that form a melodic phrase* are articulated as short separate stabs. The traditional musical term is *staccato*.

Dominance The semiotic potential of a high pitch register* combined with formal distance.* It derives from the fact that these sound features are associated with sounds that seek to cover a large territory. However, pitch level is strongly gendered and the values reverse for female voices (and other sounds considered 'feminine' in a given context): here a low pitch register* combined with loudness will realize assertiveness and dominance.

The term 'dominance' is also used in opposition to plurality,* that is, for a form of simultaneous* non-unison* sound interaction in which one voice dominates the others, whose task it then is to support* that dominant voice, although they may also oppose* it.

Duple time Duple time is a form of measured time* which is counted in units of two (ONE-two/ONE-two and so on).

Durational variety Modality scale* running from a single standard duration for all the sounds of a sound event* to a maximally varied range of different durations.

Dynamic range Modality scale* running from a single level of loudness to a maximally wide loudness range.

Emotive confinement The semiotic potential of compressing durational variety,* dynamic range,* fluctuation range* and/or friction range,* and, above all, pitch range.*

Emotive expansion The semiotic potential of increasing durational variety,* dynamic range,* fluctuation range,* and/or friction range,* and, above all, pitch range.*

Emulation A form of sequential* sound interaction in which the reactor* move repeats part of the initiator* move.

Environmental setting Environmental settings consist of irregularly vibrating or oscillating ongoing sound textures which are used as a setting for sound acts.*

Experiential meaning potential The idea that our experience of what we physically have to do to produce a particular sound creates a meaning potential for that sound. For instance, we know that we can create tense sounds by tensing our articulatory musculature. We also know that we tend to do this in certain kinds of situations (when we are tense or 'charged up', or want to appear that way). Hence tense sound quality can come to be associated with aggression, repression, nervousness, excitement and so on.

Field One of the three layers of sound in sound perspective:* if a sound or group of sounds is positioned as Field, it is thereby treated as existing, not in the listener's social, but in his or her physical world. We are not to pay particular attention to it, treat it as we would treat passers-by in the street, or trees in the forest.

Figure One of three layers in a sound perspective:* if a sound or group of sounds is positioned as Figure, it is thereby treated as the one that is, in the given context, the most relevant to the listener, the sound with which the listener must identify, or to which she or he must react.

Finality   A sound act* has finality when the end of it sounds 'as if there is no more to follow'. This is often realized by a low falling pitch (a 'full stop intonation') or, in music, by a return to the tonic.

Fluctuating time   Fluctuating time is a form of unmeasured time* which shifts between different pitches at more or less regular intervals which are too long to produce the sense of a pulse, a rhythm you could tap your feet to.

Fluctuation range   Modality scale* running from a completely steady sound to maximally deep and/or rapid vibrato.*

Formal distance   The relation between the sound and the listener is an actual or imaginary formal relation. The sound is loud as if calculated to be heard clearly by everyone in a large space, rather than addressed to just one or a few people.

Formulaic   A form of sequential* sound interaction in which the reactor move* does not repeat all or part of the initiator move* but responds independently with short, standardized 'formulas' such as 'amen', 'halleluiah', 'hear hear' and so on).

Fricative   A speech sound which involves constricting the air passages, thus producing a turbulent airstream, for example, the [s] and the [f]. The semiotic potential of fricatives derives from their 'roughness', the way they 'grate', 'hiss' and so on.

Friction range   Modality scale* running from maximally rough* to maximally smooth* sound.

Frontality   The degree to which the tongue moves to the front of the mouth during the articulation of speech sounds, for example, the [i] of *heed* is 'frontal' and the [a] of *hard* is a back vowel. The semiotic potential of frontality derives from the metaphorical extension of the contrast between 'back, down there' and 'front, up here'.

Fully constrained   See constrained.*

Fully stated   A form of sequential* sound interaction in which the reactor's* response* is not formulaic* but less standardized and more fully formulated.

Gesture   The contrast between 'gesture' and 'texture'* is essentially the same as that between sound act* and setting.*

Ground   One of the three layers of sound in sound perspective:* if a sound or group of sounds is positioned as Ground, it is thereby treated as still part of the listener's social world, but only in a minor and less involved way. We are to treat it as we treat the familiar faces we see every day and the familiar places we move through every day, as a context we take for granted and only notice when it is no longer there.

Harmonious   A form of simultaneous* non-unison* sound interaction in which the voices support each other and merge in a 'consensual' way, rather than that they clash and conflict. The musical term is consonance.

Height   The degree to which the tongue moves upwards in the mouth during the articulation of speech sounds. For example, the [i] of *heed* is high and the [æ] of *that* low. The semiotic potential of vowel height derives from the metaphorical extension of 'raising' and 'lowering'.

Hifi Hifi soundscapes allow discrete sounds to be heard from a great distance because of low ambient noise.

High key Another term for high pitch register.*

Imitation A form of sequential* sound interaction in which the reactor moves* repeat all of the initiator moves.*

Immersion When a sound is perceived as coming from all directions, the listener becomes immersed in it and is no longer able to take a more or less detached observer's position towards it.

Informal social distance The relation between the sound and the listener is one of real or imaginary informality. Loudness may increase to the point where the sound can be 'overheard' by strangers, but these strangers would not be addressed by the sound.

Initiator move The first of the two sound moves* in an adjacency pair.*

Intimate social distance The relation between the sound and the listener is one of real or imaginary intimacy or secrecy (whispering, or low, soft, breathy singing voices).

Key Another term for pitch register.*

Lax Sound quality marked by the absence of tension* so that its meaning potential relates to the kinds of situation in which we can rest, let go of aggression, self-control and so on.

Lofi In lofi soundscapes individual sounds get blurred together in a wall of sound. This 'wall' may be as close to the listener as the other side of the street or as far as the distant roar of an expressway.

Loudness The semiotic potential of loudness as a sound quality derives from its relation to the desire or need for covering distance, which arises for instance when people want to dominate a large territory. See also dynamic range.*

Low key Other term for low pitch register.*

Main pulse Every rhythmic phrase* has a main pulse, a sound made extra prominent through loudness, pitch or relative duration (or some combination of these) and carrying the key moment of the message, the most important note, syllable or other sound of the phrase.

Measure Measured time* divides the stream of sound into measures of equal duration, as the rhythmic pulses* ('beats') come at intervals perceived as equal.

Measured time Measured time is time with a regular pulse,* time you can tap your feet to. It is divided into measures* perceived as of equal duration (ONE-two-three, ONE-two-three and so on).

Mechanical repetition Repetition which does not involve micro-variativity.*

Melodic phrases Strictly speaking, phrasing is created by rhythm, but all rhythmic phrases* carry a melodic contour (even if it is a 'monotone' one) and this contour will either constitute a sound act* (gesture*) or one of the repeated motifs or patterns of a sound setting.*

Metronomic time A form of measured time* with very precise and unvarying timing, often aided or produced by mechanical or electronic technology.

Micro-variativity Minute changes occurring from time to time in sound motifs or patterns which are repeated over and over.

Modality A set of resources for indicating the *truth* of presentations*/representations,* for example for indicating as how real (some part of) a soundtrack should be regarded, or as how sincere a tone of voice should be taken. The modality of a sound event (or some part or aspect of it) is then said to be 'high', 'medium' or 'low'.

Modality configuration A presentation* or representation* may contain a mixture of high and low modality cues, as when naturalistic sound recordings and musical stylizations are combined on a soundtrack (the equivalent of combining live action and animation in a film).

Modality scale The modality configuration of a particular sound event* is realized by the values of the various modality scales which characterize that sound (that is, its pitch extent,* durational variety,* dynamic range,* perspectival depth,* amount of fluctuation,* amount of friction,* amount of absorption* and directionality*). Which of the poles on these scales have highest modality depends on the relevant coding orientation.*

Monologue Sound event involving one voice, instrument or other sound only.

Monorhythmic time A form of measured time* in which all the voices, instruments and/or other sounds synchronize their timing to the same pulse.*

Move A turn in a dialogue,* or a distinct section in a monologue* (for example a verse in poetry, a 'chorus' in popular music, a 'paragraph' or 'point' in a speech). A move may consist of one or several sound acts.*

Nasality A sound quality closely related to tension,* and usually carrying negative associations. It results from the use of a secondary 'cul-de-sac' resonator, for instance (but not exclusively) the nasal cavity.

Nasals Speech sounds which have the air freely escaping through the nose, while the oral cavity remains blocked: the [n],the [m] and the [ŋ] of *sing*. Their semiotic potential lies in the way they 'keep the sound inside'.

Naturalism This term is here used as one of the criteria used for judging the modality* of sound. In the case of representation:* the more we hear a sound as we (think we) would hear if we heard it 'live', the higher the modality. In the case of presentation:* the more the sounds are neither stylized or ritualized, nor dramatized, exaggerated or emotionalized (in other words, the more we judge them 'normal' and 'everyday'), the higher the modality.

Non-metronomic time   A form of measured time* in which metronomic timing* is subverted by anticipating or delaying the beat (known as *syncopation* in music terminology), or otherwise not strictly adhered to, for example through increases or decreases in tempo (known as *accelerando* and *diminuendo* in music).

Non-regularized time   A form of timing in which there is no standardization of one or more of the following: the duration of the measures (that is, the tempo*), the amount of sounds per measure,* the amount of measures per phrase* and the amount of phrases per move.*

Non-unison   A form of simultaneous* sound interaction in which the various voices, instruments and other sounds do not all make the same sounds (say the same words, sing the same song and so on).

Opposing   A form of sequential* sound interaction in which the initiator* and reactor* moves contrast with each other in some way, or a form of simultaneous* sound interaction in which two or more simultaneous voices, instruments or other sounds contrast with each other, as for example, in musical *counterpoint*. Note that this may either be harmonious* or disharmonious.*

Organic repetition   Repetition which does involve micro-variativity* (as does all repetition in nature).

Overlapping   Overlapping occurs when the end of an initiator move* overlaps the beginning of a reactor move* to a greater or lesser degree.

Parallel   A form of simultaneous* sound interaction in which two voices, instruments or other sounds use the same melodic contour and rhythmic phrasing, but at a different pitch level, so that they 'say the same thing', yet audibly retain distinct identities (for example, harmony lines in singing).

Personal social distance   The relation between the sound and the listener is an actual or imaginary personal relation, and hence the sound will be low, soft, relaxed and so on.

Perspectival depth   Modality scale* running from a 'flat' representation (Figure* only) to maximum articulation of the setting* (that is, Ground* and/or Field* are also used and maximally differentiated).

Perspective   The system of sound perspective divides simultaneous sounds into groups, and places these groups at different distances from the listener, so as to make the listener *relate* to them in different ways. The sound is either divided into three groups (Figure,* Ground* and Field*) or two (Figure and Ground, or Figure and Field). When there is only one sound there is only a Figure, and no perspective.

Phrase   See rhythmic phrase.*

Pitch movement   Pitch movement creates the 'melody' or 'pitch contour' of sounds. Some types of pitch movement are ascending,* descending* and saw-tooth.*

Pitch range Modality scale* running from a maximally wide pitch range to a maximally narrow one (that is, to monotone).

Pitch register* The sound quality we have in mind when we refer to voices, instruments or other sounds as high or low in character. Its semiotic potential derives from three factors: (1) the fact that, most of the time, small things make high noises, large things low noises, (2) the fact that louder voices also tend to rise in pitch, so that 'high' can indicate real or metaphorical power or status, and (3) the fact that women's voices are on average higher than men's voices.

Plain Sound quality defined by the absence of vibrato.* As vibrato is strongly associated with emotion, passion and so on, a plain sound quality derives its semiotic potential from the absence of emotion and passion (blandness, but also innocence, purity and so on).

Plosives Speech sounds produced by a sudden release of air [b], [p], [d], [t], [g] and [k]. The semiotic potential of plosives derives from their 'explosiveness' (note the difference in frontality* between the plosives, the [p] and [b] being most, the [k] and [g] least frontal).

Plurality A form of simultaneous* sound interaction in which the different sounds have different parts which are, however, of equal value and interest (melodically, rhythmically, dynamically and so on) so that there is no sense in which one can be said to dominate the other(s).

Polylogue A sound event* in which many voices, instruments and/or other sounds are heard, whether in turn or together.

Polyrhythmic time A form of measured time* in which the voices, instruments and/or other sounds do not synchronize their timing to the same pulse,* but use different, overlapping rhythms, without the whole becoming unstructured.*

Presentation Presentation occurs when sounds are used to enact meanings in the here and now, rather than to refer to something that is not present in the here and now of the communicative event. A policeman may *present* himself as a policeman through his way of speaking, his whistle, the siren of his car and so on. An actor may use the same sounds to represent* a policeman.

Provenance When a sound is imported from one 'place' (one era, one culture, one social group) into another, its semiotic potential derives from the associations which the 'importers' have with the 'place' from which they have imported the sound. For instance, when 1960s pop groups imported the sitar into their music, they did so to evoke the associations their youth culture had with India (meditation, drugs and so on).

Public social distance The relation between the sound and the listener is one of maximal distance (literally and/or figuratively). Loudness is maximal, as in speaking to or singing for a large audience without amplification.

Pulse In measured timing,* each measure* begins with a pulse, a sound which is 'stressed', made more prominent through loudness, pitch or relative duration (or some combination of these factors). The pulses mark the sounds (syllables, tones and so on) which carry the most important information of the measure in which they occur.

Reactor move   The second of the two sound moves* in an adjacency pair.*

Regularization   A form of timing in which one or more of the following are standardized: duration of the measures (that is, tempo*), amount of sounds per measure,* amount of measures per phrase* and amount of phrases per move.* Traditional accounts of poetic metre have an array of terms for regularized measures (for example, *iamb, trochae*) and regularized phrases (for example *pentameter, hexameter*).

Repetition   A form of sequential* sound interaction in which reactor moves* repeat all or part of initiator moves.* There are two variants, imitation* and emulation.*

Representation   See also presentation.* Representation occurs when sounds are used to refer to something not present in the here and now of the sound event.* A siren in the title sequence of a TV police series can be said to represent 'the police in the big city'.

Responses   A form of sequential* sound interaction in which reactor moves* do not repeat all or part of initiator moves* but respond with a different phrase. There are two variants, formulaic* and fully stated,* and responses may be supportive* or opposing.*

Rhythmic phrases   The measures* of measured sound are grouped together in phrases of up to seven measures, marked off from each other by breaks or changes in the regular rhythm of the pulses. The boundaries between phrases are also the boundaries between sound acts.*

Rough fricative   Most fricative speech sounds produce considerable air turbulence and their semiotic potential therefore lies in their various kinds of 'roughness' – in the hiss of the [s], the rolling of the [r] and so on.

Roughness   A rough sound is a sound in which we can hear other things besides the tone itself (friction, hoarseness, harshness, rasp and so on). Its semiotic potential derives from everything we can associate with the idea of 'roughness'.

Saw-toothed   A melody is said to be 'saw-toothed' when the pitch movement goes up and down.

Segregation   Sequential* sound interaction is said to be segregated when there is no overlapping* between initiator* and reactor moves.* Segregation is a matter of degree: there can, for instance, be a short or a long pause between the two sound moves.

Semi-constrained   Speech sounds are semi-constrained when their articulation involves only minor or partial constriction of the air flow, as in the [j], the [w] and the nasals.*

Semiosis The production of meaning, whether for purposes of representation,* presentation* or both. In this book interpreting sounds has also been seen as semiosis, as producing meaning, rather than as receiving ready-made meanings.

Sensory A criterion for judging the modality* of sound which rests on the emotive effect of sound, and is realized by maximum use of the means of expression that constitute the various modality scales.*

Sequential interaction The alternation of different voices (instruments, sounds) and/or groups of voices (instruments, sounds). Types of sequential interaction include various forms of repetition* and response* and sequential interaction may be segregated* or overlapping.* Sequential interaction van be dialogic* or polylogic.*

Setting Settings are (1) rhythmic/melodic motifs and patterns that repeat themselves endlessly (whether or not with very minor variations) and (2) more irregularly vibrating or oscillating ongoing sound textures.* The semiotic potential of the former derives from its relation to repetitive human action (hence the term 'social settings'*). The semiotic potential of the latter derives from its relation to natural sounds and to certain kinds of technical sound (for example, electric hums) – hence the term 'environmental settings'.* Settings serve as contexts for sound acts.*

Simultaneous interaction The simultaneous sounding of different voices (instruments, other sounds) or groups of voices (instruments, other sounds). This can be structured or unstructured,* and unison* or non-unison.*

Smooth fricative In the context of this book the [l] is considered a 'smooth fricative' to stress the semiotic contrast between the easy 'gliding' of the [l] and the scraping, grating and hissing of 'true' fricatives.

Smoothness The opposite of roughness* – its semiotic potential derives from everything we can associate with the absence of 'roughness' and with the idea of 'smoothness' itself.

Social distance Sounds are produced to carry a certain distance. This suggests a set of possible social relations between sounds and listeners which may vary from 'close' (intimate,* personal* and informal* distance) to more 'distant' (formal* and public* distance).

Social setting Social settings are formed by melodic/rhythmic motifs or patterns of sound that repeat themselves over and over, and serve as a setting for sound acts.*

Softness The semiotic potential of softness as a sound quality derives from our experience of situations in which we desire to speak softly, need to keep our voice down, are unable to raise our voice and so on (for example, intimacy, secrecy, physical weakness).

Sound act Rhythmic phrases* delimit sound acts, the individual units of meaning in ongoing sound events.* Also referred to as (sound) gestures.*

Sound event An instance of communicating by means of sound, for example a radio programme, a conversation, a song or a public announcement in a railway station. A sound event may consist of one sound move* or many.

Sound quality Sound quality may be constant, as in the case of habitual voice settings or the singing style of a particular singer; it may be specific to a type of sound event,* for example, the sales pitch of a hard-sell advertisement or the sound of classical guitar; or it may be employed to express a specific local meaning, for example a groaning sound to express dismay, or a saxophone wail to create a particularly emotive climax in a solo.

Stasis The semiotic potential of level pitch (monotone). It derives from the fact that emotional confinement* is maximal and action neutralized. The former can then for instance lead to meanings such as 'deadpan', the latter to expressing for example, the 'paralysis' of fear.

Supportive A form of sequential* sound interaction in which the reactor move* supports the initiator move* rather than contrasting with it.

Tempo Tempo is a feature of measured time* and depends on the time interval between pulses* – the smaller this interval, the higher the tempo. In most music tempo is regularized,* in everyday speech it will change from time to time.

Tension The sound quality of tenseness is created by the tensing of the throat muscles, and, by extension, is attributable to sounds with the same acoustic characteristics as tense voices (reduction of lower overtones, increased sharpness and brightness and so on). Its semiotic potential derives from the kinds of situations in which we may be tense or alert or have to exercise self-control.

Texture A more 'formal' way of referring to social setting.* Gesture : texture = sound act : setting.

Triple time A form of measured time* which is counted in units of three (ONE-two-three/ONE-two-three and so on). As most human action has a duple* rhythm, its meaning potential derives from its 'artificiality', its being 'special', 'different from the everyday'.

Unblended A quality of unison* sound interaction in which the individual voices, instruments or other sounds can still be discerned, rather than being blended together.

Unconstrained Speech sounds are unconstrained when their articulation does not involve blocking or constricting the airflow. Vowels are unconstrained.

Unison A form of simultaneous* sound interaction in which all voices, instruments or other sound sources sing, play or otherwise produce the same sounds.

Unmeasured time A form of timing in which no regular pulse can be discerned, so that you cannot tap your feet to the sound's rhythm. Its meaning potential is 'out of time', and it can therefore be used to signify the 'eternal', the 'sacred', the 'supernatural' and so on.

Unstructured   A form of simultaneous* sound interaction in which the voices, instruments and/or other sounds are all involved in the same activity but without actually working together, for example instruments tuning up before a concert, or people talking in small groups at a reception.

Vibrato   A sound quality in which the sound has some kind of 'grain', some kind of regular or irregular wavering, warbling, vibrating, pulsing, throbbing, rumbling and so on. Its semiotic potential derives from the fact that the voice wavers at moments of emotion, whether positive (passion) or negative (fear). See also fluctuation range.*

Voicing   Speech sounds which have 'tone' and can achieve a certain loudness are 'voiced', and speech sounds which cannot, and must therefore always be near-silent releases of air ([f], [h], [s]) are 'unvoiced'.

Bibliography

Adorno, T. (1976) *Introduction to the Sociology of Music*, New York, Seabury Press

Altman, R. (1985) 'The Evolution of Sound Technology', in Weis and Belton (eds) op. cit.

Aristotle, [1954] *The Rhetoric and the Poetics*, New York, The Modern Library

Armstrong, L.E. and Ward, I.C. (1926) *Handbook of English Intonation*, Cambridge, Heffer

Asaf'ev, B.V. (1977) *Musical Form as a Process: Translation and Commentary by J.R. Tull*, Ohio State University PhD Dissertation, Ann Arbor, Mich.

Attali, J. (1985) *Noise – The Political Economy of Music*, Manchester University Press

Balasz, B. (1970) *Theory of the Film: Character and Growth of a New Art*, New York, Dover

Barnouw, E. (1968) *The Golden Web – A History of Broadcasting in the United States 1933–1953*, New York, Oxford University Press

Barthes, R. (1977) *Image-Music-Text*, London, Fontana

Barthes, R. (1982) *L'obvie et l'obtus. Essais critiques III*, Paris, Seuil

Bell, P. and Van Leeuwen, T. (1994) *The Media Interview – Confession, Contest, Conversation*, Sydney, University of New South Wales Press

Berendt, J.-E. (1983) *Nada Brahma. Die Welt ist Klang*, Frankfurt, Reinbek

Berger, J. (1972) *Ways of Seeing*, Harmondsworth, Penguin

Bernard, J. and Delbridge, A. (1979) *Language as a Sign System – Linguistics in the Australian Context*, Sydney, Prentice-Hall

Bernstein, B. (1981) 'Codes, Modalities and the Process of Cultural Reproduction: a Model', *Language and Society* 10: 327–63

Blake, W. (1990) *Songs of Innocence and Experience*, Oxford, Oxford University Press

Blaukopf, K. (1960) 'Problems of Architectural Acoustics in Musical Sociology', *Gravesane Blätter* V(19–20): 180–7

Bourdieu, P. (1986) *Distinction – A Social Critique of the Judgement of Taste*, London, Routledge

Bramstedt, E.K. (1965) *Goebbels and National Socialist Propaganda 1925–1945*, Michigan State University Press

215

Brazil, D. (1995) *A Grammar of Speech*, Oxford, Oxford University Press

Brazil, D., Coulthard, M. and Johns, C. (1980) *Discourse Intonation and Language Teaching*, London, Longman

Brown, P. and Levinson, S.C. (1978) *Politeness – Some Universals in Language*, Cambridge, Cambridge University Press

Brown, R.W. and Hildum, D.C. (1956) 'Expectancy and the Identification of Syllables', *Language* **32**: 411–19

Cage, J. (1968) *Silence*, London, Calder & Boyars

Cardiff, D. (1981) 'The Serious and the Popular: Aspects of the Evolution of Style in the Radio Talk 1928–1939', *Media, Culture and Society* **2**(1): 29–47

Carroll, L. (1994) *Through the Looking-Glass*, Harmondsworth, Penguin

Chanan, M. (1994) *Musica Practica – The Social Practice of Western Music from Gregorian Chant to Postmodernism*, London, Verso

Chanan, M. (1995) *Repeated Takes – A Short History of Recording and its Effects on Music*, London, Verso

Chaytor, H.J. (1945) *From Script to Print*, Cambridge, Heffer

Chernoff, J.M. (1979) *African Rhythm and African Sensibility – Aesthetics and Social Action in African Musical Idioms*, Chicago, University of Chicago Press

Cooke, D. (1959) *The Language of Music*, Oxford, Oxford University Press

Coulthard, M. (1977) *Introduction to Discourse Analysis*, London, Longman

Crisell, A. (1986) *Understanding Radio*, London, Methuen

Crystal, D. (1969) *Prosodic Systems and Intonation in English*, Cambridge, Cambridge University Press

Crystal, D. (1970) 'Prosodic and Paralinguistic Correlates of Social Categories', in A. Ardener (ed.) *Social Anthropology and Language*, London, Tavistock Press

Crystal, D. and Davy, D. (1969) *Investigating English Style*, London, Longman

Dahlhaus, C. (1985) *Realism in Nineteenth Century Music*, Cambridge, Cambridge University Press

De Buffon, G.L.L. (1971) *De l'homme*, Paris, Duchet

Delattre, P. (1972) 'The Distinctive Function of Intonation', in D.L. Bolinger (ed.) *Intonation*, Harmondworth, Penguin

Doane, M.A. (1985) 'Ideology and the Practice of Sound Editing and Mixing', in E. Weis and J. Belton (eds) *Film Sound – Theory and Practice*, New York, Columbia University Press

Doelle, L. (1972) *Environmental Acoustics*, New York

Durant, A. (1984) *Conditions of Music*, London, Macmillan

Durant, A. (1990) 'A New Day for Music? Digital Technologies in Contemporary Music-making', in P. Hayward (ed.) *Culture, Technology and Creativity in the Late 20th Century*, London, John Libby

Eisenstein, S. (1949) *Film Form*, New York, Harcourt Brace

Eisenstein, S. (1975) *The Film Sense*, New York, Harcourt Brace

Elias, N. (1978) *The Civilizing Process – Sociogenetic and Psychogenetic Investi-gations*, Oxford, Blackwell

Elias, N. (1992) *Time: An Essay*, Oxford, Blackwell

Eliot, T.S. (1990) *The Waste Land and Other Poems*, London, Faber and Faber

Ellis, C.J. (1984) 'Time Consciousness of Aboriginal Performers', in J.C. Kassler and J. Stubington (eds) *Problems and Solutions – Occasional Essays in Musicology presented to Alice M. Moyle*, Sydney, Hale and Iremonger

Evans, E. (1977) *Radio – A Guide to Broadcasting Techniques*, London, Barrie and Jenkins

Fairclough, N. and Wodak, R. (1997) 'Critical Discourse Analysis', in T.A. van Dijk (ed.) *Discourse as Social Interaction*, London, Sage

Feld, S. (1982) *Sound and Sentiment – Birds, Weeping, Poetics and Song in Kaluli Expression*, Philadelphia, University of Pennsylvania Press

Firth, J.R. (1957) 'Modes of Meaning', in *Papers in Linguistics 1934–1951*, London, Oxford University Press

Fonagy, I. (1976) 'The Voice of the Poet', in A. Makkai (ed.) *Toward a Theory of Context in Linguistics and Literature*, The Hague, Mouton

Fonagy, I. and Magdics, K. (1972) 'Emotional Patterns in Intonation and Music', in D.L. Bolinger (ed.) *Intonation*, Harmondsworth, Penguin

Foucault, M. (1979) *Discipline and Punish*, Harmondsworth, Penguin

Frith, S. (1984) 'Mood Music: An Inquiry into Narrative Film Music', *Screen* 25(3): 78–87

Frith, S. (1988) *Music for Pleasure*, Cambridge, Polity

Frith, S. (1996) 'Music and Identity', in S. Hall and P. du Gay (eds) *Questions of Cultural Identity*, London, Sage

Goffman, E. (1959) *Presentation of Self in Everyday Life*, New York, Anchor Books

Goffman, E. (1974) *Frame Analysis – An Essay on the Organization of Experi-ence*, Harmondsworth, Penguin

Goldberg, R. (1993) *Performance Art – From Futurism to the Present*, London, Thames and Hudson

Goodman, S. and Graddol, D. (1997) *Redesigning English – New Texts, New Identities*, London, Routledge

Gorbman, C. (1987) *Unheard Melodies – Narrative Film Music*, London, BFI

Graddol, D. and Boyd-Barrett, O. (1994) *Media Texts: Authors and Readers*, Clevedon, Avon, Open University/Multilingual Matters

Hall, E.T. (1959) *The Silent Language*, New York, Doubleday

Hall, E.T. (1964) 'Silent Assumptions in Social Communication', in D.McK. Rioch and E.A. Weinstein (eds) *Disorders of Communication, Research Publications, Association for Research in Nervous and Mental Diseases* 42: 41–55

Hall, E.T. (1966) *The Hidden Dimension*, New York, Doubleday

Hall, E.T. (1983) *The Dance of Life – The Other Dimension of Time*, New York, Anchor Press

Hall, R.A. (1972) 'Elgar and the Intonation of British English', in D.L. Bolinger (ed.) *Intonation*, Harmondworth, Penguin

Halliday, M.A.K. (1967) *Intonation and Grammar in British English*, The Hague, Mouton

Halliday, M.A.K. (1970) *A Course in Spoken English: Intonation*, Oxford University Press

Halliday, M.A.K. (1978) *Language as Social Semiotic*, London, Edward Arnold

Halliday, M.A.K. (1979) 'Modes of Meaning and Modes of Expression', in D.J. Allerton, E. Carney and D. Holdcroft (eds) *Function and Context in Linguistic Analysis – A Festschrift for William Haas*, Cambridge, Cambridge University Press

Halliday, M.A.K. (1985) *Introduction to Functional Grammar*, London, Arnold

Harman, A. and Mellers, W. (1962) *Man and His Music*, London, Barrie and Jenkins

Helms, S. (1981) *Musik in der Werbung*, Wiesbaden, Breitkopf and Härtel

Herman, L. (1952) *A Practical Manual of Screen Playwriting for Theater and Television Films*, New York, New American Library

Hermeren, G. (1969) *Representation and Meaning in the Visual Arts*, Lund, Scandinavian University Books

Hjelmslev, L. (1959) 'La stratification du langage', *Word X* (2–3): 163–88

Hjelmslev, L. (1961 [1943]) *Prolegomena to a Theory of Language*, Madison, University of Wisconsin Press

Hodge, R. and Kress, G. (1988) *Social Semiotics*, Cambridge, Polity Press

Hodge, R. and Tripp, D. (1986) *Children and Television*, Cambridge, Polity Press

Jakobson, R. (1962) 'Closing Statement: Linguistics and Poetics', in T.A. Sebeok (ed.) *Style in Language*, Cambridge, Mass., MIT Press

Jakobson, R. (1968) *Child Language, Aphasia and Phonological Universals*, The Hague, Mouton

Jakobson, R. (1971) *Fundamentals of Language*, The Hague, Mouton

Joos, M. (1967) *The Five Clocks of Language*, New York, Harcourt, Brace

Kafka, F. (1978) *Wedding Preparations in the Country and Other Stories*, Harmondsworth, Penguin

Kartomi, M.J. (1984) 'Delineation of Lullaby Style in Three Areas of Aboriginal Australia', in J.C.Kassler and J. Stubington (eds) *Problems and Solutions – Occasional Essays in Musicology presented to Alice M. Moyle*, Sydney, Hale and Iremonger

Keenan, E. (1974) 'Conversational Competence in Children', *Journal of Child Language* 1: 163–83

Koury, D.J. (1986) *Orchestral Performance Practices in the Nineteenth Century*, Ann Arbor, UMI Research Press

Kreitler, H. and Kreitler, S. (1972) *Psychology of the Arts*, Durham, NC, Duke University Press

Kress, G. (1993) 'Against Arbitrariness: the Social Production of the Sign as a Foundational Issue in Critical Discourse Analysis', *Discourse and Society* 4(2): 169–93

Kress, G. (1997) *Before Writing – Rethinking the Paths to Literacy*, London, Routledge

Kress, G. and Hodge, R. (1979) *Language as Ideology*, London, Routledge

Kress, G. and Van Leeuwen, T. (1990) *Reading Images*, Geelong, Deakin University Press

Kress, G. and Van Leeuwen, T. (1996) *Reading Images – The Grammar of Visual Design*, London, Routledge

Kristeva, J. (1980) *Desire in Language*, Oxford, Blackwell

Kummerer, K. (1996) 'The Ecological Impact of Time', *Time and Society* 5(2): 209–35

Ladefoged, P. (1975) *A Course in Phonetics*, New York, Harcourt Brace Jovanovich

Lakoff, G. and Johnson, M. (1980) *Metaphors We Live By*, Chicago, University of Chicago Press

Laver, J. (1980) *The Phonetic Description of Voice Quality*, Cambridge, Cambridge University Press

Lehiste, I. (1973) 'Rhythmic Units and Syntactic Units in Production and Perception', *The Journal of the Acoustical Society of America* 54: 1102–4

Leitner, G. (1980) 'BBC English and Deutsche Rundfunksprache: A Comparative and Historical Analysis of the Language on the Radio', *International Journal of the Sociology of Language* 26: 75–100

Lessing, D. (1988) *The Grass is Singing*, London, Paladin

Lilliestam, L. (1990) 'Musical Acculturation: "Hound Dog" from Blues to Swedish Rock an Roll', in K. Roe and U. Carlsson (eds) *Popular Music Research*, Göteborg, Nordicom-Sweden 1–2: 133–45

Lomax, A. (1968) *Folk Song Style and Culture*, New Brunswick, New Jersey, Transaction Books

McClary, S. (1991) *Feminine Endings: Music, Gender and Sexuality*, Minnesota, University of Minnesota Press

McConnell-Ginet, S. (1977) 'Intonation in a Man's World', *Signs* 3: 541–59

McLuhan, M. (1962) *The Gutenberg Galaxy*, Toronto, New American Library

McLuhan, M. (1966) *Understanding Media*, New York, McGraw-Hill

Mancini, M. (1985) 'The Sound Designer', in E. Weis and J. Belton (eds) op. cit.

Marothy, J. (1974) *Music and the Bourgeois, Music and the Proletarian*, Budapest, Akademiai Kiado

Martin, J.R. (1992) *English Text – System and Structure*, Amsterdam, Benjamins

Martinec, R. (1995) *Hierarchy of Rhythm in English Speech*, University of Sydney PhD Dissertation

Martinec, R. (1996) 'Towards a Semiotics of Action', unpublished manuscript

Mellers, W. (1964) *Music in a New Found Land – Themes and Developments in the History of American Music*, London, Faber and Faber

Merriam, A.P. (1964) *The Anthropology of Music*, Evanston, Ill., Northwestern University Press

Meyer, L.B. (1956) *Emotion and Meaning in Music*, Chicago, University of Chicago Press

Middleton, R. (1990) *Studying Popular Music*, Milton Keynes, Open University Press

Miller, A.I. (1995) 'Aesthetics, Representation and Creativity in Art and Science', *Leonardo* **28**(3): 185–92

Mumford, L. (1934) *Technics and Civilisation*, New York, Harcourt, Brace

Nattiez, J-J. (1971) 'Situation de la sémiologie musicale', *Musique en jeu* 5: 3–18

Nattiez, J-J. (1975) *Fondements d'une sémiologie de la musique*, Paris, UGE

Nattiez, J.-J. (1990) *Music and Discourse – Towards a Semiology of Music*, Princeton, NJ, Princeton University Press

Nettl, B. (1973) *Folk and Traditional Music of the Western Continents*, Englewood Cliffs, NJ, Prentice-Hall

Nöth, W. (1995) *Handbook of Semiotics*, Bloomington, Indiana University Press

Oakley, M. *et al.* (1985) *Our Society and Others*, Sydney, McGraw-Hill

Oliver, P. (1968) *Screening the Blues – Aspects of the Blues Tradition*, New York, Da Capo Press

Ong, W.J. (1982) *Orality and Literacy – The Technologizing of the Word*, London, Methuen

Orrey, L. (1975) *Programme Music – A Brief Survey from the Sixteenth Century to the Present Day*, London, Davis-Poynter

Paine, F. (1985) 'Sound Mixing and *Apocalypse Now*: An Interview with Walter Murch', in E. Weis and J. Belton (eds), op. cit.

Paolucci, G. (1996) 'The Changing Dynamics of Working Time', *Time and Society* **5**(2): 145–67

Parret, H. (1995) 'Synesthetic Effects', in T.A. Sebeok and J. Umiker-Sebeok (eds) *Advances in Visual Semiotics*, Berlin, Mouton de Gruyter

Pomerantz, A. and Fehr, B.J. (1997) 'Conversation Analysis: An Approach to the Study of Social Action as Sense Making Practices', in T.A. van Dijk (ed.) *Discourse as Social Interaction*, London, Sage

Poynton, C. (1985) *Language and Gender: Making the Difference*, Geelong, Deakin University Press

Poynton, C. (1996) 'Giving Voice', in E. McWilliam and P. Taylor (eds) *Pedagogy, Technology and the Body*, New York, Peter Lang

Rampton, B. (1998) '*Deutsch* in Inner London: The Vernacular Appropriation of an Instructed Foreign Language', unpublished manuscript

Rösing, H. (1982) 'Music in Advertising', in P. Tagg and D. Horn (eds) *Popular Music Perspectives*, Göteborg and Exeter, IASPM

Russolo, L. (1986) *The Art of Noises*, New York, Pendragon Press

Ruwet, N. (1967) *Langage, musique, poésie*, Paris, Larousse

Sacks, O. (1994) *An Anthropologist on Mars*, London, Picador

Sapir, E.A. (1929) 'A Study in Phonetic Symbolism', *Journal of Experimental Psychology* 12: 225–39

Saussure, F. de (1974[1916]) *Course in General Linguistics*, London, Peter Owen

Schafer, R.M. (1977) *The Tuning of the World*, Toronto, McClelland and Stewart

Schafer, R.M. (1986) *The Thinking Ear*, Toronto, Arcana Editions

Schoenberg, A. (1983[1911]) *Theory of Harmony*, London, Faber & Faber

Schreger, C. (1985) 'Altman, Dolby and the Second Sound Revolution', in Weis and Belton (eds) op. cit.

Shepherd, J. (1991) *Music as Social Text*, Cambridge, Polity

Shepherd, J., Virden, P., Vulliamy, G. and Wishart, T. (1977) *Whose Music? A Sociology of Musical Languages*, New York, Transaction Books

Stravinsky, I. (1936) *Chronicle of My Life*, London, Gollancz

Sussex, R. (1977) 'North American English as a Prestige Model in the Australian Media', unpublished paper, Dept of Russian, University of Melbourne

Tagg, P. (1983) 'Nature as a Musical Mood Category', Göteborg, *IASPM Internal Publications* P 8206

Tagg, P. (1984) 'Understanding Musical 'Time Sense' – Concepts, Sketches and Consequences', in *Tvarspel – Festskrift for Jan Ling (50 År)*, Göteborg, Skrifter fran Musikvetenskapliga Institutionen

Tagg, P. (1990) 'Music in Mass Media Studies. Reading Sounds for Example', in K. Roe and U. Carlsson (eds) *Popular Music Research*, Nordicom-Sweden (2): 103–15

Tannen, D. (1992) *You Just Don't Understand – Women and Men in Conversation*, London, Virago

Tarasti, E. (1994) *A Theory of Musical Semiotics*, Bloomington, Indiana University Press

Thompson, R.F. (1966) 'An Aesthetic of the Cool: West African Dance', *African Forum* 2(2): 93–4

Trudgill, P. (1974) *The Social Differentiation of English in Norwich*, Cambridge University Press

Ullman, S. (1962) *Semantics – An Introduction to the Science of Meaning*, Oxford, Blackwell

Van den Berg, J.H. (1962) *Het Menselijk Lichaam*, Nijkerk, Callenbach

Van Leeuwen, T. (1982) 'Professional Speech: Accentual and Junctural Style in Radio Announcing', unpublished MA(Hons) Thesis, Macquarie University, Sydney

Van Leeuwen, T. (1984) 'Impartial Speech – Observations on the Intonation of Radio Newsreaders', *Australian Journal of Cultural Studies* 2(1): 84–99

Van Leeuwen, T. (1985) 'Rhythmic Structure of the Film Text', in Teun A. van Dijk (ed.) *Discourse and Communication – New Approaches to the Analysis of Mass Media Discourse and Communication*, Berlin, de Gruyter

Van Leeuwen, T. (1989) 'Changed Times, Changed Tunes: Music and the Ideology of the News', in J. Tulloch and G. Turner (eds) *Australian Television: Programmes, Pleasures and Politics*, Sydney, Allen and Unwin

Van Leeuwen, T. (1991) 'The Sociosemiotics of Easy Listening Music', *Social Semiotics* 1(1): 67–80

Van Leeuwen, T. (1992) 'Rhythm and Social Context', in P. Tench (ed.) *Studies in Systemic Phonology*, London, Frances Pinter   .

Van Leeuwen, T. (1998) 'Emotional Times: The Music of *The Piano*', in R. Coyle, (ed.) *Screen Scores – Studies in Contemporary Australian Film Music*, Sydney, AFTRS

Verschueren, J. (1985) *What People Say They Do with Words*, Norwood, NJ, Ablex

Weber, M. (1947) *The Theory of Social and Economic Organization*, New York, The Free Press

Weis, E. and Belton, J. (eds) (1985) *Film Sound – Theory and Practice*, New York, Columbia University Press

Welsch, W. (1993) 'Auf den Weg zu einer Kultur des Hörens?' *Paragrana* 2(1–2): 87–104

West, R., Ansberry, M. and Carr, A. (1957) *The Rehabilitation of Speech*, New York, Harper

Williams, R. (1974) *Television, Technology and Cultural Form*, London, Fontana

Williams-Jones, P. (1975) 'Afro-American Gospel Music: A Crystallization of the Black Aesthetic', *Ethnomusicology*, September 1975: 373–85

Wimsatt, W.K. (1954) *The Verbal Icon*, Lexington, University of Kentucky Press

Winternitz, E. (1979) *Musical Instruments and Their Symbolism in Western Art*, New Haven, Yale University Press

Wiora, M (1965) *Les quatre âges de la musique*, Paris, Payot

Wulf, C. (1993) 'Das mimetische Ohr', *Paragrana* 2(1–2): 9–15

Zak, V. (1982) 'Asaf'ev's Theory of Intonation and the Analysis of Popular Song', *Popular Music* 2: 91–111

Index